It's Here Now
(Are You?)

It's Here Now

(Are You?)

A Spiritual Memoir

BHAGAVAN DAS

BROADWAY BOOKS
NEW YORK

Note: Indian titles such as Baba, Maharaji, Maharishi, Swami, Swamiji, and Yogi are honorific forms of address and are relatively interchangeable. They elucidate the holiness of the person being addressed.

BROADWAY

Library of Congress Cataloging-in-Publication Data

Das, Bhagavan.
    It's here now (are you?) : a spiritual memoir / Bhagavan Das. — 1st ed.
      p.   cm.
    ISBN 978-0-767-90009-6
    1. Das, Bhagavan. 2. Spiritual biography—United States.
3. Gurus—United States. I. Title.
BL73.D375A3 1997
294′.092—dc21
  [B]   97-17510
                                        CIP

Designed by Julie Duquet

ॐ

I want to thank the living grace of my Guru, Maharaji Neem Karoli.

And to my mother, for giving me this precious human birth.

To my boyhood dog, Mimi, for showing me unconditional love.

To Wally "Famous Amos," who said to me while walking down a beach in Hawaii, "You got to get off the dime. You're one of the most interesting people I've ever met—you've got to write a book."

To Connie Church, for surrendering to existence and allowing the Goddess Saraswati to flow through her writing.

To my best friend Jay Yarnall, for his unceasing devotion to the breath and the name of God.

To Sri Tripurasundari Devi from Jivamukti Yoga Center, New York, who found me a seat to become one with God.

To my agents, John Brockman and Katinka Matson, for believing in me from the get-go.

To Lauren Marino, for grabbing me before I flew by.

To Linda Johnsen, for birthing this book with her energy.

To Umananda Saraswati, for dancing in my heart.

To Shree Maa, for the blessing of her lotus feet.

To Sri Anandamayi Ma, for filling me with the bliss of her form.

To Mata Amritanandamayi Ammachi, for bringing me home to God.

*For C.D.s, tapes, and information
on Nada Yoga Workshops, write:*

Bhagavan Das Music
P.O. Box 941
Middletown, CA 95461

AH, BHAGAVAN DAS SINGING

Bhavagan Das gets in and out of taxis with his giant body carrying a tiny baby

Bhavagan Das sits on floors to sing, closes his eyes and groans to God for hours

Bhavagan Das says Tah Dah Nah into the microphone hole talking Gandarva loka babytalk

Bhavagan Das sings the blues in Yogic Sanskrit like a perfect Virgin

Bhavagan Das sat on the street with beggars in Allahabad and Almora weeping Raaaam! half a decade crying all alone

Bhavagan Das kisses the feet of his teachers and wanders around the planet like a big yellow robed dope

If I thought I had nothing better to do I'd follow Bhavagan Das around the equator singing Bloop Bloop Bloop Bom Shankar till I had something better to do

Bhavagan Das never had anything better to do than call up Mystic Mama on the Mantric Telephone

Bhavagan Das does nothing better than sit on the ground and close his eyes and sing to his Guru

Bhavagan Das is my mother that's why I kiss Bhavagan Das' feet singing Ah Ah Ah Ah Ah Ah!

—Allen Ginsberg

Part I

Chapter I

ARRIVING IN INDIA in 1964 was like walking into a concert that had been playing for five thousand years with seven hundred million people in the band. It was the most densely populated place I'd ever been in. No empty space—just masses of human bodies. As I got off the train in Amritsar, the entry point into the country, an ocean of curious eyes stared at me: a 6'5″ blonde American teen-ager.

I had come from Lahore, Pakistan, where the streets and shops were also crowded. My compartment on the train—also jammed—was so hot and stuffy that I nearly passed out and had to lie on the dirty floor. My long body made it impossible for passengers to get by, so they just stepped on me on their way to the door. I lost count of the number of times feet stumbled across my face during the three-hour ride.

The smell of sweat and urine, the screaming babies, and the gibberish of Indian languages disoriented me so badly that I squeezed my eyes shut, trying to close it all out. I didn't have the energy to brush away the flies sitting on my face. If God were to give us a half-hour in our lives during which we could live without breathing, I would have taken mine then.

This is my first memory of India. I was at once repulsed and fascinated by it all.

I was relieved to climb out of the train when I reached Amritsar. I looked around and saw that everyone—men and women—had hair hanging down to their waists. People, everywhere, were hanging out in loose, white clothes that looked like underwear. I liked the atmosphere, and it felt safe. I decided to stay. I wanted to be a part of it all, so I gave my jeans, shirt, and boots to the first man who came up to me. I bought a bright yellow cotton cloth to wrap myself in. This was all I had on, and it felt great.

I stepped into the masses, having no idea where I was going. Something was happening—everybody was moving in the same direction. Then I saw a brilliant light reflecting off a huge, golden temple. The walls were literally plated with quarter-inch sheets of solid gold.

How could one of the poorest countries in the world afford a temple of solid gold? The irony didn't seem to bother these people; all their energy was directed toward the temple, while people were dying in the streets. This made no sense to me.

The people around me clutched flowers in their hands as tears of devotion flowed from their eyes. I had never seen anything like it. The all-pervading devotion was like a golden mist of love we were breathing in together. I felt as though I was one of them and that we were all one great heart flowing through the street. Within thirty feet of the temple we found ourselves wading through two inches of water, saturated with flower petals. We bathed our feet as we entered the temple. The marble passageways were big enough for a thousand people to walk through at one time.

Inside, incense wafted into the air as someone waved a yak tail fan before an enormous copy of the Sikh holy book, *Adi Granth*. People were reading from its pages twenty-four hours a day. Nearby, a white-bearded blind man was singing passages from memory.

Something about this temple was strangely familiar. I kept thinking, "I know this space. I could swear I've been here before. This is the space."

IT WOULD BE some time before I would grasp that there is only one temple in the world. It's an internal temple, and we each go there in our own way. What we're actually doing with our devotion is building a golden temple on a higher plane of consciousness so we can enter that inner sanctum any time and be in that space with God. The golden temple at Amritsar was an elevator, carrying me to the top floor of my own being.

I WAS SO taken with this sacred atmosphere that I decided to spend a few days there. I checked into the local dharmsala, a free place for pilgrims to stay while paying homage to the temple. Each room had a cement floor and a wooden cot with woven hemp twine to sleep on.

I had smuggled 800 rupees into India in my boot (100-rupee notes are big and have to be folded at least four times to fit in your wallet). I kept the money in a little bag around my shoulder. My room seemed secure: there were bars on the door, and I had a key. So I left my bag by the cot and went into town to get some tea.

When I came back, every last rupee was gone. It was nearly all the money I had in my life. All I had left were a few rupees in change from the tea stall.

I went to the head of the facility to tell him what happened—maybe he could help me track down the person who took it. He was a fat man with a big black beard, and he was wearing a turban. I told him what happened, and he just roared with laughter. He sat back and roared! I couldn't believe it. Who wasn't getting it? Him or me?

WANDERING THE STREETS of Amritsar, I was as lost and as broke as any beggar in India. Even worse, I didn't know the customs and couldn't understand the culture. I was in total shock. I kept going to the temple, immersing myself in the vibes of devotion, which were very strong and comforting. I didn't know what else to do.

An English-speaking Indian approached me outside the temple and introduced himself. He was the disciple of a spiritual teacher named Guru Mota. He told me about his guru.

Mota had been a worldly man, normal enough, until one night he went outside to take a pee and was bitten by a cobra. He was all alone and terrified that he was going to die. He started repeating the name of God over and over—"Hari Om! Hari Om!"—for hours, walking around in a circle. *Hari* means "infinity," and *Om* is the sacred sound of God, so it can be translated as "infinite God." When morning came, he just walked away naked, doing "Hari Om," and he never wore clothes again. He just kept repeating, "Hari Om! Hari Om! Hari Om!"

The disciple invited me to his Temple of Silence in Firozpur. Why not? I had nowhere else to go. So we took the bus together to his home and his temple.

The Temple of Silence was in the back of his house, sealed off like a prison. It was really just a room with a wooden slab for a bed, an overhead fan, a latrine, a bucket, a small pot to pour water with, and an open water spout. In one corner sat a small picture of the fat, naked Guru Mota, with a candle in front of it. That was it.

We agreed that I would do a "retreat" in this empty room. I needed to clear my head, to figure out what the hell was going on. My new friend locked me in his temple for two weeks. He would bring me food twice a day, slipping it through a space under the door. I would hear "Hari Om!" and I'd answer "Hari Om!" and my meal would appear. That was our only communication for two weeks.

Piece by piece, I began to unravel as the days passed. I finally fell apart completely and started crying—not just a few tears, but buckets full—as my life began to turn inside out.

Everything caught up with me, and my whole life came tumbling down: the continuous, bitter conflict with my parents; the vacuous life in California; the pervasive sense that something vitally important was missing in my life; and the drug holiday in Greece I had taken with an avant garde community of artists who told me that I could find good hashish cheap in India. I was a wreck.

With all that time alone, I was forced to think about the events that had led me there.

Chapter 2

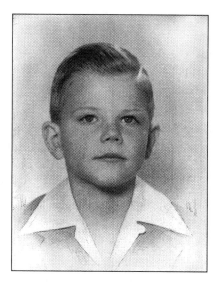

I WAS BORN Michael Riggs, and my pilgrimage began in my backyard.

I had a very intense mother who adored and worshiped me and did everything for me. She wouldn't let me do anything on my own. It was always, "Get out of the kitchen. You'll make a mess!"

I spent much of my time in the backyard of our house in suburbia, fantasizing about taking my musical and artistic talents on the road. It was the 1950s, and I didn't fit in. I liked being outside, isolated, solitary, with my bow and arrow, climbing trees, being a nature boy. Everyone else around had a mantra that made no sense to me: "I like Ike."

Eisenhower had been elected, and the postwar spirit was raging throughout the country. Everything was affordable. Imagine, a brand new four-bedroom house for $17,000. A brand new Pontiac Bonneville for $3,400 and gasoline for 12 cents a gallon. This was the American dream—you could have whatever you wanted. Incredible abundance! Suburbia was born.

My family was Episcopalian, and going to church was a regular part of my life. My father went into a trance when he prayed. He took church very seriously and saw nothing social about it. He taught me how to pray, how to feel the prayer. For Mom, church was about dressing up and going out to breakfast.

An introvert, living in my imaginative world, I couldn't connect with the American dream. I was completely obsessed by finding the meaning of life. All this modernism was superficial to me. I was interested in ancient cultures and civilizations.

When I was sixteen, I had a love affair with Dorothy. Dorothy was seventy-three years old and owned a book shop on Balboa Island. She wore flowered polyester dresses and high-heeled shoes. Her thick-lens glasses made her eyes look like those of an owl. She wore lots of make-up and had frizzed-out hair. She chain-smoked cigarettes and drank coffee nonstop.

Dorothy knew everything about every author and every book that was ever written—she just knew everything about everything! I could hardly wait to get out of school, go to the bookstore, and sit with Dorothy and smoke my pipe. There was this incredible electricity between us. She told me about Gertrude Stein, Hemingway, T.S. Eliot, William Blake, and Yeats.

Dorothy introduced me to James Joyce. I read *Ulysses* and did a term paper on *Finnegans Wake*. I knew then that I had to go to Ireland someday, to see Joyce's world and find my own Irish heritage. Dorothy really blessed me with the knowledge she imparted. While the big bands and jazz were the rage, I listened to classical and folk. And I found television to be full of slapstick and absurd, stupid people.

Once, when I was sixteen, I came home drunk at three o'clock in the morning. I pulled into the wrong garage, closed the wrong garage door, walked into the wrong house, and opened the door to my room—which I found out was the wrong room.

When I left this house I had a revelation: everything was the same. All the houses were exactly the same. Everyone had the same car, the same garage, the same floor plan—and probably similar moms and dads. I knew I had to find a place where people lived differently. I began wandering in my mind because I felt so stifled by my predictable life and the culture. I was looking for roots and didn't see any in America. I felt that there was nothing here for me.

I remember as a little boy asking my mother where I came from. Her answer was, "The stork." I was only five. I dreamt that night of storks swooping down, picking up babies, and dropping them off at different houses. Her answer didn't feel right, but if I accepted it I was convinced that the stork brought me to the wrong house.

A man called "The Greeter" had a tremendous influence on me. He was a big man, like I am now, with a beard that went down past his waist, and he had long, matted hair. He would stand on the side of the highway and wave, greeting people all day, every day.

He would beg for food. He lived in the woods in a cave in Laguna Canyon. He was a hermit and a true earth person.

As a little kid, I was completely fascinated by him and his lifestyle. He was like nothing else going on in America, and I liked that.

ॐ

AT EIGHTEEN, I left home in search of the Holy Grail. I was driven to discover something, and that something was not in America. I was determined to find it, wherever it was.

Problems in Vietnam had begun heating up. JFK was shot. I left one month later. I felt like an expatriate—tired of the American ways. I just wanted out. My parents didn't have much to say about my leaving.

I sold my guitar in Laguna Beach for $200. I hitchhiked, with the money in my sock, to New York.

One quick look told me that I wouldn't find what I was looking for in Manhattan, but I hung out for a while on the Lower East Side. I experienced the bohemian way of life and found good music and art shared by all kinds of artists.

I bought a ticket on a German freighter called the SS *Klaus Olendorf* and started my journey to Rotterdam. It cost me $160. The three weeks I spent on this boat were a very important part of my pilgrimage. I didn't speak German, and only a few Americans were on board. I had no parents, no friends. I was totally alone, and I liked it.

I spent most of my time staring at the sky and the ocean, into which my subconscious merged. Hour after hour I stared, mesmerized by the blue, tuning out the noise of the freighter. My eyes were focused on the horizon for three weeks—sky-mind, wind-mind, water-mind, star-mind. Stars, wind, water, sky—that was the mantra I was meditating, and I didn't even know it. It was my first mantra and my first experience meditating. It was occurring naturally.

We arrived at Rotterdam but couldn't get into port because of all the ice on the ocean. Ice cutters had to be used to get through—1963 was one of the coldest winters in European history.

I got to England and ran out of money, so I hitchhiked everywhere. I slept in train station bathrooms, which were filthy but warm. I'd sit on the toilet and eventually fall asleep.

I wanted to go to Ireland to find my spiritual roots, as well as James Joyce's. I ended up at Joyce's writing tower and museum. In it were his glasses and walking stick. Looking at these relics, I felt I had received a blessing and that it was a sign for me to continue my journey. His blessing gave me the green light to move on. It was as though Joyce had said to me, "Keep walking and seeing—look deep." Now I had something more to go on than blind faith.

I traveled to Scotland, where I had my first transcendental experience. I went to a place in Edinburgh called Arthur's Seat, a hill where, according to legend, Arthur had withdrawn a magic sword from a rock and been named king.

It was a very windy day and I was all alone when I went to see this rock. When I got there I felt faint and swooned, landing on my back.

I left my body, for the first time in my life, and went up to the sky.

I became a cloud, a part of the vast sky.

I returned to my body about three hours later. I wasn't afraid and felt totally relaxed.

What did this out-of-body experience mean? Had I almost died? And, if so, of what? Maybe I was hallucinating—but from what? I finally decided to just accept the experience for what it was: an experience. Today, I consider it to have been the first of many spiritual awakenings. Joyce would have been pleased with my epiphany.

ॐ

I MADE MY way to London and stayed with some people from New Zealand. There I smoked pot for the first time. Stoned, I swayed with the Indian music that was playing. I really connected with it. I knew then that I had to go to India. The consciousness of the sitar was pulling me there.

I was a musician following the muse, and the drug. My plan was to go to India, buy as much hashish as I wanted, and then take a train to Kashmir and rent a houseboat. I imagined floating around all day while the hashish smoke billowed out of my ears.

I begged my way around Europe for a year. I ended up in Spain for a while because I had to get warm. During this amazing pilgrimage through different countries, wherever I went, people fed me and took care of me out of the kindness of their hearts. I was open and ready to receive whatever was going to happen.

ॐ

BY THE TIME I got to India, I was a mess, praying and begging for answers. I felt that they were within, but I didn't know how to get there.

In the barren Temple of Silence, there was only me. My world, as I had known it, had been erased. No TV, no pot, and no girls. So I just sat very still with my eyes wide open. Then, when I finally closed my eyes, my conscious meditation began.

EVERYTHING IN INDIA was God. What materialism was to America, God was to India. Everyone was worshiping, and I couldn't go ten feet without running into a temple.

I knew that I, too, had to find God, but where to begin? What would it take for me to become enlightened? For that matter, what did enlightenment really involve? What was spiritual truth?

In the Temple of Silence, I sat for hours and hours looking within and watching my mind. I'd sail into flights of ecstasy and feel the fluttering of wings. Then I'd feel an incredible awakening of energy within me. I was breathing in the mist I remembered from the Golden Temple, the all-enveloping cloud of God's love. Then I'd realize how completely alone I was. I would burst into tears and cry for hours, sobbing and sobbing. Then I would find the peace again.

A little pamphlet on the floor described a kriya yoga breathing technique called *hamsa*. I inhaled "Ham" and exhaled "Sa," visualizing the Sanskrit letters *ha* and *sa*. I had a beautiful vision of a white swan landing on a lake in the snow. These ocean-of-light experiences were very peaceful.

For two weeks, all I had was mind, breath, and tears.

I sat in the lotus posture for as long as I could and kept turning within, looking at my interior world. I'd always come back to my breath, breathing in "Ham" and breathing out "Sa." "Hamsa" is the natural sound the breath makes as it flows in and out. Breath becomes a curtain of energy, waving back and forth. In the middle of the curtain is a gap where eternity is experienced. I was getting these little glimpses of eternity as they came through the gap in my breath.

At one point I started crying out "Hari Om!" over and over. It was like I was calling God on the telephone and getting no answer. I just kept dialing and dialing and dialing. The hours were long as I lay on my back watching the fan go round and round, waiting to hear from God. Profound moments of bliss and peace would alternate with the deepest emotional pain I'd ever felt.

Food was a big deal because it was the only thing happening in my space. So when the food came, I was in awe of it. There was so much love in the meals this man brought to me. The life force in the food and the sacredness of the preparation of the food had become God. This was the first time I experienced food as God.

One day two weeks later, the door opened. I had just had my bucket bath, and I stood still for a moment before walking toward the door. There were at least fifty women with flower garlands standing outside. They touched my feet and started worshiping me. Then they started waving camphor lamps in circles in front of me as if I were a deity or a guru. They put three leis around my neck, and I went into complete bliss. I had never been so happy. It was then that I thought I realized my position in life: I was in saint school and I was going to be a saint! The devotion offered by these women made me feel that I had finally found my purpose. Yes, I would be a saint and must continue my pilgrimage. There was obviously so much for me to learn.

But by dusk, I became deathly sick. I had dysentery and could barely move.

ॐ

I WAS TAKEN to another house, where I would be cared for by an Indian woman who had six grown sons. They took me upstairs and put me in her bed—the best bed in the house. I had a very high fever for three days.

My caretaker wore a huge gold nose ring and was constantly in the kitchen cooking. Every morning and every evening this Divine Mother would put my head in her lap and rub my brow and love me. I had never experienced such love. I was being nurtured and loved like I'd never been by my own mother.

As I started recovering, I had questions. Why was everyone being so kind to me? Why did this strange woman take me in like her own son and hold my head in her lap? When I'd look up, her eyes would smile back at mine. I felt I had truly died and come back to life. This feeling of having such a connection with another human soul was unbelievable.

As I came out of the sickness, I would sit in the kitchen with this woman. She would cook me delicious meals. It was so simple. I had become part of the family. We were all one. I knew that I was her son.

Her sons would come in and eat. Everyone was concerned about me. It was all so heartful, so effortless. So natural. I was completely reborn in that house.

This was the first time that I was aware that I had come in contact with the Divine Mother. I was healed because she gave me her energy and juiced me with her life force. Every night and every morning, she took me to her breast and made love to me with her heart. I was seeing the Divine Mother in operation. She wasn't just some mystical concept or philosophical ideal.

THE DIVINE MOTHER is the love behind life's energy that pulsates inside and outside us. She is the stone, the rock—the seat upon which we sit. She is the table upon which we lay our hand. Divine Mother is our hand; she is our fingers. She is the body of all creation. The Divine Mother breathes us, and we are her breath.

She is manifested in everything but most focused in women. In fact, women are the embodiment of her form. She can be Divine Mother the nurturer. She can be Kali Ma, the creator and destroyer. She can be Sarasvati, the mistress of detail. And she can be Lakshmi, the abundance of life.

ॐ

WHEN IT WAS time for me to go, I left Firezpur with many tears. But I needn't have cried. The Divine Mother would be waiting for me at every stop along the way.

Chapter 3

I GOT ON a bus for New Delhi in search of a Sufi saint named Rehanna, whom I had heard about from a junkie I'd gotten high with in Greece. This saint supposedly had been a woman who was part of Mahatma Gandhi's entourage.

I had never met a saint. I was excited, not knowing what to expect.

During the trip I was missing my "mother" in Firezpur, her wonderful food, and the sense of family she gave me. As the bus bumped along, I started thinking of my granny, who had adopted my mother.

Granny wore her hair in a bun and had little wire-rimmed glasses. She made meals for us that tasted like nectar—pure ambrosia from God. We ate rhubarb pie, roasted chicken, corn on the cob, okra, mashed potatoes—all fresh food. Granny was Norman Rockwell Americana come to life.

As far as I was concerned, Granny had been my mother. She lived in the house next door to ours, and until she died I lived with her, ate with her, prayed with her, and slept with her. Granny was everything to me. I preferred her to my mom, who was cool, detached, and fussy. Granny was like an Earth Mother. Her devotion to me was so intense it was profound, like I was God to her. She loved God and the Bible. Granny would rock me as she prayed to Jesus in tongues and read passages from the Bible. She would spend hours gazing into my eyes, telling me how much she loved me. I would doze off in her arms in this cloud of love, at peace, as she prayed.

One day when I was six years old, Granny was going Christmas shopping. I wanted to go with her, but she wouldn't let me. What if I saw her surprise for me? Still, I ran into the street, crying and begging her to take me with her. Granny stopped the car, backed up to the curb, and comforted me. She kissed me on the forehead and tied my shoe before she got back in the car and took off.

She was killed later that day when another car hit hers.

I missed her so much, I couldn't believe it. She had been my whole life. When our eyes met, I became her baby Jesus. No one else in my family showered me with such affection. When my granny died, there seemed to be no life for me anymore. The emptiness pushed me into an introverted state that would color the rest of my life and lead me on my spiritual quest.

THE BUS STOPPED in Delhi and I got out. Two more crowded buses would take me to the vicinity of Rehanna's small apartment complex. I was greeted by a very small woman with a cloth tied around her neck, worn like saints do. She embraced me and said, "My son, you've come at last," and kissed me on the forehead. Something happened in that kiss. It was so matter-of-fact, and yet there was a transference—an inner reality opened up to me. An incredible sense of stillness came over me. My anxieties about what to do, where to go, what to be—all of it seemed to disappear. That kiss erased an intense longing I had but was never able to name.

The little rug on which she said her prayers was her whole temple. That was all there was. She had a very small room, with no pictures on the walls.

Rehanna had a real glow. I felt happy just being with her.

I wanted to know what being a saint was. Rehanna said, "You should go to Rishikesh because that's the city of saints. You will find what you are looking for there." I wanted her to show me what to do, tell me how to live—what to do now that I had decided I was going to be a saint.

But nothing more was said. I sat in silence with her. It was the first time I experienced such stillness with another person—no anxiety to talk, to fill up space. The space was already full—of silence.

Rehanna catapulted me into a deep inner space, reaffirming what I had experienced in the Temple of Silence. Her energy was transferred to me. I understood how deeply, inwardly directed she was—she was so full that she needed nothing from the external world.

At that moment, I was completely loved. How could it be? Rehanna didn't know me. It shattered my rational mind and blew it out. Therefore, I was able to receive her blessing and the peacefulness that came with it. It was bliss.

ॐ

I LEARNED THEN that the very nature of the Self is bliss. When we experience through our senses—good food, beautiful things, wonderful sensations—we get a spillover of bliss from our own Self. Those little glimmers of happiness come from within and occur throughout the course of our lives.

ॐ

SUDDENLY, BUT WITHOUT breaking the stillness, Rehanna spoke. She leaned forward, looking deeply into the mirror of peace she had wiped clean inside of me, and whispered, "Go to Rishikesh."

I went directly from Rehanna's to the bus station. I had 50 rupees, my passport in a bag over my shoulder, my cloth, and some flip-flops. It was a very long, five-hour bus ride. The bus was small, the seats were hard. It was packed with people. There was nothing I could do except sit and take it all in.

ॐ

I ARRIVED IN Rishikesh with the monsoon rains. Nothing but water everywhere, rivers and rivers of water. Rishikesh is in the foothills of the Himalayas, so all around are sharp, jagged rocks. Hills and trees are in the landscape, and the Ganges River curves around the corner of the city like a crescent moon.

A ricksha wallah dropped me off at the Shivananda ashram. I remember walking down a dark, deserted corridor into the ashram. I opened the doors into a huge place where you do *darshan*—receive a guru's blessing and perform spiritual rituals. A few candles were lit, and a bald swami was sitting in the corner. He leapt up and hugged me.

"Welcome! You've come! Come in!"

All this attention was confusing me. Who was I? Why did everyone know me? What was going on? I felt so loved, and it felt so good that I decided not to question it.

In the ashram were pictures of a huge, fat man with lines painted across his forehead, sitting on a tiger skin. The image was surreal—very strange and yet strangely familiar. The man's name was Shivananda, and he had died a few years earlier.

Why all the pictures of this man, and why did the swamis hang garlands over them with so much love and respect? I didn't understand then that the divine could be embodied in a human being. To Shivananda's devotees, their late master was *gurudeva:* pure, radiant, divine wisdom. I didn't know what to make of it.

Later, I went to the ashram bookstore and was shocked to discover that Shivananda had written over three hundred books on every conceivable aspect of spirituality. I was given a room and settled in for the night with some of his books. As I read, the Ganges sang to me some faraway song that I felt I'd heard somewhere before.

In the morning I had a sunlit view of Rishikesh. Although there was plenty to see, I went down to connect with the river first. I wanted to experience this living deity, with which I was already in love. I just sat by her, staring at her and feeling the energy of her presence. Then I started swimming in her. I would jump in and swim all the way out to the middle. She has a strong current, which I would let carry me for miles. Then I'd get out, walk back, and jump in again.

When I was swimming in the Ganges I felt like a being was carrying me in her arms. I was embraced with loving, liquid energy and light, an all-encompassing intimacy. As I got out of the river, the Indians would touch my feet and bow to me.

The Ganges is huge, and it is the spiritual current of India. Indians bathe in it, pray in it, and cry in it. They throw the remains of their dead in it, and many choose to die in it. Yet they don't purposely swim in it because they're afraid; they're terrified of who could be out there. It was said that a very famous holy man, reported to be as old as three hundred years, had been seen floating on a corpse, using it as a raft. I saw bodies float by, but I wasn't afraid. They were a natural part of the river. The Indians would walk into the river holding onto chains anchored at the riverbank. They prayed and chanted to the river out of devotion.

The Ganges water has amazing properties. It can be bottled for twenty years and still not have bacteria growing in it, which is something scientists have never been able to explain. Everyone in India agrees simply that the Ganges is a holy river. I believe that the vibrations of the bones of the dead sanctify the river.

The Ganges was my deity while I was in Rishikesh, and to this day I still worship her. I wear her on my head inside my bun. On top of my skull I have a little glass tube of Ganges water with my guru's picture wrapped around it. I wear the sacred vibration of the river on my skull.

After I swam and bathed in the Ganges every morning, I would immerse myself in the festivities of Rishikesh. In this city of saints, holy men, and yogis, all Hindu religious traditions, as well as many spiritual freelance forms, were represented. Food was offered at all the big ashrams, of which at that time there were at least thirty or forty. All I had to do was stand in line with my bowl before the food bucket, and people would feed me and anybody else who walked up. And it didn't cost a rupee.

Imagine a nonstop, gigantic religious festival, and you're in

Rishikesh. Think of it as festive, spiritual fervor. Loudspeakers blared all over the place, garbled mantras and chanting always loud and distorted.

Pilgrims came in bands of fifty to one hundred people—old ladies and old men with bundles on their heads. They seemed so poor and yet so happy. I enjoyed watching them.

I was truly amazed at Rishikesh: ashrams, temples, restaurants, and bazaars full of every kind of religious paraphernalia you could ever imagine (and plenty you could never even conceive of: I saw a stick with a depression at the top to hold your chin up during long hours of meditation, another stick to poke into your armpit to make one nostril open and the other close).

Thousands of holy men were there, dressed in all kinds of robes. It was the first time I saw "ropeheads," yogis with matted hair. It was strange to see people with ten feet of matted hair hanging from them. After not having been combed for years, human hair becomes like an old blanket. Personally, I liked the look. And what I liked even more was that you could be naked, too! There were no rules.

All kinds of garish-looking statues of deities were there, decked out in real clothes and jewelry. People bowed before them, dropped money in the collection box, and took tilaks, red dabs of powder on the forehead.

THE TILAK SIGNIFIES the opening of the third eye, located on the forehead. By opening the third eye, the energy of light is put in the spiritual eye. What we see with our other eyes is not as important as what we see with our third eye. When you see a tilak on someone's forehead, your eyes go directly into that dot. At that moment, you put energy into the light behind the person's third eye—the inner light of the brain.

ॐ

I GOT INTO the tilak practice, applying a dab of wet red powder to the center of my forehead every morning after my bath in the Ganges. Whenever I put the tilak on I would think of Rehanna's lips. I would feel her kiss on my forehead as I placed the dot there. Emotionally, I was reenacting my sacred moment with her.

I liked the tilak ritual, but worshiping the statues seemed strange to me. They were like colorful cartoon characters, not beautiful, powerful statues. Yet I respected the devotion of the people to them. I thought all these people were enlightened. My view was that everyone in India was spiritual, and I found it unbelievable. I never deviated from this belief. I knew I was in the land of saints. I even felt it from the river.

Some people go to India and see the ragged body. I saw India's soul.

Chapter 4

THE HINDU CULTURE strongly supports people doing spiritual work, so the ashrams were like free hotels for holy men and lay pilgrims. People would often make donations to ashrams and pilgrim hostels. Even a 1-rupee donation, which was about 10 cents at the time, went a long way.

One day as I sat beside the river, a fellow pilgrim named Ravi Das stopped by and told me, "I'm staying at Maharishi Mahesh Yogi's ashram and the food is incredible. The accommodations are much better than Shivananda's. I've even got my own room." (Maharishi Mahesh Yogi, a disciple of Guru Dev, the founder of Transcendental Meditation [TM], introduced the practice of TM to the West.)

I took the ferry across the Ganges with Ravi Das. Maharishi Mahesh's ashram was built up above the water but not far—we could see it from the river.

Maharishi was sitting in a tiny room overlooking the Ganges. I watched a devotee with a bouquet of flowers throw himself on the ground in full prostration before him. I had never seen anyone do that before. All this devotion for this little, giggling man?

Maharishi had a big beard and black hair. He was rocking back and forth, playing with his beads and laughing as if the universe was one hilarious joke.

The people at his ashram gave me a really nice room. Over my bed was mosquito netting, but the mosquitoes were still ferocious. I would go to bed, pull the net over me, and then sit up to kill all the mosquitoes inside the net with me. This took at least a half-hour each night, with a flashlight.

The Maharishi people asked me if I wanted to be initiated. I didn't know what that meant. They explained that I would be given a mantra and would be taught how to meditate. I thought, "Great! This is exactly what I want." I was told to take a bath, not to eat, and to bring a coconut and flowers.

At the appointed time, I walked into a small room where Maharishi was sitting. We sat quietly for a few moments, and then he looked at me and said, "Your mantra is 'Ram,' which means 'the fire of God.' You will sit quietly every day, at least twice a day for twenty minutes, and mentally repeat your mantra over and over again. Any time a distracting thought enters, you will push it out of your mind with your mantra." He was instructing me in transcendental meditation.

Then he said, "All women are your mother." I didn't understand what he meant. At the time I didn't like my mother. I had run away from her! It became my koan—my mind puzzle.

I didn't understand then the meaning of the Divine Mother, but that day Maharishi started me on her path. To me, she is all creation that takes form in life, and she is present in all things. She is the active energy of the universe that becomes form. In the West, this energy is often called "God," a masculine God. In India, this energy is feminine—she is the mother of all things earthly and spiritual.

The Divine Mother is the fruit of persistent prayer. And praying means becoming completely lost in the feeling, letting devotion take us to her. Through prayer, a transformation occurs. The more you practice, the sooner it will come. Her essence is one of pure love. In my experience of the Divine Mother, I am in a transformed state. I'm floating in space, and I'm in ecstasy. I feel completely safe while having this incredible feeling of happiness, of eternal bliss.

Kali Ma is one of the many faces of the Divine Mother, the great divine feminine spirit. In fact, according to Hindu tradition, we are living in the Kali Age, a time of resurgence of this divine feminine spirit. Although Kali is most often presented in her warrior aspect as cruel and horrific, she is also the creator and nurturer. This is the essence of Mother love and feminine energy, as she brings worlds to birth, sustains them, and absorbs them in a never-ending cycle.

I stayed with Maharishi for two months, praying and meditating all day. My purpose was to sit as long as I could. Meditation was really working for me. The inward-drawn atmosphere of India was bringing me deeper and deeper into my mantra and closer to the Divine Mother.

(People in India are very self-contained and at peace with themselves. Their interior lives are much more pronounced than their exterior lives.)

ॐ

ONE DAY WHEN I woke up, I wasn't feeling very well. I looked in the mirror—my eyes were bright yellow.

I was extremely worried and tried to find a doctor or pharmacy. I walked toward the bazaar, asking people where to go for medicine. A little boy who came with me as a translator took me to a person sitting in front of the bazaar with a supply of different-colored bottles. This apothecary looked at me and then took out a tiny scrap of paper and wrote down a mantra. He folded the paper into a little wad and handed it to me.

"Go throw it in the Ganges," he said. He didn't ask for any money. It was all so matter-of-fact and direct.

I took the piece of paper and threw it into the Ganges, thinking, "No one will help me. This is really crazy. No one will help me." I was having an American-style anxiety attack. I was sure that I was going to die.

I walked back to the ashram in this state. When I got back to my room and looked in the mirror, I saw that my eyes were as white as eggshells. I was incredibly relieved and inspired. All I could think of was how spiritual this culture was. Everyone was spiritual. The children knew everything, the old folks knew everything, and the river healed me. I didn't even have faith, yet the apothecary's mantra still worked. If someone wrote a mantra on a piece of paper and it could heal, what would happen if I wrote it on my heart? I was inspired to go deeper with my mantra.

I didn't have much to do with the whole Transcendental Meditation scene, because I was meditating on my own all the time. I'd sometimes spend time with one swami, who sang a beautiful Krishna chant ("Sri Krishna Govinda Hare Murare He Nath ta Narayana Vasudeva"). It was so beautiful that I'd sit and sing with him. I was happy and thirsty for more, wanting to go deeper and deeper. But nobody was asking how my meditation was going or whether I was ready for the next step. I really needed to talk to someone and find out what to do.

ONE DAY WHILE I was taking a bath, someone mentioned that a saint named Tatwalla Baba lived nearby. I took the trail behind Rishikesh up the mountain a mile or two until the twisting path opened into a clearing of caves. Tatwalla Baba was sitting in front of one of these enormous holes in the rock. He glowed. The most incredible bright light was literally gleaming from his skin. And he had long, matted hair down to his feet.

Tatwalla Baba lived in a beautiful, multichambered cave that extended for several levels, like giant stairs. On one level he kept his little stove (called a *dhuni),* and on another level he had his meditation seat. He offered me a cave to live in.

I left the comfortable ashram and moved up into the hills. The caves there were primordial and beautiful. Maharishi's ashram had been so new and modern, with so much construction going on every minute. He was building huge, underground, cement caves, which was a noble effort, but his space couldn't compare with a cocoon re-cessed into a mountain. Sitting in a living cave automatically threw me into meditation. A real cave could enfold my body and liberate my soul.

Up at the caves, holy men (sadhus) hung around totally naked, taking baths in the waterfalls. Tatwalla didn't talk. He just sat and smiled. He had the most beautiful eyes—they had so much love in them. He was broadcasting love while sitting silently in his cave.

It was spring all the time in his presence. His vivid spiritual life gave life to the nature around him. The cool cave walls reverberated with the mantras resonating in his heart. "Now this," I thought, gazing at the radiant stillness, "is a real saint."

Chapter 5

I SPENT A month in my cave, meditating for sixteen hours a day. I did my mantra and practiced Transcendental Meditation. I learned that everything is inside, that nothing is outside of me but my own desires. I could chase my desires endlessly and would get nothing but more desires. And they would never be satisfied. But now, I had the breath and the word. And there is nothing but the breath and the word of God, which is "Ram." With these two elements I was able to enter an inner chamber of light and bliss. I compare it to the oneness of the ultimate, perfect sexual moment, when all is still.

With my newfound knowledge, I felt that the time had come to leave Rishikesh. So I climbed on a bus. I didn't know where the bus was going, but I had faith that God did. Another sadhu, dressed in white with long black hair, sat down next to me and took my hand like he was family. He explained how yogis and holy men traveled and how people gave them free food so they could focus exclusively on their inner practices. If you meditated a lot, people in India felt that you were doing good work that benefits everyone. You purified the psychic airwaves, so they took care of you. (It's not like in the United States, where, when people hear you're focusing on a spiritual life, they roll their eyes and tell you to get a job.) In India, being a full-time meditator is a job, which comes with a great benefits package.

When we got to Dehra Dun, the sadhu got off the bus and invited me to meet his swami. I went with my fellow holy man to a small ashram that had a little garden around it. We went in, and there sat a short, portly man with a nice belly, wearing orange clothes (even orange tennis shoes). He was a beautiful swami, with a shiny bald head. He had the same kind of glow Tatwalla Baba had. He had bright eyes and spoke perfect English. As I sat in front of him, he started telling me what to do.

"You are my student. You will stay with me. I will teach you what to do."

I was thrilled that, at last, someone would give me instruction. At the time, I had four rings on my fingers, a bell and some animal bones around my neck, and a couple earrings in my ears. He said to me, "Take those off."

I just sat there in front of him and took it all off. He gave me two white dhotis (loincloths) to wear, and I stayed with him for six months.

This was Swamiji Chaitanya Prakashananda Tirtha, and he turned out to be the best teacher I could possibly have found. God had known exactly where he was taking me to deepen my practice.

Swamiji told me what to do. I slept three hours a night and ate very little food. I had one glass of milk a day. In the evening I would eat one piece of bread and a cup of dhal (lentils).

My day began at three in the morning, and I would bathe and do hatha-yoga. Swamiji taught me how to hold the postures correctly and in what order to do the series. Then he would select one verse from the *Bhagavad-Gita* for me to contemplate all day.

He led a *satsang* (spiritual fellowship) for local devotees in the mid-morning while I sat humbly at his feet, struggling to understand the Hindi. It was an austere, but serene, existence. I thought, "Now I'm in the real Hindu world. This is how real Hindus live."

I HAD MY own little hut in the back garden. It was like living in the Garden of Eden. Jasmine flowers scented the air. Next door was a Shiva temple. I would stand transfixed, staring at the Shiva lingam (the lingam is a phallic symbol of the masculine cosmic principle). In India, you pick your own God to worship, and I was drawn to Shiva. I liked the way he looked. He was naked; he smoked dope.

Beyond appearances, Shiva is God the father—the creative force and an energy of deep veneration. He is also a male Kali—the energy of destruction and transformation. *Shiva* means "peace" and comes from the storm God Rudra, "the Howler." Shiva is a fierce divinity in the sense of the fierceness of the father. He's worshiped as the lingam, the sexual energy. He is the god of the humble—the poor, farmers, the land people. Dancers, actors, and musicians are also taken care of by Shiva.

I wish that I could tell you that I arrived in northern India with a profound appreciation for the spiritual splendor of Hindu philosophy, but the truth is that when I first got to India I didn't know a damn thing. I was dealing with the basics: I preferred Shiva to all other Gods because he had the coolest hairstyle.

I didn't understand anything other than that I should do the mantra Maharishi taught me and that I must meditate and serve Swamiji. I'd massage his feet and legs for two hours every night, from ten o'clock to twelve. When he'd start to snore, I could sneak out and try to get some rest.

In India, resting is not easy. For one thing, there was limited space. My hut had a crumbling, dirt floor the size of a closet. The bed was made from a wood frame with string cords of hemp across it. And I was tortured by bedbugs. To Swamiji, I may have been a spiritual aspirant, but to those bugs I was dinner. I'd wake up each morning with fresh welts all over my body, and my blood would be plastered all over the wall. When bedbugs bite you, they suck your blood; when you smack them, your blood splatters everywhere. But I was implacable—I fought to the last bite. I didn't get a lot of sleep, but that was okay because sleeping was not as important as meditation—a tortured body nourishes the spirit.

Bedbugs notwithstanding, I was very happy because Swamiji was teaching me all the rules, filling me in on protocol: "Don't put your fingers in your mouth. Wipe your bottom with your left hand. Don't eat while you walk." Our ashram was called Swarga Puri, City of Heaven. Swamiji and I lived alone in our little city. He was teaching me how to be a Hindu, and it felt just right.

I was in a very heightened state of awareness, alone most of the time in Swamiji's small ashram. I was continually contemplating God and the verses of the *Bhagavad-Gita,* soaking up the peaceful atmosphere.

Sometimes I would walk into town. Walking barefoot in India gave me a sense of contact with the Divine Mother. Her earth energy was in my soles. I vividly remember the smells of India—the spruce scent of the mountains, the musty odor of the ashram library and of the homes and shops in town. Everything is so old in India. It's very common to go into a tea stall that's been in business for 150 years and sit at a table where people have been drinking tea for generations. This ancient quality of India was all-pervading.

I could feel ancient India.

I could smell ancient India all around me.

ॐ

SWAMIJI HAD A fire altar on which he was constantly performing special rituals. It was mysterious, but he wanted to keep it simple for me. He'd tell me, "You don't need to know about this. It's not important for you." He'd be throwing grains into flames and reciting the Sanskrit text in front of him. I would sit there with him for hours, like a sponge, absorbing the sacred atmosphere. It all seemed so rich and sacred.

Knowledge I was gaining; food I was not. I was hungry all the time, while Swamiji ate huge meals. I wanted to excel. I was desperate to get to God. If this meant hunger pains, then that's what I'd endure.

Swamiji explained to me that I was a brahmachari and that living this strict, ascetic lifestyle would be helpful to me. Brahmachari traditionally means someone who is in a wondering state, and brahmacharya is this first stage of life when one is a student. One sits at the feet of one's guru under the tree, which is what I was doing, and he teaches. I would read stories in English that Vivekananda wrote about bhakti yoga and discuss it with Swamiji.

For the first time in my life, I read the Bible, too, from beginning to end. I was surprised to read of so many bloody battle scenes. I never understood why God was so violent until I understood that the battles are our own inner battles. It's not God; it's us.

All in all, it was a very spartan life, very simple. It was nice and clean and together. I stayed for six isolated months. It seemed to me that the folks at the Transcendental Meditation ashram in Rishikesh were so busy building their empire that they didn't have time for individual students, but I got lots of attention from Swamiji.

Swamiji taught me the ABCs of spiritual life. But the best teaching was his own experience. He was a man of immense integrity. To him, spirituality was more than inspiring lectures. He lived what he taught.

I really wanted to become enlightened, and I sincerely believed it was going to happen—I just didn't know when. It was at this time that I had an unbelievable experience at the ashram.

I'd just finished rubbing Swamiji's feet and put him to bed. I started to lie down on my bed when my whole mind exploded in light. And with the light came the most incredible orgasm throughout my whole body. It continued for five minutes. This was the most pleasurable thing I'd ever experienced in my life. Ultimate bliss.

Something changed when that happened. It was completely light, the brightest light. It was like waking up with the sun rising right in your face. The bliss was incredible, like a sexual orgasm that kept going from my head down to my toes and back up again. Every cell in my body came to attention. God was making love to me. I knew it was God, and I just wanted more. This was why I was here. This was it. I felt and saw God.

I got so excited, I didn't sleep that night. I went outside right away and sat down in full lotus position, wrapped in my blanket, as still as I could be. I entered the inner space.

ॐ

PEOPLE THINK THAT the experiences mystics describe are metaphorical or mythical. They're not. They are literal, physical experiences.

You can either read about these things or you can start a spiritual practice, beginning with something as simple as the basic yoga techniques Swamiji Prakashananda taught me. You can have extraordinary experiences yourself.

The Sanskrit word *prakashananda* means "bliss of divine light." Swamiji gave me the direct experience of his true inner nature that night. But his greatest gift was yet to come. He would take me to my guru, Neem Karoli Baba.

Chapter 6

THE PATH TO enlightenment is not a group trip. It's between you and God. This means you've got to go inside. The fewer external distractions and the more concentration you have, the easier it is to get there. When beginning an inward-directed practice, it's essential to spend some time in isolation. I did so in the

Temple of Silence. Although I didn't know it then, that was my beginning.

I don't see voluntary isolation happening in the West. Going inward is such a basic concept, but I don't see it happening much in our "New Age" today, aside from the occasional Tibetan-sponsored retreats where you do one practice for three years. We need to start going inside, even if we go for only three days. You retreat from the external to the internal. Until you learn to go inward, you will never know who you really are.

Until you have enough time and devotion to do a long retreat, pilgrimages are a good substitute because you never know whom you're going to meet.

ॐ

ONE MORNING SHORTLY after my blissful experience of feeling God, Swamiji came in and said, "We're going on a pilgrimage!"

A rich devotee drove up in a big, four-door, standard Indian car. Swamiji rode in the front seat and I rode in the back. Swamiji sat on a doily so as not to pick up vibrations from anyone else who might have sat there before.

We drove into the mountains to Ranikhet, where the wealthy devotee had rented a big mansion. Swamiji did a lot of spiritual practice there. One of his practices was to stop shaving, which is considered a significant austerity. I knew that one day soon I was going to have to shave my head and wear orange robes, but for now I still clung to my long hair and beard.

So I was in Ranikhet, in a beautiful mansion with comfy couches all over the place. I was instantly bored, but I was finally being offered good food. They had brought a cook, and I was off my diet of just one glass of milk a day.

We left Ranikhet a few days later and continued on into the Kummon mountains. We ended up in Naini Tal, which is about 7,000 feet up in the foothills, two and a half miles from Delhi. It had been one of the main hill stations for the British, who would hide up there when it got really hot in the plains. It looked like a Swiss chalet. (Today it's a big tourist attraction.)

There was a Muslim graveyard about two miles outside of town. On top of it was built a temple called Hanuman Girdi, the Fortress of Hanuman, where we stayed. All the temples in India are dharmsalas, waystations for pilgrims, with rooms for pilgrims and saints. We had a nice little room in the back.

I walked into the temple, where a twenty-foot tall, bright orange, papier-mâché monkey stood, opening up his chest. Inside his chest was a huge cavity with a piece of glass like a TV screen, and inside the TV were two little dolls. The boy doll had blue skin and the girl doll had fair skin.

This monkey was bizarre to me. People would worship this diety?

This monkey god had a long tail, and a big club in his hand. A fellow pilgrim explained the monkey by telling me the story from the *Ramayana*. The boy doll was the avatar Rama, who came to earth thousands of years ago to rescue the planet from the demon king Ravana. The girl doll was Sita, Rama's wife. When Ravana kidnapped Sita, the pure-hearted Prince Rama rushed to rescue her, but he couldn't do it alone. The monkey king's general, Hanuman, who was the son of the wind, volunteered to help. He jumped across the ocean from the southern tip of India all the way to Lanka, where Ravana was holding Sita captive.

Ravana was trying everything he could think of—from offering the most alluring presents to making the most blood-curdling threats—to persuade Sita to marry him. But in her heart Sita never, for one moment, stopped calling out to Rama.

Hanuman immediately returned to India to inform Rama that he had found his wife. A military expedition was quickly organized. Ravana had all kinds of advanced technology, including flying chariots, but Rama and his band of monkeys conquered Ravana and set Sita free.

Hindus understand that Sita represents the human soul, captured by the demon of egotism, tempted by all the allurement of the world and yet terrified of the disappointment, disease, and death that always come with it. Though she's held captive in the demon's garden, the soul never forgets her true husband, Rama—God himself.

The yogic meaning of the story is that God loves the soul more than anything, but he can't rescue her alone. He needs the help of the son of the wind—the breath. When God and the breath become allies, they're able to free the soul. Calming the breath makes the body calm down, and then the mind becomes calm. When the mind is calm, you are able to sense God's presence in your heart.

The mythological meaning is that when a devotee loves God, like Hanuman loved Rama, there's nothing he or she can't accomplish with God's grace—even jumping over the ocean.

For thousands of years, Hanuman has been honored from one end of India to the other because he was the perfect devotee. If you look in his heart, you will always find God. Every moment of his life, with every breath he took, Hanuman chanted the holy name: "Rama, Rama, Rama, Rama!"

Next to Hanuman was a skinny sadhu. I liked his outfit better than Swamiji's. In India, different regiments of sadhus wear different types of uniforms; it's the spiritual equivalent of the air force, navy, or marines. Swami Prakashananda was in the bald-headed, orange-robed corps. But this sadhu was with those who wore the homespun white dhoti and blanket, with long matted hair and beard. I took note immediately: a branch of renunciates that didn't have to cut off their hair!

The sadhu was a muni, a yogi whose practice of austerity includes complete silence. For the previous twelve years, whenever he wanted to communicate, he would jot his thoughts down succinctly on a small chalkboard. His name was Hari Das Baba.

I told Hari Das Baba what I was doing and showed him the hatha-yoga postures I'd been practicing. I was showing off, and he was acknowledging me and gently correcting me. We sat up and talked most of the night. He wrote in perfect English on his slate. I didn't know it that night, but we would become close friends for the next six years, and very soon we wouldn't need the slate at all. Our conversations would become telepathic, thought to thought. It was easy to connect with him that way.

The next day Swamiji and I fasted and did a special purging practice. We drank huge quantities of salt water and made ourselves vomit it all back up. Yogis do these types of inner washes to purify their digestive and respiratory systems. Then I'd walk past the temple and see the monkey statue again. I thought it was so hokey, but at the same time there was something compelling about the image: God as an animal tearing open his heart to show us the pure divinity within. I sat with the statue for a while, then went outside to drink salt water and throw up again.

I was getting good at these cleansing techniques. I would stick a thick string up my nose and pull it out of my mouth. I would swallow rags and pull them up again, churning my stomach one way and then the other, and then scrape my tongue clean. I showed Hari Das Baba how I did these kriyas, and he helped me perfect my technique.

I sensed a little competition between him and Swamiji. Swamiji was a scholar, a book man, while Hari Das was the real thing, a cave yogi.

My practice for six months had been as Swamiji's servant, the run-and-fetch man, getting him tea and biscuits and then eating the scraps off his plate. I understood this form of practice. It's good to learn how to have a serviceful attitude, forgetting ourselves and focusing on making someone else comfortable. That's the one thing that all the great saints I met had in common: humility. They all had to have been in my place at one point in their lives.

We set out the next day back to Ranikhet, where we had rented a bungalow. We drove down the road into a valley called Kanchi. It was beautiful, sun swept, dipping from about 5,000 feet to 2,000 feet. A big river cut right through the valley. Near the bottom we noticed a temple off to the left. Swamiji asked the driver to stop by the tea stand and looked at me and said, "There's a saint here that I want to see." That was the only time I'd heard Swamiji use the word *saint.* He was still a saint in the making himself.

The temple was on the other side of the bridge. It was actually built over the cave of a very famous baba who had lived there earlier and was a highly advanced master. I peeked into the temple and there was Hanuman the monkey again, staring back at me from the wall. His face reminded me of my dog, who used to look at me in just the same way. It made me feel welcome. We rang the temple bell. Swamiji touched his head to the floor, and I did the same. (I didn't really feel anything, but I was concerned with protocol.)

I followed Swamiji down to another complex of cement buildings a short distance away. Five doors led into empty rooms. In the second room was a wooden cot, and sitting there was a little old man, wrapped up in a blanket, twinkling. It was like looking at a big, brilliant diamond in the sun. There was actually a visible light around his body. His name was Neem Karoli Baba, but his devotees called him Maharaji, "Great King."

I was completely awestruck. My mouth dropped open. Swamiji was really excited. I just stood there by the door and watched this saint. He was completely inwardly directed, and yet he carried on a conversation and laughed. His blanket kept slipping down, and he'd throw it back up.

It would fall down again, and he would throw it back up. He was moving his body continually, fidgeting like a monkey, scratching, looking around.

Swamiji bowed before him. When I went to bow, I felt so big that I stumbled over myself. I went right to his body and put my head on his leg. Maharaji threw his blanket over me and popped me on the head. At that moment, I had the same experience of light I had with Swamiji, the same sexual bliss. My whole body went into orgasm. It was even more intense this time because behind the light and physical bliss was total love. I'd just met the love of my life.

When I came back into my body I was very emotional, and I started to cry. It was embarrassing. Tears poured out of my eyes. Swamiji smiled. I realized that I still hadn't put Swamiji's seat down for him; I was holding his rug in my hands.

I put the carpet down, and then Maharaji moved over and signaled Swamiji, "Come here, sit next to me." I put the seat down next to Maharaji on the bench. Swamiji sat next to him. Maharaji was counting his mantra on the knuckles of his fingers. Swamiji took his hand. I was watching Swamiji worship him. Swamiji was so happy. They seemed to become one. I was beside myself with joy.

I knew at that moment that the romance was over with Swamiji. My mind was racing, and my entire being was quivering. I had to conceal my feelings.

When we got up to leave, Maharaji called after us, "Take *prasad* [food blessed by God], take *prasad!*" The devotees took us back to the Shiva temple, sat us down, and put leaf plates in front of us. There were ten hot, greasy puris (Indian fried bread) on each plate, with lentils and potatoes.

The last thing I wanted to do was eat. I was choking with emotion. Swamiji insisted, "Eat, eat. You must eat his *prasad.*"

The first bite was the most delicious food I had ever tasted in my life.

Suddenly it was as if I hadn't eaten in a year. I ate all of it effortlessly, even though I had a very small stomach since I wasn't eating much food in those days.

Afterward I gravitated right back to Maharaji's room. He said something to a man in Hindi, and the man looked up at me and said, "Maharaji says you love him very much." Tears flowed out of my eyes. I sobbed and sobbed. Maharaji was very happy. I ended up with my head on his leg again, and he was hitting me on top of the head. I was beside myself and couldn't stop crying.

Swamiji and I went back to the bungalow in Ranikhet the next day. I could not get Maharaji out of my heart. Twenty-four hours a day he was on my mind. The only thing that comes close to something like this is falling romantically in love. I just wanted to see him again and again; I wanted to know everything about him. But I was feeling terrible because of Swamiji—it was as if I were being unfaithful. What more can I say? I was swept away. This had never happened to me before or since.

Then Swamiji said to me, "It's time for me to initiate you. Tomorrow morning I'll give you a mantra."

He got up early the next day to make the appropriate offerings to the fire. I brought the offerings of flowers and fruit, just like I'd done with Maharishi. Swamiji gave me a mantra of the Divine Mother.

From Swamiji's perspective, we were back to our life together, but I was feeling distant from him. He didn't measure up anymore. He was a great man, he had no flaws, but I was in love with someone else. This situation was like being married to someone for a couple years and then meeting the person of your dreams. I struggled with the conflict of not wanting to hurt Swamiji but felt that I must be with this other person.

A major Hindu festival called the Kumbha Mela was coming up, and I knew Swamiji wanted me to go with him. He was going to initiate me into sannyasi, the renunciate tradition. He planned to name me Swami Shanti Prakashananda Tirth, which means "The Peaceful Abode of the

Light of Bliss Consciousness." I would become a swami and wear orange robes.

But I didn't want to wear orange robes and be bald. I wanted to have long hair and wear white, like Maharaji's disciple Hari Das Baba.

ॐ

WE WERE BACK in Dehra Dun in the ashram, and Swamiji could sense what I was going through. I was dissatisfied. I wanted more food. Swamiji had a goat brought to the ashram, so I had more milk. I was being pampered. Suddenly I got a new bed and was given three meals a day. This special attention was making me feel even more guilty. I was given new clothes and a new blanket. But regardless of all this, I couldn't stop thinking about Maharaji.

I had no money, but I still owned a diamond ring my father had given me when I was fifteen. I went to the bazaar and pawned it for 50 rupees, about $5. I was planning my escape. Swamiji went to bed at midnight and usually got up three hours later, which meant that I could slip out at two.

I didn't sleep that night, and I was trembling. At two o'clock, I started creeping out of the ashram. Each step took a long time. Just as I reached the Shiva temple next to Swamiji's house, I sensed something near me. I turned my head, looked down, and there were Swamiji's feet.

Swamiji was in his slippers, standing right in front of me. I threw my head down to his feet and started sobbing. Swamiji just stood there with this beautiful smile on his face and said, "I know. I know."

He'd known all along that I would be leaving. I had assumed he'd be hurt. But Swamiji was a real *sadhaka* (practitioner). He was established in his own divine light. There's no pettiness or jealousy in the light of the self. He simply smiled and gave me his blessing.

I caught the train to Naini Tal and walked up to Hanuman Girdi, and there was Hari Das Baba, expecting me. I said, "What's going on? Who is Neem Karoli Baba? I can't stop thinking about him. I've been crying for two weeks."

Hari Das Baba matter-of-factly wrote on his slate, "He is a great siddha," and erased it. A *siddha* is one who has attained perfection. Then he wrote, "He has opened your heart."

Chapter 7

Neem Karoli Baba had opened my heart.

All I wanted to do was be with Maharaji, my guru. And Maharaji seemed delighted to see me. I was so happy to be near his body. He had the most beautiful fragrance you've ever smelled. It was like the top of a newborn baby's head. It took me out of my senses.

He gave me a beautiful room by the river and a nice wooden cot with no bedbugs. And then he started making fun of Swamiji. He said, "So what did Swamiji feed you?"

"One glass of milk a day."

Maharaji gave out a deep belly laugh. Then he asked, "What did Swamiji eat?"

I said, "Ten chapatis and four helpings of dhal."

Maharaji ordered his people to give me a blanket and cloth to wear, and lots of food. I sat right in front of him all the time. I was so high being with him. I was ecstatic.

He'd be kibitzing with other people, just hanging out talking about day-to-day things.

"How's the wife?"

"How's the car?"

"How's the child?"

He never talked about anything spiritual, but I worshiped him. There was no difference between worshiping Maharaji as God and worshiping the Divine Mother.

ॐ

THERE ARE TWO energies: the Father and the Mother. The Father is the formless and the Mother is the form. We worship God the Father, but we don't give God a form. We don't know what God looks like. But the Mother is all form. So worshiping Maharaji's body as God was worshiping the Divine Mother. Maharaji was "Ma."

ॐ

I GOT A little picture of Maharaji and made an altar in my room. Now I had God. I knew without a doubt that Maharaji was God. I would sit in my room in front of his picture and meditate when I was not sitting with him in person.

Nobody knew where Maharaji was from. He just showed up around 1955 or so in the Kummon mountains. Some people claimed to have known him for fifty years. There was always this mystery around who he was, where he came from, and how old he was. He looked like he was anywhere from eighty to a hundred, but he moved like a twenty-year-old man. He was not feeble in any sense. You got the feeling he could pick up a whole mountain and hold it up in the air. Many thought he was an incarnation of the monkey god Hanuman. Some said they'd seen his body grow really huge, and others claimed they'd seen him shrink down very small. And then there were those who swore they'd seen him with a tail.

Maharaji kept me with him continuously for six months. I went everywhere with him. When he traveled in a car, I'd be in the back seat while he rode in the front. We would make the rounds of all the different devotees' houses. There were always feasts. I gained twenty pounds those first few months.

Everyone was always so happy to see Maharaji. The moment he'd arrive, the festival would begin. All the mothers would get the pots of curry going, and the food would start happening as the tea was poured. It was all so happy and festive! I went from being in a cloistered monastery to living a total lay life in one leap.

Maharaji was completely in the world, just like Jesus. He was in the bazaar all the time, mingling with his devotees. He would walk through their houses and eat everyone's food. I was barefoot, had my white clothes on, carried my blanket—I felt so at home. Whatever state Maharaji was in, he was constantly repeating "Ram" (God) all the time. He never stopped.

Everywhere, everyone flipped over him. When Maharaji would walk into the bazaar, people would fold down around him. They were on the street with their heads at his feet. "He's here! He's come! He's come!" All the businesses shut down instantly, and everybody ran out in the street. All the kids raced after him.

There was no form to this holiness. That's what was so strange. There was no temple, no organization. He just constantly kept wandering. And eating. I remember going to a wedding with him. He consumed five or six different huge meals, one after another. It seemed impossible to eat that much food, but he'd relish each bite. Then someone else would bring him a tray of heaping plates, an eight-course meal. He'd eat the whole thing and then start the next one.

The night after the wedding, he had me brought to him, and I sat in the room with him all night. He just lay there. I sat up against the wall meditating, and then he started to snore. The moment Maharaji started snoring, I fell into this incredible bliss. Then he'd stop snoring and sit up. I'd come out of it. Then he'd lay back and start snoring again, and the bliss would hit me intensely. I don't know what went on that night, but something extraordinary happened to me. Some transference occurred vibrationally from his body into mine. It was one of the most unforgettable nights of my life. We were alone—without a translator. We were in the bridal chamber. His soul was making love to my soul. I use sex as a metaphor because I can't think of any other way to convey how powerful it was.

It was our wedding night. He impregnated my soul with Ram; he inseminated the name of God into my heart. He poured the essence of his being into my being. The snoring was his *prana,* his life force, penetrating mine. No words can convey the bliss of the union between a realized master and his devotee.

So now I had Maharaji—my God, my love. I would meditate on him all the time. I'd get into this deep state where there would be no thoughts, just peace and joy, and I just wanted to stay there forever. I was always wanting to dive deep. When I was sitting in front of Maharaji, in a split second I could go off into the deepest meditation. But he would always bring me out of it! He'd let me go for a little bit, five or ten minutes, then he'd hit my head. "Take tea! Drink tea!" He'd break it. I don't know why. I didn't want tea—I wanted him!

The time came for the Kumbha Mela festival, where Swamiji was supposed to initiate me. This festival occurs every twelve years. Twenty to thirty million people come together to honor God and receive his blessings. Participation shows intense devotion, and the blessing one receives goes far beyond one's daily, spiritual practice.

Kumbha means "pot," and *mela* means "fair." It is believed that there is a pot of nectar in the sky; when the planet Jupiter enters a certain constellation every twelve years, the nectar in that pot overflows. The nectar drips down from the heavens into the guru's heart and then comes out of the guru's heart to feed the people spiritually. Heaven and earth merge.

Is the nectar real? As much as one believes and experiences it, yes. Yogis and saints say that the nectar can be felt and tasted. I know I felt and tasted it.

Kumbha Mela is one of the most amazing events. It's like a hundred thousand Rishikeshes in one spot, a party that goes on for three months. Millions of holy men and saints are there, including some of the most unusual sadhus. Mantras and chants hum on the airwaves through the loudspeakers. And hundreds of elephants parade. The Indian army is there, with jeeps and soldiers to set up latrines and direct traffic. Thousands of campfires burn with sadhus, yogis, and different holy men sitting in front of them. Maharaji alone had set up camp with thirty tents.

Kumbha Mela was like a living Ripley's "Believe It or Not." Sadhus with steel chastity belts. Holy men who had been standing for ten, fifteen years. They never sat down. They'd lean on a swing. Their legs would get grotesquely swollen, like those of elephants. I saw many,

many yogis with withered arms. They gave one hand to God, holding it straight up in the air until the whole arm atrophied. They'd make a fist and not let go, even as their fingernails grew out of the other side of their hands.

And there were huge wooden carts, a city block long and with 20-foot-high wheels, filled with all sorts of deities—even temples are built on them. As these monsters went rolling by, elderly men and women would purposely throw themselves under the wheels, believing they'd be instantly liberated by dying on such an auspicious occasion. Heaven is coming down to merge with the earth, so if you can die at this festival, you will die in heaven. What could be better?

As misguided or weird as this seems, these people were very serious about their spiritual lives. What struck me was the commitment to sacrifice one's body to know God. At this festival, the river of commitment washed over me and made me realize how much I loved God and why I was born.

I was in heaven. I was at the holiest of holy festivals, and I had a real guru. Now I was going somewhere. I was on the highway in my car. I had a tankful of gas and a credit card with unlimited credit because my guru was the richest person in the universe. He was one with God; he was in God all the time. I knew he was God and knew I didn't have to search anymore.

I visited all the different camps at the Kumbha Mela festival and danced all the dances. People had *kirtans* (songfests) that lasted for weeks on end. Some groups had been doing the same mantra nonstop for forty or fifty years, chanting the Hare Krishna mantra or "Om Namah Shivaya." Then I met the Ram Namis, a whole village of people whose entire bodies were tattooed with the divine name "Ram," from their foreheads to the palms of their hands to the soles of their feet. They wore peacock feathers, and all their clothing had "Ram" printed on it. They did Ram dances and chanted "Ram, Ram, Ram."

In the midst of all this chaos and sublimity, Maharaji turned to me and said, "I'm going to initiate you." I was ecstatic. I was going to be formally initiated by Maharaji!

ॐ

HE INITIATED ME on the actual day the pot in the sky spilled its nectar. This is when tens of millions of people take the sacred bath at Prayag (present-day Allahabad). Maharaji told me to beg for food for him. I went through three or four different lines and filled my *kamundalu* (a gourd hollowed into a water pot) with food.

I brought him an enormous amount of food. He could hardly wait; he voraciously ate it all. I guess he ate all of me, all the thoughts and feelings that were holding me back from God. He was very pleased. Food was the key.

Maharaji gave me a new spiritual name: Ram Dass. I told him, "I don't like that name!" It didn't feel right. He was quiet for a moment and then said, "Okay, your name is Bhagavan Das," which means "Servant of God." (He kept the name Ram Dass in reserve, and a few years later passed it on to another Westerner.)

Then we took a boat out onto the Ganges. There was a full moon, and the pot was pouring out the nectar. It was time to take the sacred bath. We jumped out of the boat. Millions of people were in the river. I started swimming far into it. Everyone was afraid that I would get carried away by the current. The water was like nectar. It felt like I was taking a bath in milk. It wasn't water—it was bliss-light. I was taking a bath in pure devotion. The river was filled with millions of flower petals. Everyone was bathing and praying and tossing flower petals. It was ecstasy!

But, as great as that moment was, my meeting with Anandamayi Ma was the pinnacle of the Kumbha Mela for me.

I HAD HEARD about Anandamayi Ma, India's greatest woman saint. She was widely known, and many of Maharaji's people were planning to see her. I bought a rose for her and found her tent. Inside, at least ten thousand people were having a huge kirtan. It was packed, and I couldn't get in, so I just stood outside looking in at her.

From afar she looked like a small white egg of light. I was so transfixed by what I was seeing, I couldn't move. Then, to my utter amazement and shock, the egg of light started getting bigger and was floating toward me.

I know this is hard to believe, but what I saw next was Anandamayi Ma floating out of the tent above all the people. She just moved like a ray of light beaming herself in front of me. As she walked to me, her energy moved in a way that seemed to make her float. Her huge aura, like a white luminous egg, encompassed her body. I had never seen anything like it in my life.

She held out her hand. I put the rose in her palm. Then my knees gave way and I sank down to her feet. When my head touched her feet, I felt as if I was going into the center of the earth. I thought I had linked up with the soul of the earth because I had connected and felt a total oneness with everything.

At that moment I realized enlightenment.

I was free from everything in the external world.

I moved my head up, and she looked at me and smiled. Then she turned around and floated back into the tent. She was like a star that had come down from the sky and then receded back to heaven.

Why me?

Who was I to get such a blessing?

Anandamayi Ma was my touchstone. All my life and all my love was in the rose I offered her. When she accepted the rose, she accepted my devotion, and I was free.

Enlightenment is the beginning of the journey, not the end. It took one moment for me to realize God, but it would take twenty-five years for me to begin actualizing Him.

The next day, I went to see Anandamayi Ma again. This time I sat directly in front of her. It was near the end of her life. She was probably about eighty years old, a large woman who wore only white. Anandamayi Ma never claimed to be anything but a child. She always referred to her body separately: "Whatever this body wants." Her state of consciousness was numinous.

She said to me, "What is your name?"

I answered, "Bhagavan Das."

Then she asked, "Who is your guru?"

I was learning to speak sadhu. When you speak sadhu language you put 1,008 *Sris* in front of your guru's name to show how much you respect him. *Sri* means "Respected Sir."

I answered, "Sri Sri Sri ek sah Sri Neem Karoli Baba." This means there were 1,008 *Sris* in front of my guru Neem Karoli Baba's name, and there were more at the end.

The moment I said *Neem Karoli Baba*, Anandamayi Ma leaned backward, raised her hands, and laughed blissfully. She was so happy.

ॐ

So at the Kumbha Mela I got my spiritual dad and mom. I got Dad first, Neem Karoli Baba, when he initiated me. Mom, Anandamayi Ma, was the living embodiment of my deity, the Divine Mother.

I folded up after that. I went into a fetal position in a corner and pulled a blanket over my head for about ten hours. The previous forty-eight hours had been beyond my wildest imagination. It took hours for my body to assimilate what had happened. Maharaji and Anandamayi Ma were so much one and the same. Their consciousnesses were identical. It was too much to grasp. But Maharaji was happy that I saw Anandamayi. Real masters don't get upset when you visit other saints because real masters don't see other beings as separate from themselves.

The people at Maharaji's camp wouldn't let me in the kitchen because I was a foreigner, an untouchable. Just by walking in the tent I was polluting the food they were preparing. The women would scream and yell at me when I walked by. Maharaji heard about it. So he took my hand and pulled me into the food tent. He wanted to show them that I was okay. They calmed down after that.

I spent every spare moment at Maharaji's feet. Holding his feet, I would fly through the universe. I would go through the most remarkable states of consciousness at his feet. I held them as long as I could. I would just drink the love that poured out of him. It put me in an altered state of consciousness.

I got high being around him. Everyone was filled with love. Everyone was so beautiful. There were no power trips around Maharaji. There was no politicking in his aura. He would say, "Give the man a hundred rupees." Someone would give him a hundred rupees. He'd say, "Take care of him. His mother's in the hospital." Whatever Maharaji spoke was done. I believe it was due to the absolute and utter faith Maharaji had in the name of God.

Here's an example of how he operated. A devotee named Larry Brilliant, who would become one of the cofounders of the famous humanitarian organization Seva, met Maharaji in India just before Maharaji died. Maharaji said to Larry, "You're a great doctor. You will eradicate smallpox in India."

Although Larry was a doctor, he knew nothing about smallpox. He kept thinking about what Maharaji said, and when he came back to America he thought, "Maybe I'll just call up the World Health Organization." Larry told the man at WHO that smallpox was going to be wiped out because his guru had said it would.

The man asked, "Who is your guru?"

"Neem Karoli Baba."

"Okay. Come on over." And it actually happened. Within half a year, smallpox had disappeared from India.

Another time, Maharaji asked a young devotee, "What happened with your medical exam?"

He answered, "I failed it."

Maharaji shouted, "You didn't take my name? Why didn't you pray to God?"

It comes down to simple faith. Sincere devotion to your guru is sincere devotion to God.

Maharaji had absolute faith in Ram and repeated his name all the time. With Maharaji, it was always, "Don't ask me. Ask God. I can't do anything. Go ask Hanuman. Hanuman does it all—he's the commander in chief. Talk to God about it."

Still, people were always barraging him with their problems. This person was sick, that person couldn't afford the dowry for his daughter's wedding, somebody's business was failing. Maharaji would shake his head very seriously and sigh, "What to do? What to do?" Often he wouldn't say anything more, yet people's problems would mysteriously disappear.

The Kumbha Mela lasted three months. I stayed there with Maharaji's feet on my head the whole time.

Then I realized that worshiping him was not enough. I could no longer get high on just his juice. I had to generate my own. But how?

Chapter 8

I KNEW I couldn't learn to fly by myself as long as I continued riding on Maharaji's magic carpet. So with money he gave me, I got on the train and headed toward Madras for no other reason than just to go. I was following a feeling. I should point out that I didn't think before I did things then, and I still don't today. I do things and I think about them afterward. I move from my intuition. Nothing is premeditated. I have no agenda, and I have no plan.

I was sitting on the train wearing the sandalwood paste marks sadhus wear to advertise that they worship Hanuman: a big red teardrop in the middle of the forehead, two huge white strips on the cheeks, two on each arm, six on the chest, and two on the back. I was covered in ashes, wore a sacred thread over my chest like the Brahmins (priests of the *varna* caste), went barefoot, had on a white dhoti, and tied my hair on top of my head in a knot. A tiny picture of Maharaji fit in the small bag I carried. And I had my mantras. That's all I owned. So I sat on the train and stared at Maharaji's picture all the way to Madras.

The temples were so big in Madras! In southern India, temples are huge and elaborate. They are shaped like jagged pyramids and filled with long halls, carved lions, statues of deities, and burning torches. What I appreciated most was that there was no tea in southern India—they drank coffee! And since I love coffee, I felt at home. The food, though, was extremely spicy and made my eyes and nose run.

One of the most famous temples I was told to see was Tirupati, at "The Seven Hills of Lord Vishnu." This is located in the state of Andhra Pradesh, north of Madras. The seven hills were originally sacred to the seven sages and the Goddess. The statue there is of Venkaeshwara (Lord Vishnu) appearing as the charming cow herder Govinda (Vishnu's incarnation of Krishna as a boy). I hiked up the seven hills and dropped into the vortex of devotion swirling around Krishna. It was like wading into a pool. I started to move with the pilgrims, and suddenly I was swirling in the frenzy of devotion.

Here I began kissing the ground as a spiritual practice. I would take a step, kiss the ground, murmur "Om namo Bhagavatay Vasudevaya [I bow to Lord Vishnu]," stand up, say "Om namo Bhagavatay Vasudevaya," bend down, touch the ground, repeat the mantra, stand up. I did this for eight to ten hours, and it altered my consciousness. I went into the inner light of the heart of the deity by approaching the formless reality and projecting an image onto it and crying, "Out of your mercy please let me love you! Become a mirror for my devotion so I can see myself in you."

I didn't understand any of this philosophically at the time. I was simply lost in the *bhava,* the divine mood. I was experiencing the truth of tantra: Only God can worship God; only Goddess can worship Goddess. You become what you worship, and then you worship yourself.

On top of one of the hills was Tirupati, the grand temple citadel, which had not changed much since ancient days. Thousands of pilgrims arrived every hour on the hour, asking for boons (spiritual gifts and blessings). They sacrificed their hair. Thousands of barbers lined up in stalls, and freshly cut hair was lying everywhere in big heaps. The devotees offered their hair, and their prayers were answered.

Intention, commitment, sacrifice, faith, and devotion—together these produce real effects. Too often we underestimate the power of thought. Thoughts manifest. Your life is what you think it is. That's why meditating and disengaging from the thought process helps free the self. The devotees believe, "I will give my hair, my beauty, my good looks to Vishnu, and he'll have compassion for me and help me out." And he did.

The temple was so big that I was dwarfed. I stood under massive carved columns twenty-five feet tall, surrounded by thousands of pilgrims waiting in line to go through the giant doors.

The ceremony in front of the temple was intense. It was as though I had found the one place in the world where God really lives. The music, chanting, prayers, vast number of people—oh, the enormity of it all! I couldn't go to this place just once. There was too much to see and too much to feel. But, most important of all, I had to find out what it meant to me.

I entered a turnstyle machine set up by the initiated priests who, with the power of the mantra, keep the river of liquid shakti flowing. After many hours of repeating mantras in line, I was finally inside the doors. Everything got dark. The giant stone walls, dark with soot, reminded me less of a cathedral than a fortress. I couldn't see the end of the corridor. It was so long, with a cavern of blackness backlit with flickering torches. The ceiling had to be at least thirty feet high.

Devotees that we were, we all had little boats in our hands made of leaves, containing offerings of food and flowers. Around me clusters of families were waiting together, everyone chanting, "Govinda, Govinda, Govinda, Govinda!" Thousands of people were chanting around me. "Sita Ram, Sita Ram, Sita Ram!" "Radhe Shyam! Radhe Shyam!" Everyone was trying to drown out everyone else with their own favorite name of God.

It was musky and damp, and everyone was dripping with sweat. I was drenched, too, as I was pushed along in the line.

There was no way out. I was totally trapped in the enormous crowd. I was like a snake in a bamboo reed: there was no reverse gear; I could only go forward. I had no choice. I was being pushed toward God.

ॐ

IT WAS GOING to happen. I was going to see God.

As it got darker and darker and sweatier and sweatier, I could smell everyone's bodies and all the crushed flowers under my feet. Sonorous sounds of the sacred prayers being chanted by the Brahmins came from both sides of the corridor. Imagine, a hundred Brahmins on each side, chanting in unison—a really unearthly sound echoed in the chambers of this castle of God.

The Brahmins have shaved heads except for a tuft of hair they leave on top of their head. This tuft allows God to pull them up to heaven.

Many were naked from the waist up and wore huge diamond earrings and lots of gold.

Finally I came out of the darkness and into the golden light. God was tall, fifteen or twenty feet, and made of one solid black, carved, basalt stone. Vishnu was covered with gold. The Brahmins had melted down everyone's jewelry and stuck it on the statue. Tirupati is the richest temple in India. Those who can afford it give all their bracelets, necklaces, rings—all their gold—to God, and their desires are fulfilled.

The atmosphere was very intense within five feet of God, like the New York Stock Exchange on the heaviest trading day. The chaos was part of the worship. Yet in the midst of the craziness was a deep sense of peace, like in the eye of a tornado.

I was standing in front of God with my offering in a basket when one of the priests took it to the feet of the Lord. Then he picked up another offering and placed it in my basket before handing it back to me. The priest kept the rupees from the basket as his salary.

Now I had shakti, the energy of God, in my basket. I had offered my devotion, and someone else's devotion was returned to me. All of us are linked in the eyes of God, and the love we offer him flows back and forth among us all.

The line suddenly jagged, and right in front of God was an empty space. It was the first I'd seen in many hours—a genuine miracle! The statue of Vishnu was very big, scary, and mysterious. Although it was black, it was really bright. And the intensity of the light was all the greater because I'd spent hours in the long, dark halls. Now I could either go into the light or look away from it. The moment I looked away, I would experience the next mind moment in a softer way. I held that empty space as long as I could. How long could I hold the vision of God? As long as I wanted. Then I closed my eyes, bowed, and said, "Enough, God. Thank you," and shuffled out of his presence.

You see, I was constantly dying and being reborn, moment to moment, in different states of consciousness. All states were impermanent, so it didn't make any difference which frame of consciousness I assumed. None was better than any other. No state was higher than another state because they're all just states, passing away. My egotism, my clinging, and my hopes had to die. It was a spiritual death and a choiceless situation. This death was reaching out for me. How was I going to face it? Why not dance into its embrace?

The moment of sacrifice should be a time of great rejoicing. I was sacrificing the moment: my petty thoughts, my petty feelings, my plans, and my desires were sacrificed into the absolute stillness of God.

Standing in that empty space, with all humanity, I stepped into eternity. It was just me and God. I was in total awe. Tirupati is majestic, how I always wanted God to be: rich beyond my wildest dreams, powerful, and big. The flickering torches created a magnificent presence. The statue seemed like a door, behind which was whatever I desired. I visited that temple so frequently that I felt as if I lived there.

ॐ

IN THE TIRUPATI pilgrimage center, I lived in a little hollowed-out rock cave in the back of a restaurant. I had Maharaji's picture, a little oil lamp, and my blanket to lie down on. I was constantly practicing my initiation mantra that Maharaji had given me: "Gayatri," which means "May I be the light." It is an ancient mantra of the sun, considered the most sacred of all the mantras. It is usually passed down from father to son. Maharaji passed it down to me, but it would take me twenty-five years to realize that Maharaji was my real father.

I was overwhelmed by it all. At Kumbha Mela I'd gotten my spiritual mother and father, who had given me my spiritual name and sacred mantra. Now, God had taken form. Everyday, three times a day, I was swept into the mass of devotion with everybody else in the temple procession. I was experiencing, for the first time in India, a very powerful form of God in a temple. This was as close to an organized religion as I'd experienced in India. There was only one deity here to worship: Vishnu. Everything is done for this God—the sacrifice of hair, handing over precious gold jewelry, the leaf boat devotion. The whole temple centers on the presence of this God. When I stood before him, I saw this idol breathing. It was like standing in front of a real person.

For the next three months I lived in my small cave in an altered state of meditation, and all my time was spent in line to see Vishnu. After the darshan with Vishnu I was mentally exhausted. I had to sit and breathe as the whole universe vibrantly moved through me. While I was trying to recover, people were having a party, dancing all around.

I felt about Tirupati the way I'd felt about the Ganges River. Both of them spoke to me. They were living deities, powerful and mysterious. I was devoted to them and I loved them. And just as I had swum and bathed in the Ganges every day, I demonstrated the same devotion to Vishnu and his temple. Each day, I stood in line for hours with my offering, waiting for the miracle of an empty space.

After living at Tirupati for a couple months of absolute devotion, I met a rich devotee from Madras who wanted to be my patron and give me lots of money. That was fine with me. He said, "I will give you whatever you desire. What do you want?" I hadn't even cut off my hair and still Vishnu was granting me a boon. God is so gracious; there is no limit to his love.

I didn't really want anything—that was the problem. My rich patron insisted. Finally I decided it would be fun to go to Ceylon (now Sri Lanka). Soon I was looking out the window of an airplane.

The plane landed in Colombo, and I went directly to the Ramakrishna mission. It was the one Hindu retreat in an otherwise Buddhist country. The library had the entire Pali Canon, the complete story of Buddha's life and a transcription of every sermon he ever gave. I read the entire canon—all three hundred volumes translated into English. It took me two days to read each volume.

I began having out-of-body experiences at this temple. I would lie on my bed, and the next thing I knew I was on the ceiling looking down at my body. I would float out of my body and go traveling, see things and talk to people, and then get thrown back into my body. It was at once an unusual and exciting experience. But I don't know how it happened or why—I had no control over it. It was a magical power that just came to me.

I could hardly wait to slip off each night. I was flying all over the place. It was like the sensation I got just before I had an orgasm—really, this was how exciting it was! I would sail up to the ceiling and look down at my body. I just loved it. I guess you could say that I was cashing in on my meditative experiences, having learned how to focus my mind. This experience showed me how normal consciousness is just the tip of the iceberg and how vast the ocean of human awareness actually is.

I stayed at the ashram for a couple months. I ate huge Indian eighteen-course meals that put me to sleep for two hours. I then cloistered myself in my room devouring the Pali Canon. Later I would go to the temple and chant. I was still wearing ashes and had matted hair.

Beautiful Sinhalese women would come to the temple with their hair decorated with flowers. Seeing them struck a chord. While my soul was crying out for God's love, my body was crying out for a more tangible embrace. I needed to wrap my arms around a woman.

At that point I didn't know about tantra. I thought that I had only one choice: either God or a woman. One or the other. I didn't know I could balance the two. I felt it was time to take a vacation from God.

Chapter 9

ON WENT MY blue jeans; out came the mats in my hair.
I washed off my ashes and went searching for a girlfriend.
I ended up in a nightclub called the Tropicana, which was
a bar set up as a whorehouse for sailors. I got a job singing
there, doing two shows a night. As a bonus they let me
sleep on the piano.

My new name was "King Pleasure." Having a natural ear for music, I played Beatles songs I had heard in Greece on the guitar with a five-piece band behind me. This way of life was so different from what I'd been living. I really enjoyed it.

It rained a lot in Ceylon. I would spend my afternoons in the botanical gardens, sitting under my umbrella in the rain and watching the water in puddles. I would meditate all day, then go back to the bar at night and start my first set. I was on at midnight and 2:00 A.M. Many times, while I was singing, people would throw beer bottles at me, so I'd have to duck and keep playing. Fights would erupt and guys would get smacked through the wall. It was that kind of bar.

But the girls were nice to me. I met a beautiful, blonde Swedish girl who spoke English, and we would go out and climb thirty or forty feet to the tops of eucalyptus trees. It was balmy at night. We'd just sit there, talking and hanging out. The trees would sway like a boat on water. We spent a lot of time in this romantic swing, but she wasn't prepared to consummate the relationship.

In the earliest morning hours, after the bar shut down, I'd be sitting on the top of the piano like a yogi. I was surrounded by thirty beautiful women of the night. They'd be filing their nails, combing their hair, and nursing their drinks. They all liked me a lot, but none of them would have sex with me. I was their child. They were sweet to me and treated me as if they were my mothers.

"All women are your mother." The curse of Maharishi Mahesh Yogi had dogged me all the way to Ceylon!

I went to Ceylon for sex but never got laid the whole time I was there. I got tortured. The Buddhist scriptures talk about hungry ghosts—desperate spirits with huge empty bellies and mouths too small for food, floating around in the atmospheres, tormented by desires they're never able to fulfill. In Ceylon I was a hungry ghost. I could truly see Maharaji's humor in it. I could see him laughing. This is what happens when you play hooky from God.

The *Ramayana* describes Ceylon as an island of demons. Actually, lots of wonderful people lived in Ceylon, but at the Tropicana I was working for gangsters, real-life demons. It was an ugly, violent underworld. They finally paid me the salary they owed me. I'd been waiting for this money to get back to India.

When I woke up the following morning, the money was gone.

I was completely disillusioned with the world and knew I had to get back to my spiritual roots. But there were no Hindus in Ceylon. So, since I couldn't get back to India, I plunged into the Buddhist world. I guess Maharaji wanted me to discover what Buddhism was about.

ॐ

I HEADED FOR the Tooth Temple, the sacred temple in Kandy where the Buddha's tooth is preserved. It is a genuine relic. In fact, the tooth is so powerful that it creates a power *yantra*—the physical form of its energy.

The Buddha's tooth! The light from it was intense. If that much light was reflecting off Buddha's tooth twenty-five hundred years after it was extracted, imagine how much light must have come off his whole body while he was alive! The thought blew me away.

In Kandy I wandered out into the jungle behind the temple at all hours of the day and night. I've always been a nature mystic. Nature is very warm and revealing to me. I can get completely lost in the woods and have a great time. This is because I've learned to override my sensations (like the fear of being lost in the jungle in the dark) with my breath.

No matter how afraid or panicked I become, the moment I sit down, connect with my breath, repeat God's name, and invoke my guru, I'm instantly peaceful. The thought "I am lost" is gone. I am found. I instantly find my true Self. Until I do this, I'm lost and in a panic, like a mouse running around the bottom of a bucket, like a *jiva* (an individual soul) without Shiva (God). Once I connect with the Divine Being, which is the immensity of creation, and fold my hands and salute, I become free at that very moment. In the gesture of adoration, praise, and genuine bowing, I get the energy to jump out of the bucket.

Late one night I heard music coming from the jungle and saw lights floating in the darkness. A huge procession was plunging through the forest. I ran out to see what was going on and hid behind a tree. There was elephant after elephant after elephant, crowds of people marching beside them. They were carrying torches, beating drums, and chanting and ringing bells. I was so overtaken by the power of it all that I dropped to my knees. Several people spotted me, put garlands around my neck, lifted me up on top of the lead elephant, and started blowing their trumpets.

I was at the very head of the parade. I rode the elephant into the dawn.

It was the most incredible ride of my life. Riding an elephant is like gliding, with a lope to it that's extremely sensual—it was undulating. I was so still and solid and strong, yet I was moving through space. Elephants are very intelligent animals. I was experiencing the being of the elephant, experiencing it thinking of me. And then I was thinking elephant thoughts while the animal's ears waved like fans in a breeze.

My elephant was so accommodating. I felt I was sitting on a moving tree. I sat really straight. I imagined myself as Indra, the king of gods, riding his elephant across heaven.

The jungle parade was noisy, wild, and bizzare, yet it was perfect. Asians use chaos to catch the part of the mind that's squirrelly and wants to go different places. It's like meditating in front of the TV: sirens are wailing, guns are blasting, and victims are screaming in that unreal world in front of your eyes, yet one is completely unaffected.

I felt in the presence of my guru. Maharaji was there, orchestrating the whole unfathomable procession. He wanted me to meet Ganesh, the elephant-headed god who reaches out with his trunk to remove every obstacle. He tramples the jungle to clear a path. Ganesh led me straight to his mother, Parvati, who is the Mother of the Universe. That morning I rode Ganesh into the sun.

Still dazed by the magnificence of the elephant parade, I left for the Buddhist monastery in Colombo and was introduced to Ananda Maitreya, one of the most famous monks in Ceylon in the Theravadin tradition. The goddess Annapurna blessed him with the supernatural power to feed as many people as he wanted to feed. His begging bowl was never empty. It was always full of food.

Ananda took me under his wing and really liked me. He was especially interested in Neem Karoli Baba. He wanted to know about all the miracles Maharaji did. I would always laugh and describe Maharaji's antics, as well his warmth, love, and generosity.

This monk was very innocent and childlike. He had big ears and was a sweet, funny man obviously very well respected in the community and well connected.

The Buddhists had a forest monastery in Kandy. I was allowed to go there and have a retreat with all the monks.

I was doing a lot of chanting and devotional *puja* (offering to a deity) to Maharaji's picture, which was my practice. Whenever I would do this, the young monks would come by and want to get into the practice with me. They were starved for devotion. Some schools of Buddhism are so austere that the monks are desperate for anything that will make them feel something. I saw it in their eyes.

I felt badly for these analytical young Buddhists. As I watched them interact, I realized that the heart really was the answer. I couldn't analyze my way to enlightenment. I had to open my heart. I remembered what Haris Das Baba had written on his slate when I returned to Maharaji as a devotee: HE HAS OPENED YOUR HEART.

ॐ

I WAS TRAPPED in Ceylon for six months. Not only had my money been stolen, but I had no visa. I was crying, "Ram, Ram, Ram." I wrote to Hari Das Baba who went to the visa office many times and finally got permission from the government for me to reenter India.

I took the ferry to Rameswaram. When I got off the boat I was wearing regular civilian clothing, with my hair combed back. One of the first people I ran into was a sadhu I knew. He had a long tilak on his forehead, his matted hair was tied up in a bun, and ashes were smeared all over his body. It took him a while to recognize me.

He said, "Bhagavan Das! What are you doing? Why are you dressed like this? Where is your dhoti?"

I felt a wave of shame and guilt. I changed immediately, got rid of the Western clothes, and put my dhoti back on. I was a sadhu again. My vacation from God was over.

ॐ

ON THE WAY back to my guru I visited Sri Tiruvannamali, the late Ramana Maharshi's temple. I stayed there for about a month. The temple is built on a huge hill. Everyone thought of Ramana Maharshi as a *gyani,* a master of the path of knowledge, but in reality he was *bhakta,* a fervent devotee of the Divine Mother. He worshiped her in the form of the hill—real-earth shakti, divine female all-pervading energy.

I ended up staying in a cave on the hill with an alchemical yogi named Garuda Baba. Ramana had told him that he should devote his life to

Garuda, the eagle of Vishnu. If he did, he would be able to live on air. So when I met him he was a "breatharian." That was his thing. He was extremely skinny. I never saw him sneak a meal the whole time I was there. He did drink water.

It was Garuda Baba who first taught me to feed on the sun. He showed me how to hold my left hand up to the sun and draw the shakti down into my heart. In the heart is a mouth that can digest solar energy. Your lungs become lips and you eat air. I would do this with Garuda Baba. We would situate ourselves in the forest so that the leaves of the trees blocked the direct sunlight. We would focus on the softer light of the edge of the sun. That's where we did *tratak,* staring at one point with unwavering concentration. This is the beginning of meditation.

I think many Westerners are frustrated with meditation because they don't realize that you can't just sit down and meditate. First comes the need to learn to concentrate. One must practice being completely absorbed in something without thinking of anything else. You can't skip this first basic step.

Garuda Baba looked like a bird and jumped around like one. He was crazy and wild. He had a gawky look and a beaky nose. He was an adept of Surya Vidya, the yogic solar science. I started fasting with him, taking only water, as we did hatha-yoga and drank from the sun. The sun is a window.

I preferred hanging out with unorthodox yogis. I felt they were somehow more real than the monks in the ashrams because they were so radical. These yogis were willing to take chances—they were not interested in making themselves comfortable. I'd walk down to the ashram for the music program, then go back to the top of the hill and eat light with Garuda Baba. I stayed with Garuda for two weeks before I moved on.

I continued my journey from there to Pondicherry, Sri Aurobindo's ashram, because I wanted to see the Mother. She was a French woman named Mirra Alfassa who had moved to southern India to become Aurobindo's disciple and wound up becoming the Mother of the Universe. Everyone in India respected her. She was a great saint.

The Mother rarely gave darshan. She would see people only on their birthdays. I wrote her a letter and said, "You are my Mother, my everything, my all, my more. I must see you now. You are my birth and death." I got a letter back from her saying, "Dear Son, I will see you on Sunday at three."

This was a good lesson—to know what I wanted and to be specific about it. When I was clear about my goal and determined to do whatever it took to achieve it, the Divine Mother gave it to me.

That Sunday afternoon a little man with a long white beard, who had probably been with Mother for thirty or forty years, brought me to her room. The moment he opened the door I was completely blinded by the golden light. I couldn't see anything. I literally stumbled into the room.

There was nothing there but the Mother of the Universe sitting in a chair. I dove into full prostration before her. I had a rose I bought for her. She said to the little man, "He's really a big one, isn't he?"

I gave her the rose and she just looked at me. I felt light pouring out of her eyes.

She smelled my rose and touched it to her heart before handing it back to me. It glowed with light. That was all; the darshan was over. I moved back out the door.

I spent the next week alone with that rose. I kept it next to Maharaji's picture. I didn't know what to do with it, so I dried it, crushed the petals, rolled them in cigarette paper, and smoked them. I got very high from that rose cigar.

AT PONDICHERRY I read the life of Milarepa, the great Tibetan mystic and ascetic. Every page of the biography opened up like a panoramic movie scene in my mind. I felt like I was in Tibet. I wanted to become like Milarepa.

It was very hard for me to find a balance between my spiritual life and material desires. It was an ongoing struggle. I'd immerse myself in the worldly life, as I did in Ceylon, then experience a strong sense of disgust.

I'd tell myself, "I've got to get back to the Pure Land. Why did I ever leave?"

Then when I'd be back in the Pure Land, I'd feel, "God, it's so boring here. The food's lousy. There are no pretty girls. It's not fun."

But for now, the Pure Land was beckoning again. I was off to transform myself, using Milarepa as a model.

Chapter I 0

I LEFT PONDICHERRY with a person I had met by the name of Surya Bhakta, a very comical man. Like my friend Garuda Baba, Surya Bhakta was a devotee of Surya, the sun god. He was a San Franciscan who had found his way to India on the hippie circuit. He had signed on with a guru named Surya Premananda, who was a disciple of my own Swami Prakashananda. So in a sense, Surya and I were related.

We headed north together so I could introduce him to Maharaji. When we got to Bombay, Surya said there was an incredible old lady there who really knew how to make an awesome bhang *lassi* (hashish milk shake), so we took a detour to find her.

We checked into a five-star hotel (Surya had lots of money from America) and then set out to find the old woman. She ground up this concoction on her millstone, round and round. We both drank huge goblets of the frothy, green brew. I thought the effect would last a couple hours. It turned out to be a three-day trip. We went back to the hotel and it was really coming on strong. I lay on the bed staring at the ceiling, while waves of color rippled over me. My body was in total euphoria. This was a very unusual drug trip. I relaxed and went with the flow. I was having a very blissful time.

The next thing I knew, I smelled smoke. I jumped up from the bed and saw billows of smoke coming from the other room. I ran in and found flames shooting out of the closet where Surya had been performing his puja.

PUJA IS A physical act of worship, and many people do it every day. It involves engaging in a relationship with God with the physical focusing of the mind. Usually on a table or altar, incense, water, candles, fruit, and flowers are offered. The devotee stares at a picture or statue of the diety, bows, and repeats a mantra over and over again.

ॐ

I MANAGED TO put out the fire, leaving the thick red carpet soak-ing wet and Surya's altar destroyed. I opened all the windows to let the smoke out. This was India, so of course no one bothered to investigate. Surya Bhakta, however, was nowhere to be found. I had no idea what had happened to him or how the fire had started.

I spent the next couple days wandering the streets of Bombay. I finally found Surya Bhakti in front of the hotel. He was dazed and dirty—truly a sight. He explained that while I was in the other room semicomatose on the bed, enjoying my trip, he had opened the window and looked onto the waterfront below. The harbor was filled with warships. Adrenaline surged through his body as he realized that the Indian military had tracked him down! They knew he had secrets of sun worship and were planning to invade the hotel! In a desperate panic, Surya Bhakta burned all his notes, pictures of his guru, and all the puja articles he was using in the closet so the esoteric secrets entrusted to him couldn't be stolen. Then he took off, frantically fleeing the CIA and the naval intelligence officers, who were no doubt right on his heels, leaving me there with the fire!

Surya ran out, hopped into a taxi, told the driver to go as fast as he could, and then handed him 300 rupees. The taxi driver finally dumped him off at two in the morning at the outskirts of Bombay. Surya forgot his passport and all his papers in the taxi. He'd also given the driver his entire bankroll.

In this wigged-out state, Surya stumbled over a hill and found himself surrounded by brilliant lights, ear-shattering noises, and horrible mon-sters. Clearly they were all demons out to get him because he was an initiate in this sacred knowledge of sun worship. He had to hide! He raced away and found a deep creek.

He broke off a reed, went under the water, and lay in the mud all night breathing through the reed. He waited until he thought it was safe and then made his way back to the city.

Now that he'd sobered up, he realized he'd been in the middle of a movie set. It just so happened a movie crew had been filming that night. I thought this was all very funny, but he didn't see the humor because he was still lost in his paranoia. He was living in this CIA reality that didn't exist.

Surya Bhakta and I were a team now, an odd couple. He was a very short Jewish man with wild hair that stuck out like a clown's. He carried a staff and wrapped the top of his head in a kerchief. I wore my rope hair and my beard.

RATHER THAN HEAD straight back to Maharaji, Surya and I decided to go to Nepal. I had never been there before and had heard that good hashish was very easy to buy there. I also thought it would be an interesting place to visit. Surya had more money wired from America for our journey.

We took a long overland trip through Patna into Nepal. The country looked like something from a medieval fairy tale. It was so different from India. Everything about Nepal was from the Middle Ages: bullock carts everywhere carrying hay, wrinkled people in medieval outfits sitting in the carts, glowering.

At that time there were no cars in Nepal. Everyone carried possessions on their backs, piled stuff on their heads, and walked around in dirty rags. The heart of Kathmandu, the capital of Nepal, was a musky bazaar with millions of shops. The temples had pagoda-like roofs, showing the Chinese influence.

We were able to rent a room in front of Pashupati Nath, which is the main Shiva temple of Nepal. The floor was a very cold cement slab. Kathmandu is freezing in the winter because it's about 5,000 feet above sea level.

Nepal was not all goodness and light. We came across a lot of witches, demons, and burning grounds. The witches would curse people, and everyone was afraid of them. Very powerful, very malevolent women would go to the cremation ground to collect human bones and then write people's names on the bones and bury them. I became fascinated with this dark energy.

ॐ

THE SPIRITUAL PATH gives you a choice to use your power for either good or evil. Many are tempted to use it for evil—that's human nature. We must overcome this temptation. This is why the spiritual life is called the razor's edge. The more realization you receive, the more power you're given. But if you don't remain humble and compassionate, you may find yourself slipping into some very deep, dark spaces. And kindness is essential.

The Lord's Prayer says, "Forgive us our trespasses as we forgive those who trespass against us." Jesus wouldn't have put that in the most famous prayer in the world if he hadn't known that a hundred times a day we need to let go, we need to forgive. When we do, the next moment arises fresh and clean. There's no victim; no one did anything to anyone. And most important of all, one must forgive oneself, too.

The nature of human existence is stuck in time, and we are constantly given new moments. With every minute that passes there is another minute ahead of us. That's why there's never any cause for despair, ever. There's always a new moment.

You might blow it one hundred thousand times. But if you get it the next time, who cares how many times you blew it? It's important to remember this in spiritual practice and to learn from your mistakes and strive for the greater good.

You might think that you're getting higher and higher when, before you know it, you're doing business with demons. Once they give you power, they want something for it. You have to pay for it—nothing is free. It's like an inner realm mafioso saying to you, "Okay, we're going to make you famous, we're going to give you psychic powers, we'll make all the girls adore you, but we do want a little something in return—your soul."

It's better to always go for love as you constantly let go of the power. I don't care what you're promised, keep laying down any spiritual gift you may receive with humility. Let your kindness to others be your power.

Love is so effortless to give and is so much of who we are. It's amazing how wonderful and simple it is and how often we overlook this spiritual power, which we are all born with. It's the one spiritual power we can use ceaselessly without worrying about it leading to a downfall. We all want to be so profound and so big and so great that we don't realize that love is the only way.

This is what tantra is—when the mundane and the spiritual are completely woven together. Then there's nothing to lose, nowhere to go, because you're always there. The moment is the present.

Seizing each moment means you're fully aware and present in the now. When the presence fills you, you can truly come from a place of compassion. It's no longer "What can I get?" It's "What can I give?"

Don't filter your feelings through mindsets about how you want things to be or how you think things should be. However you think it is, that's how it is for you. Knowing this is important because it enables you to function compassionately. That's what I was learning in India: how to be a kind person.

ॐ

SURYA AND I stayed in Kathmandu for several weeks, and he got me even deeper into worshiping the sun, a form of spiritual practice that made total sense to me. The sun is the source of life, the sustaining force of our solar system, the supreme deity.

I would meditate a lot, and then we'd go out to worship the sun. We'd sit, sunbathe, and close our eyes to see the inner light of the brain. We spent a lot of time gazing at the sun through tree leaves—just as Garuda Baba had done. Surya Bhakta loved the sun passionately. It wasn't just a ball of gas to him; it was a living, conscious entity he could communicate with.

We'd hike to Bodhnath or Svayambudnath, the Monkey Temple, so we had a selection of shrines to visit. I was becoming fascinated with Tibetan Buddhism. In Nepal, half the population is Buddhist and half is Hindu. The two traditions are married there. They've got Shiva lingams on top of Buddhas and Buddhas on top of lingams, all mixed together.

The Monkey Temple in Kathmandu is extraordinary. Legend has it that long ago the bodhisattva Manjushri took his sword and cut the valley in half, creating a huge lake (a bodhisattva is one who forgoes nirvana to benefit other sentient beings). Then Manjushri drained the lake and a huge mountain, Svayambudnath, rose up out of the valley. At the top of the mountain is a temple that's home to thousands of wild monkeys that jump on you and snatch the glasses right off your nose and try to undo your watch. Warning: they bite. That's one good reason to carry a walking stick in Nepal.

We also spent time in a huge Tibetan temple that was the home of a fifty-foot-high Buddha. At least a thousand steps led up to this temple, where there were hundreds of butter lamps and many Tibetan chanters. This temple was filthy, but it had soul, so much shakti. The Tibetan chanting drew me in.

I'd never heard low Tibetan chanting with the drums. It carried me to something familiar that I couldn't understand. All I knew was that I was a Hindu holy man dropping into Tibet on top of a mountain in Nepal.

I hiked all over the Kathmandu valley with Surya. Then we'd stop in a tea shop and sit against the wall for several hours, sipping tea and repeating our mantras.

I did lots and lots of *japa,* which involves fingering and rubbing each bead on a string as you say your mantra. Maharaji did continual japa on his fingers. His right hand was always moving. He counted the different knuckles in his fingers while doing his mantra; he counted each of the joints as he repeated his "Rams," twenty-four hours a day.

Maharaji said "Bolo Ramanama Sukhadayai," which means "Chant the name of God with a concentrated mind and it will bring you bliss." With japa there are three ways to do this. You begin by moving your fingers over the prayer beads, repeating the mantra—in my case, "Ram, Ram, Ram, Ram." The next level involves repeating the mantra inaudibly. The mouth moves but no sound is uttered. Then you say your mantra in your mind only; the mind becomes a prayer wheel.

Japa was my whole spiritual practice—repeating the name of God and doing the beads. The *Bhagavad-Gita* says, "Of all austerities and sacrifices, I am Japa." Japa is the supreme sadhana in this age. The mantra definitely brought me an incredible focus and stillness and transported me out of fascination with form. It seemed to cut away the glamour of the external world, bringing peace. The idea was to just stay with the breath and the name of God. That's what I was doing most of the time. We would walk, and I would work the beads. So with every breath came the name of God. I was amazed at how my practice brought me such stillness, focus, and peace. To unite the soul with the name of God fulfills all desires.

I was so involved in my new Buddhist practice that I was in no hurry to get back to Maharaji. Not yet.

IN 1968, KATHMANDU was where the hippie scene was happening. While the whole town was filled with thousands of temples with continuous Hindu prayer and worship (with a Buddhist overlay), hippies from all over the world migrated there, with their loud music and long hair, to buy drugs. For $200 a month you could live like a king. This included buying all the drugs you wanted and renting a nice house.

While Buddhist monks said their prayers on top of the very sacred Monkey Temple mountain, the Beatles' hit record "Abbey Road" blasted throughout Kathmandu. Suddenly this seventh-century culture was being thrust into the twentieth century. It made for a strange mix to see junkies and bizarre hippies walking down the road with this ancient background—they looked like animated characters to me. It was an ongoing party. I stayed as far away from all the international hippie chaos as possible. Everywhere I looked, people were tripping on LSD. Amazing numbers of young people were there. The atmosphere created by it all was very intense.

Anyone could just walk into a store and say, "Morphine," and they'd be asked, "How many?" There was no better backdrop for drug tripping and sex than the picturesque medieval town of Kathmandu surrounded by the gorgeous Himalayan Mountains, the mountains of eternal snow.

There was a store down by the square called the Eden Hashish Store. Its slogan was "Let us take you higher." People could choose from fifty different kinds of hashish and twenty kinds of marijuana. People could sit down and sample whatever they had to offer while drinking tea. And they could buy as much as they wanted, even carry out a duffel bag of the stuff. It was legal. And since drinking was not allowed, India and Nepal were strong marijuana cultures.

GENERALLY SPEAKING, THE conventional Hindu attitude is that drugs are a lower path. It's looked upon as something that's okay for some sadhus to do, but the pure sadhus don't.

Drugs are used in the Aghora tantric tradition, which is a *tamasic* (dark) *sadhana* (practice). The Aghora idea is not to let the drugs get hold of you but for you to be able to move through the intoxication. It's like taking a massive hit of LSD and being able to answer the door, talk on the phone, drive the car, go to the store, and buy milk.

One has to conquer the intoxication, like Lord Shiva, who swallowed all the poison in the ocean but held it in his throat so it didn't enter his body. That's why Shiva is called Nilakantha, which means "Blue Throated." His throat is swollen and blotched from the chemicals he holds there. The point of all this is that at the moment of death you may be groggy, you may be in terrible pain, or you may be starting to faint, but you have to hold on to a clear state of awareness and die in full consciousness. When you practice staying completely clear during intoxication, you're preparing for a conscious death.

I want to be honest about the part drugs played in my spiritual development, but I also want to make a serious point: drugs are a very dangerous path. You definitely have to have protection. The way you protect yourself is with the love you have for your guru—then the guru watches out for you. If you don't have divine guidance and protection, drugs can kill you.

This is why the essence of spiritual life is truly the guru. It's not a popular position in the West anymore since we've had so many guru scandals, but it hasn't for one moment stopped being true. If you want to learn Ayurveda, you have to have a guru. If you want to learn to meditate, you need the guru.

If you have a real guru, a *Satguru*, then you're protected. If you don't—if you try to go the direct route without a guide—then you don't ingest the drug, the drug ingests you. Drugs are shakti. By definition, the guru is a person who, like Shiva, can hold the shakti. You can get addicted or even overdose if you're not using drugs worshipfully. I had some very good experiences with drugs, but I don't recommend them to others because most people in the West want the poison—they don't want Shiva. And they don't have elders to show them how to use poison in a sacred manner.

Drugs can be useful spiritually because they're so dangerous and terrifying. Some people need terror to break their mindset. Whether it's the terror of having a baby, the scary night all alone when you get lost camping—whatever the terror is—that's the moment of breakthrough into the now.

People of all cultures have used drugs spiritually. We have our shamans in the modern world: our oncologists, our neurologists, our gynecologists—all whom we trust. And what do they give us? Drugs. The whole world runs on caffeine, tobacco, and aspirin. Food can be a drug, as can too much spice or fat. Whatever the drug of choice happens to be, it has to be used correctly.

In every culture people have always wanted to change their consciousness. And people will always find a way. You can't stop them. You can try—you can put them in jail. Still, people will alter their consciousness in any way they can. Fortunately, there are many safer ways to raise your consciousness than experimenting with drugs, and most gurus in India prefer more conservative routes. Doing your meditation, japa, and hatha-yoga is a slower path, but the effects are more lasting, and you run less risk of frying your nervous system. Without a doubt, self-discipline pays for itself in the end.

SURYA AND I decided to walk to Tibet. We'd heard the Chinese were building a new road through the mountain passes. So we headed for Tibet with our clothes and our blankets. During the entire trip we slept outside. We were so cold that we barely slept—we just shivered.

We had been begging for food all along the way. Close to our destination we came up over a bend in the road. We could see the whole night sky lit up with lights like a city, and we were both thinking, "Oh boy, tea! Biscuits! Food!" Then we came over the hill and there was a huge, fifty-foot-high picture of Mao Tse-tung, with hundreds of lightbulbs around it and generators running the show in the middle of the mountains.

It was surreal.

It was Chinese.

The Chinese military informed us in a very serious tone that we shouldn't go any farther. They gave us tea, and we again slept outside. I didn't get to go to Tibet, but I didn't mind because I had God.

I BELIEVE THAT we can either allow ourselves to be attacked by physical sensations or rise above experience. I was walking barefoot in the Himalayas in the snow, freezing and absolutely miserable. I tried to rise above the experience so that it would no longer be a problem. I was exhausted, freaked out, and lost. So what? I had God's name.

Knowing where to place faith is crucial. Put faith in money? The money's stolen, and you're in trouble. Put faith in your partner? When your partner walks out, you're in trouble. But put your faith in God and you no longer define unpleasant sensations as painful. Many poor people in Nepal don't own shoes, but their faith in God is indestructible. So who needs shoes? Actually, we were enhancing our spirituality by practicing austerity.

Austerity is practiced so that one may gain freedom from the confusion of everyday life. The more you have, the more you need. The less you have, the less you need.

As your inner life expands, your outer life becomes less demanding.

At this point you start experiencing life on a much different level. With enlightenment comes a richer life.

The simple, enlightened life is profound, as you're able to live in the eternal now. Without the necessary austerity, you can get caught up in the "gonna-wanna-should-could" reality, sadly never experiencing the present moment.

Today, spiritual aspirants don't want to practice austerity. They want to realize God while living in their cozy homes, having their mystical visions between wine and cheese parties. Austerities are good for you—they make your mind strong and help you develop your inner strength. It's something we all need because our culture has made our minds so soft. We are weak and vulnerable.

ॐ

WE TURNED AROUND and headed back to Kathmandu. Once, around three o'clock in the morning, we were walking down a very narrow street, like a corridor, between buildings. Suddenly, out of nowhere, a pack of wild dogs came hurtling straight at us. They were mad, rabid, Nepalese dogs, covered with sores and frothing at the mouth while they howled and snarled.

In a fierce battle, we beat them back with our walking sticks. It was a terrifying fight. I was on one side of the street and Surya was on the other. Together we triumphed!

Dogs are wild in Nepal. They live on the flesh from the burning grounds. They look like they're possessed by demons and run around in large packs. Nobody goes out in Nepal after dark because that's when the demons are out. "Close the door! Lock it up!" But I was a night walker, and it was the only time I could get some peace. No one would bother me, and I could get fresh air. But that night the demons almost got us.

We ran across some travelers from Europe, French and German, who were a destitute bunch of street people. I went out and got a huge pot—the biggest pot I could find—and a little kerosene stove. We didn't have much, but we managed to start making food, and before I knew it I was feeding everybody.

They'd all come to our room for free food. Maharaji, my guru, was feeding them through me. It was amazing that I could do this. They were so hungry, and watching them eat sated me. I loved them, gave them soup, and told them stories. It took the desperation out of their eyes. It was a humbling experience as my heart opened. I could feel my chest expanding, and I felt so full of love.

ॐ

THE MORE WE share, the more we receive. Indians believe that's the way of Lakshmi, the goddess of wealth. If you want Lakshmi, abundance, and money to come to you, you have to be like Lakshmi's husband, Vishnu. Vishnu is the preserver, the one who takes care of all beings. So become like Vishnu and take care of people. Then Lakshmi will come to you so you can continue being like Vishnu. That's the secret of drawing her energy into your life.

Chapter 12

I COULD HARDLY wait to get back to Maharaji's feet.

Finally Surya and I reached Kanchi, and Maharaji blessed the two wandering pilgrims. For him, though, it was as if I had never been gone. If you were out of his sight, you were out of his mind.

Maharaji was unique: he had no agenda and was constantly in eternity. He didn't react to things the way most people did because he didn't have any social consciousness. He just existed in this vast space. And he was always in two places at once. He was always in this otherworldly God place, yet he was always in the physical realm.

Maharaji never talked to me about anything spiritual and rarely gave me any directions. I would just sit and be there with him, and in his presence I'd get a huge burst of energy to continue my practice, which I was still learning.

I stayed at the temple in Kanchi. Maharaji would visit the temple, and then he'd mysteriously vanish.

There were no appointed tasks. Most of my time was spent as a hermit in a retreat space. My goal was to sit as still as I could, as long as I could, while staring at the wall. I had seen a painting of the Zen patriarch Bodhidharma staring at the wall, which had given me similar aspirations. I wanted to be like Bodhidharma. So I stared at walls. I had a little picture of Maharaji, a candle, and the wall. I couldn't afford a stick of incense.

Surya returned to America. He had been so crazy in all his adventures that I was relieved when he left. The last time I saw him, before he left India, he was in Delhi. He was burning a hole through his third eye on his forehead with a bundle of lit incense because voices had told him to. I watched in horror before I said goodbye. All I wanted was my peaceful life at Kanchi.

I got back into cooking at this time. I had a little stove in my house and cooked for Maharaji. He loved to eat my food. Feeding my guru was one of the highlights of my spiritual life. I would make rice pudding for him and put my whole being into that pudding, and then Maharaji would eat me.

I wanted to disappear into my guru, but my guru was the one who was always disappearing. No one knew where he'd go. I think he vanished into all of us. When he'd return, he'd tell me, "Bhagavan Das, you were up at dawn doing puja, you were missing me very much, you didn't eat enough while I was away, it was good that you helped Neeti Arora with her crippled son. . . ." Connecting with Maharaji—who had the power to know everything I was thinking and tell me everything I had done in the last forty-eight hours—was unnerving for my ego. I felt I had no control. My mental censor was powerless.

ॐ

HOW CAN SOMEONE outside me be able to be in me? Only if they are me. So who was I? I asked myself these questions and came to understand that this is the reality of the atman, the Self. And it's the Self that everyone has. It's my true Self and your true Self—the individual, inner Self. This atman is one with God. It is and partakes of the nature of God, and it is that place inside of you and me that is omnipresent, omnipotent, and omniscient. It is the *omkar* of the *nada,* the voice of God, the hum of creation. When I listen to the music inside my head, that fine ringing in my ears known as the *nada* (which everybody hears) is the *omkar.* The *omkar* is what our soul rides on. It is the sound current of God; this is the sound of the ingoing and outgoing breath.

The atman dwells in the heart as the sound of "Om." When I'm very still, in solitude, when there are no other sounds present, I hear the sound of Om.

Maharaji was the physical body of the vast inner reality of the atman. He read my mind like an open book to remind me that I was no more separate and independent than the fingers of a hand. He'd tell me my innermost secrets, and I'd be astonished and a little afraid.

The reality of who we all are, and of what Maharaji was, can really scare the ego if it's invested in its own little universe. The whole cosmos around us collapses like a house of cards when the guru huffs and puffs and blows it down. The guru is the big bad wolf. He's come to eat us. If you're not willing to offer him the pudding of your being, it can be scary. You need to give your whole self to him, inside and out. Only through that surrender can you come to understand the power of atman.

The concept of the Atman comes from the ancient sages of India: the Rishis. They lived a simple, family life in the forest and spent their days in meditation and spiritual practice avoiding distractions whenever possible.

MAHARAJI PERFORMED A miracle a minute. Food, money, a trip to the hospital—whatever the people needed was taken care of.

One time I brought Maharaji eight apples. He put them under his blanket, and he had no other apples. Then he started giving out the apples, and I counted as he did: one, two, three . . . thirteen . . . forty-eight. I carefully counted. From the eight that I gave him he had created forty-eight apples.

Another time, a man came to see Maharaji because he had only one rupee. The man said, "Maharaji, this one-note rupee is all I have—I need more."

"Give me your rupee," said Maharaji. He took the man's rupee and put it in the fire of his cooking stove.

"What are you doing? That's all that I had!" screamed the man.

Maharaji took a pair of tongs, and I watched him pull numerous one-hundred-note rupees out of the fire and give them to the man.

Maharaji hid his miracle attainment—that was his illusion. But the miracles were so common that it got to the point where I hardly paid attention to them anymore. It was so matter-of-fact. They were the background of reality. Whenever questioned about them, he would answer, "I did nothing. God did it."

Once, I borrowed a friend's Land Rover and drove up to see Maharaji in Vrindavan at a small spiritual gathering. It was beautiful, as they usually were. Everyone was happy and fulfilled.

Suddenly, Maharaji jumped off his tucket (a low wooden bed) and announced, "Let's go to Agra!" Everyone leapt up to escort him out. I thought he'd get into one of the other cars and I'd follow behind. He looked over at the Land Rover, hopped in, and slammed the door shut. I got in, and soon we were driving down the trunk road from Vrindavan to Agra. On Indian roads, including the national highway, were cows, ricksha wallahs, dogs, wild goats, and even chickens on the loose! It was extremely dangerous, and fatal accidents were not uncommon.

I was going about forty-five miles per hour, which is pretty fast in India. Maharaji looked over at me and said, *"Jaldi karo, Jaldi karo!* [Go faster, Go faster!]" I inched it up a little. Then Maharaji yelled, *"Jali, jali, jaldi karo!"* and I went a little faster. He didn't seem satisfied, so I floored it all the way to Agra. As the speed increased, we were going so fast that I could barely hold onto the steering wheel. The jeep lurched recklessly on the bumpy road.

Then the strangest thing happened. I looked over at Maharaji's seat, and there was nothing but his crumpled blanket. I held onto the wheel with one hand and held up the blanket with the other—and there really was nothing there! I swore to myself that I would never drive that fast again.

I thought, "This can't be happening; this can't be true." But there was nothing I could do but let go of my ideas of how the moment should be. And by letting go, I broke through. I realized that at any given time, there was only the moment. No more. No less. Only the moment.

And then came the rush. My whole body started pulsating with ecstasy. It was an unbelievable experience, like being in two universes at once. The moment was here now, and so was I.

I don't know how long it lasted (it's an hour and a half to Agra) because I was in eternity. I looked over again, and there was Maharaji sitting next to me, wearing his blanket, chewing his Rams. "Ramramramramramramram!" We pulled up in Agra. Maharaji threw the door open and leapt out of the car just like a monkey.

Maharaji was a Ram transmitter. He sounded like a siren. "Ramramramramramramram!" One of the attainments of great saints is that they become transmitting stations. They go on the air. It's a cosmic channel. Maharaji was broadcasting blessings every moment of the day. "Ramramramramramramramram!" It was his siren call in another sense, too. I'd be attracted to the shore of his blanket, but the boat of my ego would shatter on the rock of his being.

Maharaji was so much larger than life that it was hard to see him as a human being, and yet he was so human. The bliss and love I'd feel being with him was so incredible that I'd forget about whatever problem I had. It was like Dad had come home from work and was laughing and tossing me in the air and absolutely everything was okay.

But the feeling of euphoria would slowly wane after Maharaji left. I'd hang on to it effortlessly for three or four days, but after that I'd have to intensify my austerities.

MY REGIME IN Kanchi was to wake up at three in the morning, make a small fire, and go down to the ice-cold river. I would take my clothes off, dive in the water, and grab a rock at the bottom of the river and hold on as tightly as I could while I held my breath and mentally chanted, "Ram, Ram, Ram. . . ." When I couldn't hold my breath any longer I'd climb out and sit on a rock and go into meditation. I'd be so numb I could sit really still. It was great. I always saw the river as

Ganga. All rivers in India were the sacred Ganges to me, so I worshiped them as Mother Ganga. Consequently, I got the blessing of the Ganga.

WHATEVER BLESSING YOU ask for is the blessing you will get. If you look at your guru as God, you get the blessing of God. If you see your guru as a human being, you get the blessing of a human being. Whatever the guru is to you is what the guru is. This is such a profound point, yet it is often overlooked because it's right in front of your face.

My mind was always overriding my emotions. "There's more here. There's secret mantras I need to know. My guru isn't teaching me enough! The Tibetans have the answer! I'll find it with the Tibetans!" The key to spiritual enlightenment is solitude. You're there with yourself with the loneliness and all the feelings you feel. All you've got is the name of God. Is it enough? How do you make it enough? Is there more?

Part of me was perfectly content to sit alone with God. But another part seriously craved magical powers. I wanted a flying carpet. I thought it would be more fun than a motorcycle. So I was able to persevere in very strict austerities in part because of my desire for supernatural powers.

I'D LEAVE THE riverbank when the cold finally hit me and go back to the solitude of my room and chant to Maharaji's picture. I would chant, chant, and chant, raise the energy, and then go into meditation with it. When the energy would drop, I'd chant again. This was the ongoing practice, running on the gasoline of constant devotion. That, too, was the grace of the guru—grace that gave me the faith to find out who my guru was, start a spiritual practice, and stick with it.

I had the privilege to go into deep inner states for weeks on end with no one to demand that I take the garbage out, find a job, or drive the kids to school. I didn't have to do anything to make money because there was no external world for me.

For six years, literally everything I needed was brought to me without my even having to ask. I didn't need much—an occasional meal, a piece of cloth to wrap around my loins.

YOU DON'T NEED TVs or movies or gossip or cocktail parties when your inner world is activated. You're so filled with stillness that there's no room for mental agitation. But as I would later find out, most people don't have the luxury of nurturing their inner life twenty-four hours a day without distractions. Even in India, where I did have this luxury, it was inevitable that my concentration would slip and my inner dialogue would start chattering.

How do you make friends with the inner dialogue? Through meditation, prayer, and constant repetition of your mantra. These are practices we all need to participate in. But the majority of us don't. We don't realize how powerful we are in affecting all creation with our feelings. Once people realize what an impact their feelings have on the atmosphere around them, they can become a living prayer wheel.

I live in a constant state of prayer; no matter what I do I'm in prayer. You become a living prayer wheel by repeating the name of God and synchronizing it with the breath. It's "Ma" on the inhale and "Om" on the exhale. Fueling this with faith and devotion, a divine atmosphere is created.

Maharaji was a living prayer wheel. All the great masters are.

ॐ

ONE MORNING I came out of meditation, opened my eyes, and everything I saw in my room was light. I wasn't on drugs, I was totally straight, but I felt as if I was hallucinating. I saw it all as pure consciousness. Everything was alive with divine awareness, pulsating with energy and light. I didn't know what to do—I was terrified!

I had to pee, but I couldn't even stand because everything was God. I crawled out of the room on my hands and knees.

Once I was outside I peed out the whole universe. My urine was totally holy, and the ground was holy. I started drinking my urine and rubbing it all over me because it was the nectar of God.

I bowed to the earth, and the light started glowing from the rocks. Everywhere, I saw light and consciousness and God. I couldn't move from that spot outside my house because I was looking at the light coming off the leaves of the trees and experiencing to the core of my being how things were permeated with consciousness. I curled up in a ball, unable to move all day and night. I was in an absolute state of awe. The next morning, a temple monk found me and was really concerned. I couldn't even talk because this monk kneeling over me was God. I was touching his feet and worshiping him.

I lost all identification with my body and my mind. I was insane. Hari Das Baba came over and fed me with his own hands and took care of me the whole time. He was feeding God because my body was now the entire universe. Everything was me and everything was so holy, so sacred, and I was in such awe over everything. I was kissing everything in my room. I was kissing my own hands. I was in absolute wonder at the consciousness of everything around me.

The room was vibrating with energy; everything was alive. The cement walls in my room were alive, my bed was alive, my blanket was alive, the lint was alive.

After being in this state for two weeks, I snapped back into my body and there was the room. And it was just a room. And there was my body. And it was just a body. It was a terrible let-down, not to be God anymore! But my faith, which had been strong before, was now unshakable. I was going to do more chanting, meditating, and practicing austerity until I regained that state, and next time, I would never let it go!

But things never work out like you plan. . . .

Chapter I 3

SHORTLY AFTER MY profound firsthand experience with pure consciousness, Maharaji took me by surprise. "Go to Delhi and stay with Major Rikki," he said.

I didn't know who Major Rikki was or why Maharaji wanted me to go to him. Maharaji repeated, "Major Rikki, Major Rikki, you've got to stay with Major Rikki!"

I had always hated Delhi and didn't want to go, but the guru's instructions are the will of God, so how could I have not followed the orders of Neem Karoli Baba? I was given the major's address and took off for the bus station.

It's a tremendous austerity to live in India, but the most severe penance of all is to ride an Indian bus. People from New York or Amsterdam or London think they know how awful public transportation is. They're wrong. No Westerner can possibly imagine how cramped and uncomfortable Indian buses actually are. You wait in line for several hours, sometimes several days, to get a ticket. The buses are so packed with people, you have to struggle to expand your chest wall to breathe.

Delhi was a huge, wild, crazy city with traffic signs and cows in the street (not that anyone paid more attention to the traffic signs than they did to the cows). And everybody wore pants.

I was living in my mythological world and found this Westernized version of India very distasteful. I was a sadhu, a holy man, so of course I carried deep resentment toward "worldly" people—in other words, toward everybody else.

I wanted to live only with holy people in a holy environment. And here I was in smelly, dirty Delhi with millions of cow-dung-burning campfires. The sun was hidden behind a green-gray sky. Sometimes I couldn't even see ten feet in front of me, it was so polluted. And drivers didn't use turn signals, they just leaned on their horns. Imagine five hundred thousand cars honking simultaneously, in an all-enveloping cloud of diesel fumes and smoking dung, and you're starting to get a feel for Delhi.

Major Rikki lived in a fifth-floor apartment in a huge suburban tract. It was an unattractive cement block house. Major Rikki was a big, forceful military man, Indian born but very English, who had a waxed moustache sticking out and always wore his army uniform. He chain-smoked State Express No. 555 cigarettes, ate meat, and drank. When at home, he would sit in his underwear in front of Maharaji's picture in his bedroom, with an ashtray on one side and a bottle of scotch on the other.

At Rikki's place, one was always expecting Maharaji, or anyone Maharaji sent. There was no official notification because when I was in India there were few telephones. All communication was done telepathically or by mail. When I arrived, I told him, "Maharaji sent me to stay with you." He made me feel right at home.

Major Rikki and I got along well enough, but I was on edge—cautious and disturbed. What could Maharaji be thinking, sending me to live in this degenerate atmosphere?

Major Rikki also had a big stack of *Playboy* magazines, which I eventually gave in to reading. I couldn't resist the temptation. As soon as I was given the opportunity, I gave in to all of it. I was masturbating to pornographic magazines, smoking State Express No. 555, and listening to Major Rikki boast about his military career. I hadn't touched any alcohol, though—I was the sadhu in the house, after all. But why in the name of God did Maharaji send me to this hell realm?

Every night, I'd peek into his room and see Major Rikki in front of his picture of Maharaji, rocking back and forth, puja lamps lit, smoking, drinking, and carrying on long Hindi conversations with Maharaji. Sometimes he'd be yelling. I didn't understand a word. I thought Major Rikki was totally mad.

For the first time in India, I started to question Maharaji. I didn't see how any of this was furthering my spiritual development. In fact, it was seriously hindering it.

ॐ

MAJOR RIKKI WAS the head of an army outpost in New Delhi. One day, some years earlier, Maharaji had appeared sitting placidly in front of the gate to the army complex. The guards told him that he'd have to move because they couldn't get the cars or trucks through. Maharaji loved to sit in the middle of the road—any road. He was always holding up traffic. It was one of his little idiosyncracies. Anyway, the soldiers ordered him to leave, but he wouldn't get up. They tried to force him, but he wouldn't budge.

The soldiers told Major Rikki that some old baba was sitting in front of the entrance, stopping traffic. Major Rikki, who was in love with his own power, said, "A baba! Throw him in the brig!" So they picked Maharaji up and carried him into the jail and locked him in a cell. When they got back to the gate, Maharaji was there in the middle of the road again.

Major Rikki himself came out, confirmed the reports of what happened, and became a total devotee of Maharaji, worshiping him as God. Until then he did not believe in God at all. Although he wouldn't give up his Western vices, his life was changed forever through his spiritual practice and ongoing relationship with Maharaji.

ॐ

ONE AFTERNOON, A few weeks after arriving, I was lying out on the veranda in Major Rikki's apartment, the one room where the sun comes in, thinking about how badly I wanted to be back in the mountains. I'd just finished masturbating to one of the Playboy bunnies and I hadn't had a chance to wipe myself off when there was a loud knock. Maharaji's voice boomed from behind the door.

I was beyond the beyond. I was wiping myself with one part of my dhoti while touching Maharaji's feet with my head, totally embarrassed, ashamed, and flipped out of my twenty-year-old mind. Maharaji strolled out into the room, happy as can be, chuckling away. He sat down on Major Rikki's bed, and Major Rikki began rubbing Maharaji's feet and laying his head in Maharaji's lap. Maharaji was blessing him, and they were having a great time, like old pals.

Major Rikki was like a little kid on Christmas morning, crying and hanging on to Maharaji's feet, still smoking nonstop. I couldn't believe it. The room reeked of booze and cigarettes. Maharaji was oblivious to it all.

What I didn't realize was that devotion was all that mattered.

Judgment was not an issue.

Finally Maharaji turned his attention to me. He said, "I can do anything with you that I want. I have total control."

"How?" I asked, still flustered.

"Because I have the key to your mind."

"What?"

"I am your guru."

"Yes, you are."

"You have to do everything your guru says. You must obey."

"Yes."

He said, "Leave India. Go back to America."

I started crying, "No, no, no! I'm not going back to America. I will not go. There's no way I'll go back! I'm just beginning my practice! I'm going to stay here and realize God!" I was frantic and scared, and the stress and indulgence of the past few weeks came pouring out.

I didn't know that Maharaji had purposely brought me to Major Rikki to show me my shadow side, because he knew in time I'd drink, take drugs, and have lots of sex if given the chance. I was an American, not an Indian. To become a part of the American culture again was my karma. But could I maintain my devotion, actualize tantra, after I returned to the material world?

Maharaji said, "You're ready. You can't become any more of an Indian. Be devoted from America."

Did I pack my few possessions?

No.

Make travel arrangements?

No.

Say farewell to my sadhu friends?

No.

I disobeyed my guru and ran away.

I fled to Bodh Ashok Vihara, a Buddhist temple, which was the only other place I knew in New Delhi. I had stayed there briefly a few years earlier when I was very ill. At the time, a Cambodian monk named Dharma Wara had healed me with colored water. I was so sick with a high fever that I couldn't move. Rats were crawling over my body but I couldn't even lift my hand—I just had to watch them. It was a terrifying experience. Life is terrifying, particularly when you add death to it, when you put the whole picture together and stop avoiding reality. During that experience I learned that unless you're willing to go into the terror, there's not going to be any realization. The only way to find peace is to go through the fear.

The rats never hurt me. There had never really been any danger—only fear. Dharma Wara would come in and mop my brow. He had me drink colored water, and he watched me.

He was really healing me with the sun. Different-colored bottles were filled with water. As the sun came through, it would vibrate the color into the water. It's not scientific, but in India people aren't interested in what's scientific. They're just interested in what actually works. The colored water must have worked, because I got well very quickly.

NOW HERE I was again. This time I was in trouble because I didn't know where to go. As I sat by the well, a Buddhist monk came over and gave me a small brass *vajra dorje,* which represents a thunderbolt and is the symbol of Tibetan Buddhism. The thunderbolt is the divine, inde-structible weapon of Lord Shiva. It also represents the indestructible nature of the mind. This magical weapon always hits its mark. For me, receiving the vajra dorje was a sign that I should follow the Thunderbolt Path. I was sure that the Tibetans would have answers.

I kept telling myself that Maharaji hadn't taught me anything. I needed more advanced practices, more secret mantras. How was I sup-posed to progress on the spiritual path if Maharaji just sat there grinning at me but wouldn't initiate me into advanced techniques? I needed a new teacher, a guru who understood me and saw my full potential. Or so I made myself believe.

Wesak, the major annual Buddhist festival, was only a few days away. The monk encouraged me to take refuge in the Buddhist teachings and communities. He looked so peaceful. I started thinking about how much I needed a change and how all the Hindu stuff was getting to me. He led me to a nearby temple.

So I took refuge on Wesak, the anniversary of the day Buddha achieved final enlightenment, a very auspicious day. Buddhists came from all over the world to take part in the huge festival.

Dharma Wara and I spent some time together again, and he named me Anagorika Dharma Sara. *Anagorika* means "Homeless One"; *Dharma Sara* means, "The Essence of the Buddhist Teaching." I thought, "Ah, everything is new again." Now I was a Buddhist. That Hindu stuff was too confusing. All those garishly painted statues! Thank God I'd escaped!

I liked the Tibetans a lot. They were fun to be around and weren't vegetarians, so I started to eat meat again. I started feeling much health-ier.

The Tibetan pujas were colorful and beautiful. I loved to listen to the monks chant. I was in a Tibetan refugee camp, a self-contained Tibetan universe, completely different from the Indian culture around it. It felt especially spiritual and holy to me. Unlike the Hindu community, where only the sadhus were holy, in the Tibetan community lay people are considered as holy as the monks. This was a new idea that I found appealing. They were all in it together.

After the festival, I caught the 1:00 A.M. bus back to the temple where I was staying. I got off at my stop but still had to walk a couple miles off the main road. It was a still, full-moon night. I felt so happy. I was alone, walking down the road through the Muslim graveyards. It was eerie, but I felt so comfortable, like I'd found my niche in the world. I had a new name and could feel Buddha's blessing pouring down on me.

I turned a corner and went into a state of total terror. Hurtling straight at me was a dog with two heads, with four eyes blazing insanely, howling manically with both mouths! I did my whole Nepalese "scare the dog" trick—I yelled and threw a big stone. The stone bounced off its body like a cotton puff. The dog lunged at me and took a huge bite out of my leg. Then, as suddenly as it had appeared, the monster dog vanished into the darkness.

Welcome to Tibetan Buddhism! I was in shock. A slice of my leg was missing, and blood was streaming over my foot. I hobbled as quickly as I could to the temple. Dharma Wara came out and put the colored water on my wound and wrapped my leg in cloth. I went to bed shaking and finally fell into a troubled sleep.

When I woke up the next morning, my leg was completely healed. There wasn't even the faintest trace of a scar. Had Dharma Wara really cured such a serious injury overnight? Who—or what—was the dog? Had the whole thing really happened? There wasn't a scrap of physical evidence, only a residue of fear in my mind. I pushed the experience out of my thoughts because I couldn't begin to fathom it. I didn't know what any of it meant—the demon dog, the full moon, the Muslim graveyard. It was overwhelming.

I WAS A Tibetan Buddhist now, so I headed for Darjeeling, where the main Tibetan exile community was set up. Darjeeling is very much like Kathmandu—a high mountain city. I liked the mountains in India, but the plains were too hot and crowded. It was cool up in the mountains, and the winding streets were incredibly scenic. I was just like a tourist, appreciating everything.

I walked around Darjeeling saying a new mantra. It was the refugee prayer "Namo Buddaya, Namo Dharmmaya, Namo Sanghaya," which means, "I take refuge in the Buddha, I take refuge in the dharma, I take refuge in the community of saints." A Nepalese man overheard me chanting and said, "You must come visit my Lama."

The man took me to a little Buddhist village called Samdamp Tarje Ling Gompa. *Gompa* means "Place of Meditation." Inside the main building was an extraordinary man sitting in a box. His name was Kalu Rinpoche (Lama Kalu), and he looked like a monkey. He had a huge head, like a space alien. He had big hands and long, skinny arms stretching down to his knees (this is one of the signs of a living Buddha). He sat with his back really straight.

I started asking the people about him. They told me Kalu Rinpoche never laid down. He'd been sitting up for twenty years. He was doing a special kind of meditation training, which I later took up—the practice of sitting up all night meditating. (If one is going to do this training, it helps to have a wooden box, just big enough to allow sitting in the lotus position. There's no room to lie down, and if you lean over or slump back, you get so uncomfortable it wakes you up.)

Lama Kalu was wearing a sleeveless, day-glow-orange shirt, and he was doing japa. Watching his hand dance over the prayer beads, I realized I'd never seen anyone do japa with their left hand before. I was from the right-hand, Hindu tradition where the left hand is considered impure because it's used to wipe your bottom. Hindus consider the left hand dirty and the right hand clean. The Buddhist way made more sense because one could grant boons with the right hand and still keep the japa going.

It was 1967, and I was the first American whom Kalu Rinpoche had ever met. He put his hands on top of my head and said a prayer. His blessing was like a tangible substance. It was almost as if his breath became a bird that grazed the top of my head with the tips of its fluttering feathers.

Kalu Rinpoche was the lineage holder of a very esoteric Buddhist sect called the Shangpa Kargyupas lineage. He was a great yogi whom the Tibetans consider the Milarepa of our age.

Lama Kalu had recently arrived in India from a twelve-year meditation retreat in a cave outside Bhutan. He never slouched. I never saw his back less straight than a board.

Sitting in the hall, I felt as if I'd been time-warped into another universe. In fact, I'd just stepped into Tibet, magically transported to Darjeeling courtesy of the Chinese army. My hosts fed me Tibetan tea, which is basically salty, buttery, tea-flavored soup. It tastes better than it sounds. But what impressed me most was that I was considered instant family. They adopted me as one of their own.

Lama Kalu loved my name, Dharma Sara. "Oh, Dharma Sara! Dharma Sara's very happy." He'd look at me and beam. He looked so happy to see me, and he'd say, "Milarepa, Milarepa." I was wearing white robes and had hair down to my shoulders, which reminded him of the Tibetan yogi Milarepa, my hero! I felt incredible peace. I thought, "I've finally found my meditation teacher." But a twinge of guilt remained in my mind, which I eased by telling myself, "Well, I can't really leave Maharaji but, uh, yes, Maharaji sent me here! Obviously he sent me to get the real secret teachings from Kalu Rinpoche."

Lama Kalu officially initiated me in the Chenrezig mantra, "Om Mani Padme Hum" ("Now all powerful is the light of essential nature; now all powerful is the light of the lotus"), and he gave me his prayer beads. He told me to do the mantra for twelve years to develop the power of compassion. It wound up taking me longer than twelve years, but I did as he said. I was so excited about this mantra that I did it night and day. The sound "Hum" awakens the kundalini, the life force at the base of the spine. I really got into the power of the mantra because that's all the Tibetans did. Mantras were their whole trip. I realized I'd finally found my path, which was the *mantrayana:* the path of the mantra.

I got the full blessing in the mantra because Lama Kalu was able to empower me. He would eventually come to America in the late '70s, open over forty centers, and have many followers before he died.

ॐ

MANTRAS HAVE TO be given by a guru. I was initiated in a mantra by a guru who was completely realized and breathed his realization into the mantra. The moment I got the mantra, the mantra awoke within me. The mantra started doing itself through me, using me as a vehicle. I allowed myself to be used by the divine shakti. I surrendered to it, having full faith that I was floating safely in an ocean of compassion.

I felt so much love, but I was torn. I was sure Maharaji had sent me to Kalu Rinpoche because I needed a meditation teacher. I was sincerely asking, "What do I do?" My problem was that Maharaji had no handles. Your hands would just slip off his blanket, which filled the entire universe.

Maharaji seemed so expanded all the time. There was really nobody there. It was the most amazing experience being around someone who's completely immersed in the Godhead all the time. And yet we carried on normal conversations. He was in two places at once: here and there.

But he sent me to Lama Kalu so I could learn baby steps to get to the state Maharaji was in.

I didn't realize then, as I do now, that the ultimate teaching was given to me by Maharaji the first day we met. He had looked up and said: "You love me."

He was right. It all comes out of love.

I was confused about which guru was better for me. I finally worked it out in my mind by convincing myself that Lama Kalu was my meditation guru and Maharaji was the guru in my heart. I put the small picture of Maharaji in my little meditation cabin.

ॐ

LAMA KALU WAS constantly demonstrating the importance of compassion. You've got to be kind to people, he stressed. Spiritual life begins and ends with loving kindness. This is so different from the American way. Everyone is so power hungry in the West: power seminars, power lunches, power milk shakes. Power will eat you. It will burn you, and it will dry you up. It will suck out all your juices. Power will destroy you unless you have a pot to hold it in. The pot is your spiritual practice. And when your pot overflows with loving kindness, your spiritual practice is real.

Real spirituality isn't about getting high; it's about getting down. We're already high and we're already spiritual—we just need to get here. We need to arrive in the present. That's where faith is; that's where devotion is.

It all comes back to the "Om" in the mantra.

"Om" contains everything. The beginning and the end.

"Om" is now.

Chapter I 4

ONE DAY I decided to take a walk in the woods to do my practice. I hiked far, found a beautiful stream and a huge rock to sit on, and went into deep meditation, "Om Mani Padme Hum." It was idyllic, a spot where many of the great saints had sat.

Lost in my meditation, I suddenly felt a blow to my

body and a very sharp pain. I opened my eyes and found myself surrounded by twenty or thirty people, including many young children,
with stones in their hands. They had appeared from nowhere. They
started shouting angrily at me in Nepalese. All I could think of was that I
must have been sitting on their rock. When I felt a rock shoot by my
head, I realized they were stoning me. They were serious about killing
me. I jumped up and yelled, but the stones kept coming. I was completely surrounded by demons.

DEMONS ALWAYS COME to interrupt your practice, but demons
are not real. They're projections from the nature of the mind, like
Milarepa said. Don't give them reality. Take them back into the causal
plane, which is the atman or Self covered in bliss. The subtle or psychic
plane is the mind, and the material plane is the body. Sometimes the
reality of the material plane simply asserts itself.

THESE PEOPLE INTENDED to kill me, but I rejected the outcome.
Pulling my white robe around me, I walked out of the woods as quickly
as I could, repeating "Om Mani Padme Hum" with the conviction of
my concentration. Big rocks soared by like missiles. I could hear them
whistling by, barely missing my ears. I held onto the mantra and kept
walking, barely ten feet ahead of my attackers.

I walked steadily and kept the mantra going, not letting up on the
japa. I stayed on it, walked straight, and finally reached the highway,
thinking that if we were out in public, the mob would disperse. But no
such luck—they were gaining momentum and drawing more people

into the frenzy. Everyone was hurling stones. Unbelievably, none of the rocks actually hit my body.

I was walking down the highway with forty people behind me, aiming rocks at my body. I could feel the rocks through the folds of my cloth—they came that close. I could feel them pass a millimeter from my head. I visualized the back of my skull cracking. I was scared, but I kept the mantra going.

I owe my life to that mantra. I experienced the power of the word of God. Terror tantra: Can you hold the inner space in the face of imminent danger?

I finally got to the monastery. The mob continued after me and chased me up the stairs. The next thing I knew, Lama Kalu was standing on the top stairs with his robes flying in the breeze and his *mala* (string of beads) in his hand. He simply looked at the crowd and held up his hand, and my attackers ran backward as fast as they could.

I put my head on Lama Kalu's feet. I was so shaken. I went back to my room, panting in front of Maharaji's picture, thinking, "Did this happen because I left Maharaji?"

The next day, Lama Kalu explained that there had been a sadhu in the mountains who was stealing children. He would take them down to the plains and break their arms and legs, deforming them to use them as beggars. Since I was dressed in a white dhoti like the Hindus, the village people thought I was that sadhu. That morning, the lamas dyed my dhoti Buddhist red. Lama Kalu tied my hair up on top of my head himself, wrapping a ribbon around it, and looked at me and said, "Dilgo Khyentse." Dilgo Khyentse was a really famous lama who was tall like I am. So I turned into a lama overnight.

Everyone spoke Tibetan, and I didn't understand what they were saying. The monks spoke only a few words of English here and there. I would go into a dharma hall with fifty monks and they would mumble and grumble and chant mantras as they walked around with vases of peacock feathers. Then they tied strings on me. I would just sit for eight to ten hours every day, just being there, not understanding a word but still being a part of it just by my presence.

IT ALL COMES down to presence.
Being present in the moment.
And love.

SHORTLY AFTER BEING chased by the villagers, I woke up to find the monks very excited. They created much fanfare because Dudjom Rinpoche was coming to town. I had no idea who he was. The Tibetans' explanation was terse: "Famous lama. Holy lama." Yet another "His Holiness." The monks decorated the grounds with many prayer flags.

"He's the highest Buddha, the greatest saint!" they were saying. When he showed up, I thought he was a woman. He looked and acted like an old grandma. He wore his hair in a bun and had no facial hair.

I joined the monks and stood in line with a *kata*—a white cloth offered the lamas as a token of respect. They usually bless it and hand it back like prasad. The little Tibetan man walked up the steps smiling and stood in front of each person to receive the cloth. When he came to me, he stared up at me straight in the eyes for five minutes.

The whole world dissolved. My mind came to a total standstill. Time and space ceased to exist. There was nothing anywhere but light. I didn't exist; he didn't exist; the cosmos didn't exist. All that existed was light. Then he brought my mind back and hung the *kata* over my shoulders and walked on.

Afterward, Lama Kalu explained that Dudjom Rinpoche was the reincarnation of Padmasambhava, the lotus-born guru who first established Buddhism in Tibet. He was also the head of the Red Hats, the most ancient and magical of the Tibetan sects. He was married, had many children, and had a special gift: he was able to transmit the true nature of one's mind by looking at you. He held me in his gaze and carried me with him into the state of enlightenment. It was up to me to hold on to the state after he averted his eyes.

Not long after, I was given the Padmasambhava initiation by Tarthang Tulku, who's part of Dudjom Rinpoche's lineage. I was given a thangka (a cloth painting) of Padmasambhava. But every time I'd look at it, the face would turn into Maharaji's.

You might think that this was all in my imagination. Perhaps, but often the internal stuff is more real than the external stuff going on around you.

ॐ

LAMA KALU WAS sponsoring a special retreat in which about thirty monks had been sealed into small cells where they saw no one for three years, three months, and three days. Food came to them through a flap in the door. It was easy for me to stay up all night meditating because the worship never stopped.

At two in the morning I would hear human thigh bone trumpets from the lonely cells, as well as human drums. These were sacred sounds coming from sacred instruments crafted from old monks' bones and skin. When the monks died, their bones were dried and hollowed out to make trumpets and drums. A tight sheathe of the monks' skin covered the tops of the drums.

At three, the bells would ring again and I would hear the lamas chanting. Sometimes I felt as if the monks were only half in my world.

Part of them was off in the psychic universe, communing with the Buddha and conquering the demons that lurk behind our thoughts, with their sacred vibrations and profound sounds. The monks' souls cried out over the spiritual airwaves to protect us all. As I meditated, I was embraced by this haunting music.

It was always important for me to have long periods of solitude. But I also needed a city trip every couple months. I liked having the opposite states because I could test the level of equanimity I had attained in the city, where I was faced with human desires. I was able to see to what extent I lived in a meditative state and to what degree I was engaged with the senses.

CAN YOU HOLD the nondual vision when you visit duality? How much does it cost you?

It becomes a mixed bag. Mingling with the world is how you develop compassion. The more people you can love, the better off you are. How many strangers can you see as God?

First you have to establish the peace of God in your own heart. That can be accomplished only in solitude. You have to face your fears. You have to come to terms with the internal dialogue constantly going on in your head.

Everybody gets to star in their own movie. Sometimes, though, the movie stinks, and you start looking for a way out of the theater of your mind. The way out is never around—it's always through. Whatever you're doing, go through it. And sanctify it. It's not really your movie anyway. God is producing and directing it. So enjoy your bit part.

ON ONE CITY trip, I went to the bazaar in Darjeeling, where I ran into Zina Rachaevsky, a Russian princess I had met in Athens. She was definitely a star in her own movie. She said to me, "Michael, you must come to my house and meet my lamas." They were like her pet dogs.

The princess had two lamas living in her garden house, getting good meals in exchange for the sense of spiritual glamour their presence cast over the house. I was having dinner with them the first time I heard the Beatles' album "Revolver," which had just come out.

It was very intense for me, sitting on the windowsill listening to the Beatles, watching the mist change, and living in a Tibetan fairyland of dragon clouds and maroon-swathed lamas with clanging bells. It was as if the Beatles were somehow being piped back into the Middle Ages.

I was far away from America and couldn't have been happier.

Chapter I 5

I WAS FASCINATED with Kalu Rinpoche's lineage. I
had visions of all the great Tibetan masters: Naropa,
Tilopa, Milarepa. But the Tibetans were always talking
about a great living lama they called the Karmapa,
who lived in Sikkim. So of course I wanted to go see

him, and I also needed to do some traveling, to have some adventures.

Sikkim is an extraordinarily beautiful Himalayan valley with terraced rice fields, emerald-green mountains, and snow mountains behind them. It is a breathtaking, luscious landscape. My ride dropped me off, signaling, "Rumtek, Rumtek. Up that way." The Karmapa's Rumtek monastery was about five or six miles farther up another road. I bowed and kissed the ground, threw my pack over my shoulder, and repeated my mantra all the way there.

About halfway to the monastery I noticed a blazing light in the distance shooting directly at me. I walked toward it, saying, "Om Mani Padme Hum!" Finally I reached the huge white gates, about thirty feet high. I bowed and sat down, staring at the bright orange-gold beam of light that seemed to emanate from the monastery. The gates opened, and two Tibetans came out with a large teapot. I pulled out my skull cup, and they filled it up and walked back inside, leaving the gates wide open. (The skull cup, made from the top half of a human skull, is an important article in tantric worship. It is a reminder of death and impermanence. When it is used as a food bowl by a yogi, all the offerings turn into nectar. The body of the yogi becomes the deity worshiped, and the skull cup holds the soma, which gives immortality. Death is transformed into eternal life.)

I stared up at the huge square temple and saw that the mysterious light was coming from the roof. Near the source of the beam I could make out a solid gold eight-spoked Tibetan Wheel of the Law, with a deer carved on each side. I stared up at the light, saying, "Om Mani Padme Hum!" feeling incredibly blissful. I could hardly wait to see the Karmapa.

Several young Tibetan boys came out (I discovered later that they were reincarnations of great masters from the past) and escorted me in through the side entrance of the temple. I climbed up ten stories of stairs to the roof, saying, "Om Mani Padme Hum!" On top of the roof the light was sitting in the chair. It was the Karmapa's shirt, blazing orange-yellow on his chest. He was laughing at me.

I threw myself down in full *pranam* (laying flat on the ground) and felt ecstasy rippling over my back in waves. Then I felt someone lifting me. I looked up and was blinded by the orange-yellow light, behind which was a face. He had fat arms and a big smiling face, and a light was coming off his bald head. I crawled up to the Karmapa, and his pudgy hands came down on my head. I felt warm honey being poured over my soul.

The Karmapa asked me where I'd come from. I told him I'd come from Kalu Rinpoche. He promised he would initiate me the next day into the Vajra Yogini mantra—the Thunderbolt Naked Goddess mantra. It is the Tibetan yogi mantra that makes *tumo,* or mystic heat. (With this mantra you can fill your body with mystic heat as you get warm on the bliss. This way, you are able to meditate for long periods of time in the cold.)

I had so much shakti moving through my body that night that I couldn't sleep. I decided to meditate and do my mala instead. I sat in the room and closed my eyes, saying, "Om Mani Padme Hum!" All of a sudden my mind turned into a blue-sky dream. It was a beautiful, crystalline, azure sky—like the sky at dawn—with no taste of a cloud. It was translucent.

A ring of light shot out of the sky straight at me. I saw the Karmapa flying in the ring, carrying a crystal mala in one hand and holding a black hat on his head with the other hand. It was incredibly real, but for months afterward I kept wondering, "Why was he holding on to his hat?"

Much later I learned that the black hat was given to the 8th Karmapa, Mikyo Dorje, centuries ago. It had been woven in the celestial realm from the pubic hair of one hundred thousand *dakinis,* little celestial fairies. It held the power of the dakinis, so when the Karmapas wear this hat it activates the liberating power of the Tibetan spiritual lineage. Lineage is very important in Eastern religion because it is the conduit through which the energy of divine knowledge travels from century to century.

The next morning I was totally in love with the Karmapa. The young monks who brought tea were like peacocks: they didn't walk—they sort of flew around, up and down the stairs and through the corridors. They seemed to be flying because their robes were always flapping like goose wings. The lamas took me to the rooftop for another visit with His Holiness the Karmapa.

The Karmapa was so huge, like an Arabian sultan sitting on a grand flying carpet, with nothing but sky behind him. It was very much like my dream. I could see a black crown hovering above his head as I was sitting in front of him, but not with my physical eyes. I would later realize that dakinis were flying around him all the time.

I know this sounds like a fantasy, but they were there. In India I learned that "far out" experiences can be very real. I was already used to rocks talking back to me and trees saying hello—birds and cobra snakes, too. This was and always had been part of my reality. I had been a "nature boy" as a child, and The Greeter hermit from the woods had been one of my heroes.

ॐ

THE DAKINIS ARE very subtle, petite, naked fairies with tiny human-bone necklaces around their throats. They flit around like humming birds in the air and inside your mind. They whisper things and do favors for you by enlightening you. Once you are empowered by your guru, the dakinis you already have are then awakened by your guru's dakinis. They help you realize the truth that already exists within you, and at the same time they protect you from knowledge you're not prepared to receive (like information that would harm you or others). In spiritual practice the truth is revealed only when your soul is ready. How do you prepare your soul? Faithfully. Continue your practice.

ॐ

As THE KARMAPA sat reading aloud from a Tibetan text, he kept looking at me. I felt as if my body had turned into a giant pot and he was pouring a substance into me. He was filling me with the sounds that were coming from his mouth. These were sacred teachings spoken in a language I couldn't understand. These sounds were turning into deities: hundreds and hundreds of tiny vajra dakinis falling into me from the sky like snowflakes. They each had a little skull cup and a *khatvanga* (a trident with a skull on top of it.) Each had three eyes, and they were naked and had beautiful breasts. Light emanated from their yonis (vaginas).

The Karmapa gave me the Vajra Dakini mantra, which is basically the yoga of inner heat, or *Tummo*. He tied a ribbon around my neck and blew on the knot. I could see blue vapor come from his mouth that congealed around the knot. Finally, he put his hands on my head as if he were sealing up the bottle, putting the lid on the pot.

I had to leave the next day because I only had a two-day visa. I asked the Karmapa if he was my guru. He said, "No, no! Lama Kalu will teach you everything." The pure golden Buddhahood of the Karmapa was just awesome. He was dripping with golden shakti. He was the father, the king.

I did the Vajra Dakini mantra for the next twelve years. Vajra Dakini is the dancing, naked, sixteen-year-old red dakini covered in flames. She holds aloft the knife that cuts off the ego, and she drinks from a skull cup the hot blood of ego. She dances on the corpse of a demon, naked, in the full bloom of youth, dripping with shakti, three eyes staring into the ten directions of space, tongue hanging out, fanged, blood dripping from her chin.

I felt that it was time for me to move on. There was a small town nearby in the Sikkim valley with a huge Chinese population that the Tibetans call Kallingpong. I had heard about a Chinese yogi called C.M. Chen who lived in Kallingpong and had written hundreds of pamphlets in English. They were about the red and white *bindus,* the points where the identity of the individual soul and the universal soul is realized, where all living beings unite, the central channel—really esoteric stuff. Since I was near Kallingpong I decided to track him down.

The street urchins knew the old Chinese yogi, who always threw things out the window. He had been living in a hermitage in the center of the bazaar, having taken a vow not to leave his room for twenty years. He had a very hot puja going. His puja table was a shrine, alive with worship. It was multitiered, like a staircase, and elaborate with numerous offerings in different states of decomposition. All the offerings had mildewed. Spider webs were growing over the altar, fruit was rotting, an incense bowl was jammed with hundreds of used incense sticks, and grains of rice were dripping off the side. But there were also fresh flowers, fresh cakes, and fresh fruit. It had butter lamps on it, too. His puja table was truly an art form of worship. For years he had come to this table with his prayers.

Yogi Chen told me he had met the Karmapa in Tibet when the Karmapa was sixteen years old. The Karmapa had said to him, "Come here." Yogi Chen went up to get his blessing and the Karmapa said, "Kiss me." So Yogi Chen kissed him and got such a blessing that he had been in retreat for the last sixteen years doing heavy-duty *vajrayana* practice ever since. (Vajrayana is pure tantric worship using everything as the path, with an emphasis on mantra and inner visualization. It is the path of the guru and Enlightenment can be achieved in one lifetime.)

He'd gone to Tibet from China many times when Tibet was still largely accessible, back in the 1930s, and he had gotten many potent esoteric teachings.

Yogi pulled out several vajrayana texts and started translating them for me so I would know how to perform the dakini practice correctly. He told me what mantras to say and what to visualize as I said the mantras—the whole puja.

TIBETAN BUDDHISM IS really profound because it uses the imaginative quality of the mind to visualize. You create an inner art world, and with it you're able to give substance to the worship. It makes your worship much more interesting and detailed and becomes a science of the mantra, the yantra, and the tantra. The mantra is the mind of the deity, and the yantra is the body, the holder of consciousness that allows the mind to concentrate. The yantra is a geometric diagram that holds the subtle, universal energy form of God.

I STAYED WITH Yogi Chen for two days. His room was like a huge cave with books piled to the ceiling. He'd open his window and throw all kinds of sweets and fruit and money into the street as part of his puja offering. That's how he got to be so popular with the local children.

Yogi Chen ended up in Berkeley in an apartment building on Shattuck Avenue in the early 1970s. I used to visit him there. He would go down to the pet stores and buy hundreds of dollars worth of fish and birds and perform a ceremony out in the woods and let them all go. That was the lifestyle of Yogi Chen.

AFTER SEVERAL MONTHS on this traveling retreat, I headed to Darjeeling again. There I met a beautiful brunette, Gay, and I fell totally in love and lust. Gay was a very classy, intelligent, wealthy, beautiful, Jewish woman. She had an incredible light around her—she was a beautiful Ma.

I'm not sure how she ended up in India or why she had come. She was the photographer who took the shot of me that's in Ram Dass's book *Be Here Now*. We were taking a walk one day and she just took the picture. Then she invited me into her parlor for tea, which I knew could lead to a lot more. But I was a renunciate. Except for when I was at Major Rikki's house, I'd stayed true to my path. I wanted to protect myself, so I ran back to the monastery as fast as I could, reciting "Om Mani Padme Hum!"

The next day Gay showed up at the monastery with arms full of gifts for Lama Kalu. The next thing I knew I was sitting next to her. Lama Kalu did mantras over our heads and blessed us. I interpreted this to mean she was my dakini and he was giving her to me. With her I would learn to do tantra and the visualizations in the sex act.

So I went home with her. At that point I didn't understand that sex could be a spiritual act. I was moving on pure lust. But she initiated me and taught me tantric sex.

THE WHOLE IDEA of tantric sex is to take the kundalini, which is the dormant life energy from within, and bring it up through the body to the third eye. Think of the kundalini as a coiled snake moving up the spine. The man refrains from ejaculating, or holds his seed, to do this. As this is occurring, all the chakras (energy centers in the body), are vibrating with energy. This is done while breathing and saying the name of God as you make love to and worship your partner. You bathe in the bliss of her orgasm—that's the blessing she gives you.

ॐ

GAY AND I wound up in bed together for two weeks.

I tried to stay centered in the sex act with my mantra. I would do my puja while we were making love, and she was my living diety.

I would go into a deep visualization if I didn't come. As long as I could stop before I ejaculated, I could use the sexual energy to transcend the act with the power of my mantra, my breath, and my movement. I'd sit up straight with her on my lap because if I lay down it was hard to hold the seed. Sometimes I succeeded and sometimes I didn't. Sometimes I would go off completely—it was pure sex, have an orgasm, and goodnight! Other times I really got it, and every time I did, it was because of my effort to stay focused.

ॐ

THAT'S THE BEST you can do: stay conscious and stay focused. Say, "I'm going to repeat the mantra, the name of Ma, with every stroke of my penis. I'm really going to stay on it." You forget, come back. You forget again, come back again. Hold the seed and allow the woman to come and bathe you in the bliss of her orgasm. That's the blessing she gives you.

Chapter 16

OF THE TWO highest saints I met, Neem Karoli Baba and Kalu Rinpoche, neither of them let up for a moment with their mantras. For Neem Karoli Baba it was "Ram, Ram, Ram . . ." and for Kalu Rinpoche it was "Om Mani Padme Hum, Om Mani Padme Hum. . . ."

THE MANTRA IS completely liberating because it helps us focus from "I am the body" to "I am." The "I" turns in on itself. In effect, the ego becomes transmuted into the form of the deity. Your own purified mind becomes the guru, which means that you're always in direct connection with your inner guide. Staying on the mantra while you're having sex, while you're eating, while you're working, while you're doing anything, will keep you in touch with yourself and your true purpose.

Spiritual practice is like a boat. Before you can ride in the sea of enlightenment you have to get in the boat. But you have to have faith. If you don't have faith, pray for faith. Raise the sail and pick up the wind of your own breath. Follow it back into your heart with the mantra. Return from where you came and you'll go right back into the Mother Light, the ocean of consciousness.

When you do sadhana, your spiritual senses awaken and you can actually see God, hear God, touch God, taste God, and feel God. Unless God is so real you can smell him, you're not going to have the depth of devotion that's necessary to carry you through spiritually dry periods. When it's dry, when nothing's happening, when there are no ecstasies or visions, you need to persevere with the practice. You've got to have faith.

This is where satsang comes in. We need to gather together and celebrate. We keep celebrating the puja, intoning the mantras, and each person's inspiration infuses every other person. We share our longing and our process of awakening. This carries us to the next level.

ॐ

I WAS HAVING wonderful satsang with Gay. But I could see that she was getting attached to me, and I knew I needed to leave. I was still on the road and had to stay on the road because I wanted to be free.

I left without telling her. I folded up my bed pack and got on the bus to Deer Park outside Benares, where Buddha taught his first sermon. I don't know how she figured out where I was but she showed up a few days later, crying because she wanted me to be with her. I knew it wasn't what I was supposed to be doing. I blessed her and embraced her, and she left. I never saw her again, although I would always be grateful to her for what she taught me.

I had temporary lodgings in a small house where I made a huge puja table. I began a three-day puja to Maha Kala, the god of death. On the second night at about two in the morning, I was doing the ritual recitation and playing my bell and drum. I picked up a human thigh-bone trumpet, intoned the mantra of Maha Kala, put the trumpet to my lips, and blew as loud as I could. I wanted to see if he would come. I wanted to see if he was real. Or was this just hocus-pocus magic? If he was real, having a dialogue with death would be incredible. I was definitely setting up a challenge. I was terrified.

While I was blowing the trumpet, a gust of wind slammed open my door. My window burst open at the same moment. Maha Kala came into the room.

He was a huge, blue-black demonic-type deity. His body was fat and outlined with flames. He had six arms. His hair was standing up in all directions. He was a full, wrathful Tibetan deity.

He was dancing wildly. I could smell the fire. The energy in the room was terrifying. I was petrified. Every hair stood on end.

He asked, "What do you want?"

Until that moment I hadn't really believed that when you use these ancient rituals to invoke the gods, the gods really come. So when he asked what boon I was requesting, I was completely unprepared. The only thing I could think to say was, "I just called to see if you would come." He disappeared instantly.

ॐ

I WANTED TO continue my immersion in Buddhism and so traveled to Bodh Gaya, the spot where Buddha became enlightened.

I took the bus to the town of Gaya, which is about ten to fifteen miles from the center of the Buddhist world. I arrived at eight in the morning and walked from town all the way to the temple doing full prostration the entire way. I would do a prostration, get up, take a step, and do another prostration. I was bleeding all over by the time I got to Bodh Gaya, and it had gotten so late that the temple was closed. But I was blissed out from the exertion of doing the prostrations and repeating "Om Mani Padme Hum" thousands of times. I fell down in exhaustion at the temple door. A great peace swept over me. I cuddled up into a ball off to the side of the doorway and fell contentedly asleep.

At dawn I walked out into the field behind the temple to answer the call of nature and had to beat off the wild pigs coming to eat it before it hit the ground. I could hear the Muslims calling God from the minarets in the mosques nearby. "Allah hu Akbar! (God is great!)"

The Maha Bodhi temple is an incredible space, very high with heavy doors, and inside is a solid black stone Buddha, totally peaceful. I sat down, feeling the love of Buddha emanating from every stone in the temple.

I did one hundred thousand prostrations there. I found myself a spot outside the temple and all day and night I practiced, face to the ground. I'd say, "Om Mani Padme Hum," stand up, put my face to the ground, recite "Om Mani Padme Hum." I would watch the Tibetans walking around the temple with prayer wheels—twenty-four hours a day, this circle of devotional energy spinning clockwise around the temple.

There was a beautiful Tara murti built into the inside wall of the temple that I fell totally in love with. Tara, the Tibetan form of the Divine Mother, was unmistakably alive. I would do a lot of puja to her and light candles and bring gifts. The granite slab she was carved into was worn down into a crescent from the millions of foreheads bowing down before her. Every time I would put my forehead there, I'd repeat her mantra, "Om Tare tutare turey swaha!" which translates loosely as, "Oh Goddess, take me across. Save me from this ocean of birth and death. So be it." (Tara's body is green, and when you look at nature, you can, with the eye of faith, see her everywhere. Known as Kyan Shih Yin in China, she carries a vase of divine nectar and is the loving compassion of the Buddha.)

It took me about a month to finish the prostrations. Many times I'd be walking around the temple and I would actually see dakinis flying around its pinnacle. I was amazed to see these fairy beings, these miniature goddesses.

ॐ

I USED TO talk to the Bodhi tree, under which Buddha achieved full realization. It became the Mother to me. I wanted to worship the Buddha, yet I was strongly drawn to Shiva. But then and always it was the Mother of the Universe who drew the full force of my devotion.

I liked the simplicity, the silent feeling, of the Buddhist temples. They were so different from the chaotic, beggar-ridden Hindu temples. My shakti was in full throttle in Bodh Gaya, and I was sleeping only two or three hours a night, if that, sitting up. I was constantly on the prayer wheel, doing thousands of "Om Mani Padme Hum" and vajrayana mantras. I did numerous prostrations. Before me I would see the *mahasiddhas,* the great Buddhist masters of India, sitting on lotus petals in the air. They were always half naked and wore bone ornaments. They seemed to be the perfect bridge between Buddhism and Hinduism.

I was 1,000 percent at home in India, wandering pennilessly, living wholly on the overflowing grace of the Divine Mother. But, like Maharaji, she wasn't going to let me stay. Her plan was to ship me back to America to learn lessons so bitter that they couldn't be taught in India.

But there was another scene in Mother's play that would have to be acted out first. The principal player had just flown in from Harvard.

Chapter I7

ALTHOUGH I WAS spending most of my time at the temple, I couldn't help but see that the villagers outside Bodh Gaya were being ruthlessly exploited by the local *mahant*, the headman who controlled the village finances. Everybody worked for him. He owned the villagers' houses, so they were at his mercy, but he wasn't paying them much for their work. I decided to leave the temple and confront him. What's the point of having spiritual power if you don't use it to defend the poor and oppressed?

I found him sitting in his luxurious home on a tiger skin rug, surrounded by religious paraphernalia, beads in his hand. No doubt he thought of himself as a spiritual man. Many of the world's worst tyrants have considered themselves deeply religious.

I lit into him like an Old Testament prophet. "You hypocrite! You're pretending to be godly while you're cheating the people! You're a fraud!"

I was full of self-righteous fury, and my new role as defender of the downtrodden felt good. Thrilled with myself, I headed back to the temple and continued my prayers at the Bodhi tree.

The next day, I received a "Quit India" notice from the government. I had messed with The Man, and he was going to make my life miserable. I had fourteen days to leave the country.

No one would talk to me. The clerks at the post office wouldn't even hand me my mail. The word had gotten out: anyone caught so much as telling me the time of day was an outcast.

So much for being the champion of the people!

I went into hiding. I hid out in the caves of Vulture Peak, where Buddha gave the Prajnaparamita Sutra. According to Zen Buddhists, one day, instead of giving a lecture, Buddha held up a flower and didn't say a word. They say it was his greatest sermon.

I found a comfortable, dry cave with a southern exposure and dropped into silent meditation. These were dry limestone caves tucked back in the mountains, permeated with the tranquil vibration of meditation. I hid there for a couple months, leaving only when I went down to the springs to bathe. As I walked on the road I would look down at the dirt and realize, "Buddha's feet walked on this road. Buddha's feet!" And then I'd drop to my knees and cry. Living there was a very profound experience for me because I had a lot of love for Buddha. It was amazing to live in the same caves that monks had occupied for centuries.

I watched my breath all day and went out begging at night. I'd always do well because my begging bowl was a dried-out human skull. As soon as people saw it they would throw food in. They would say, "Here, eat and leave!" I always got fed fast.

Being an outlaw holy man was tough on the nerves, though, so I decided to cross the mountains from Bodh Gaya into Nepal. I slipped past the border patrol—I had no visa. Near the Svayambudnath temple I found a homey cowshed and made myself a bed of grass and hay. When I laid the blanket down, it was heaven!

I'd walk around the temple all day long. I was into keeping the mantra going, or maybe the mantra was keeping me going. I felt the sacredness of all forms. I was living in a mandala, a heaven on earth, in this magical land where every human being was deified in my consciousness.

One day as I was walking around the mountain I met a French girl with long black hair and sparkling eyes. We had great rapport, even though she never said a word the whole time I knew her. She started following me around the mountain, and then she came home with me. I hadn't had any sex in a year and a half. It was a beautiful connection. She was completely silent. I never learned her name. We just had this intense sexual connection—that was enough.

Kathmandu was starting to become a hippie hangout by this time, so there were more travelers in town. I met a beautiful Swedish girl named Ingrid, a seventeen-year-old blonde, in a tea shop, and somehow I ended up with both girls. It was an amazing trip. I'd have the blonde on one side and turn around and have the black-haired girl on the other side. I thought, "God, these mantras really work!" I started feeling like I was Padmasambhava and these were my two young dakinis. It was like taking time out from the harsh asceticism and relaxing in a moon bath of dakini energy. I felt like a king in my cowshed kingdom. I had my sadhana and four beautiful young arms to wrap myself in. Life was absolutely perfect.

I guess my contentedness caught the attention of one of Divine Mother's many faces: Kali Ma, the goddess of destruction and renewal. "Aha! Bhagavan Das is happy! Well, we'll just have to do something about that!" Since when have happy people made any significant spiritual progress?

I WOKE UP one morning with my girls and my cows and found a Danish hippie standing over us. He said, "There's this guy in town giving everyone LSD. Everybody gets eight hits. His name is Richard Alpert."

I knew what LSD was because I'd heard of Timothy Leary and Richard Alpert. News about these two renegade college professors with a mysterious new mind-altering drug had made it all the way here, to the seventh century. I was excited because I'd always wanted to try LSD. I knew I had to meet this guy.

I got dressed and headed into town. There was a restaurant called the Blue Tibetan where foreigners often hung out. People would go in, roll hashish cigarettes, and connect with each other. I sat at a table against the wall and ordered some tea. I'd been in there for about ten minutes when this big, gangly, bald-headed American walked in the door. Another Westerner and a short Indian man followed. All three had on brand-new, freshly pressed, clean clothing. They stood out like color characters in a black-and-white movie.

They looked at me as they walked by and then sat down at the back. Richard Alpert had his back to me and a tape recorder on the table next to him. Beside him sat Harish Johari, the Indian man, and across from both was David Padwa, the other American. They kept staring at me, so I got up and walked over.

I sat down next to Richard, who was fiddling with his tape recorder—checking the batteries, popping them in and out, pushing the buttons—and never acknowledging me. He seemed so nervous. I thought, "This is truly one of the most uptight persons I've ever met."

Harish, who looked like Hanuman, the monkey god, said that he'd heard about me. Folks in that area called me Dharma Sara, my Buddhist name. I mentioned the LSD, and they invited me back to their room for a hit. They were staying at the five-star hotel in Kathmandu called the Soalti, built by one of the king's sons. Fifteen stories tall, it was the largest building in Kathmandu, and it overlooked the entire valley.

My hosts offered me room service. I could have anything I wanted, so I ordered a peach Melba.

And so we began the "forum": a male power head trip. Talk about male bonding. It was this incredible ongoing philosophical talk that went on all day and night. It was so intense! Harish would roll hash cigarettes to keep things flowing. We discussed what was going on in America, kundalini and sexual energy, God, and the Divine Mother. It seemed as though we talked about everything. Richard and David were two intense Jewish intellectuals. It was an unbelievably diverse dialogue among the four of us about the mysteries of the universe, including Hinduism and Buddhism. We talked about *The Tibetan Book of the Dead* and about different states of consciousness. Then there was the book *Serpent Power*, which dealt with kundalini yoga. What did it all mean? We were all over the place in our conversation.

But the crown on the queen was LSD. Richard was convinced that LSD was the spiritual soma, the nectar of immortality, the spiritual substance that comes through alchemy. In that alchemical state, the drug produces an incredible vision, a heightened awareness, a sense of timelessness, and an opening into another dimension. Richard had come to India to find out about this soma and what came after it.

The next day, Richard offered me hits of LSD and STP, another psychedelic drug. I took them both and was launched on a forty-eight-hour trip.

Right away I started getting paranoid. I felt that I had to get out of the building. I couldn't deal with the sheetrock walls and the thick carpet. I was too far from the earth. My soles needed to touch the soil. Richard and I took the elevator downstairs to the bar area near a swimming pool. I sat down at the end of the pool and watched the sunlight reflect on the water. The water turned into the Ganges, and I started feeling happy.

Suddenly, all my energy flew into the sky. My legs locked into the lotus position, my back straightened, and the sun worship I'd been doing kicked in.

I stared into the sun, both eyes wide open, from ten that morning until the sun set in the early evening. I traveled with the sun all the way across the sky. I heard this extremely powerful "Ommmmmmmmmmmm!" coming out of the sun, and I plunged deeper into the sound. I slipped through the sun into a huge black hole and realized suddenly and completely that God lives behind the sun. The sun is his door.

Then I was in another dimension. It was black, peaceful, and absolutely immense. I was totally free. I had the choice at this point to drop my body. I knew I was free, liberated. I wasn't afraid. I had the choice to stay in that state or to come back.

The sun was starting to go down.

I had only another hour to make the most important decision of my life. I really wanted to go. I was absolutely ready to plunge every last cell of my selfhood into that eternal glowing molten core of bliss. Yes!

"Come back!" Maharaji's voice startled me so much that I lost my focus.

"What are you doing here?" I said. I was angry. "I'm a Buddhist now!" The sun slipped beneath the horizon, leaving me behind.

It was disappointing to return to earth. Everything had been so bright. Material reality seemed like a photographic negative in comparison. I looked over at Richard. He had the biggest head I'd ever seen. I thought, "God, it would be incredible to have his head as a skull cup. It would be twice as big as the one I have now." I reached over and put my hand on top of his head to see how it would feel holding it upside down in my hand. He was looking at me intensely, as if he wanted something from me. He looked like he wanted sex. He made me uptight because he was so pushy, in my face.

But Richard was also an intensely charismatic man. He was totally into me while I was totally into the LSD. I felt like I was being licked like an ice cream cone. He was licking me up and down. He was fawning all over me without touching. Richard was flipped out, like I was God, completely ecstatic in his adoration of me.

Even with all his neuroses, I loved Richard. He was like an angel with the most exquisite eyes I've ever seen, and he was balding. And he had the most beautiful soul: all golden. I was quite taken by him, even though he was gangly and somewhat geeky. He had a lot of pencils and pens in his pocket. And he had a strange edge about him that I thought came from the professors' world. He was also a psychotherapist. I could feel that he had a lot of conflict between his mind and his feelings. This conflict came out when he wasn't high.

He was always lying down when he could. He wasn't one to sit up and listen. He took in data and information lying down. It was his favorite way to be. I was practicing a lot of yoga and training my body, so I was usually in an upright position.

When he was high, he was the most flowing, beautiful person I've ever seen in my life. He was funny and smart. When he wasn't high, he was in his head all the time. While I was tripping I saw that he was interested in me not only as an experiment.

As if he'd been sent by central casting, a Hindu Brahmin got into the pool and started chanting the Gayatri mantra, the mantra of the sun, the mantra my Guru Maharaji had given me. My vision was starting to return, but everything had this light behind it—an aura, a pulsation. Everything had light.

The next thing I knew we were in the water and the pool was full of Ganges water. I couldn't say the Gayatri mantra. All that came out of my mouth was "Om." Everything was Om. Everything was sound that had become light, and then the light became form. This revelation was blowing me away.

Richard started playing with me like a kid, and we were going under water together—splashing and moving together like two dolphins. I got out of the pool and was still sitting there when the Hindu man who'd been doing the Gayatri mantra came up to me, bowed, touched my leg, and sat there trying to talk to me. I couldn't say anything except "Om." It was the only word that would come out of my mouth. That was the beginning and the end—there was nothing more to say. It was all so simple and complete.

I looked down at myself. The bottom part of my body was a man and the upper part of my body was a woman. I had breasts, and my hands were really thin and long. I was a hermaphrodite. This was a major revelation!

David Padwa came down carrying a beautiful Kashmiri shawl, warm and light. It was like a cloud. I put it on and started a slow promenade, like a deity walking with my two attendants, Richard and David, one on each side. With each step, not just my voice but my entire being said "Om." My voice seemed to come out of the soles of my feet and my fingers.

We walked in the entrance of the Soalti Hotel. It was like walking into America, except there were all these Nepalese people standing around in hotel uniforms. When I walked past they all saluted me, touching my feet.

It was strange being in the suite again. I felt strong hotel vibrations. I could hear all the toilets flushing; I could hear the water running through the pipes in the walls; I could feel the vibrations of all the people who built the hotel—I could even feel the vibrations of the people who built the beds. I really wanted to go back to the seventh century, to the cows and the smell of cow shit, to the feeling of the earth beneath my feet.

At that moment I really wanted to run away. Maharaji had told me to go back to America. I had refused, so America had come to Nepal.

Harish started singing a really low, humming chant. I could hear the "Om" in the hum. I realized he knew what I was feeling and was trying to comfort me by tuning in. He could see I was freaking out, and he was teaching me how to deal with it. I felt peaceful as I began to chant with him. I realized everyone had a sun in their heart that was radiating out an "Om." Everyone has the sound, though in some it is louder than in others. But if you chanted "Om," like a tuning fork, everyone would start to vibrate the sound. The whole world would be swallowed in the sound of reality.

I felt I was a captive in this room with these guys. This wasn't a suite, it was a cell! My mind was coming out of the "Om" into a paranoid space because I didn't know these people. Except for Harish, they were American. They kept me in this cell because they were scientists studying me.

Richard was observing me, writing notes and trying to figure out my mental condition. I could tell by looking at his body that all his energy was in his sex center. I put my hands on his heart and started breathing "Om." Then I went from his heart to his throat and had my hands on his forehead. I could feel the energy move up from his lower body into his third eye. I gave him the "Om Mani Padme Hum" mantra at that time. We chanted it together for a couple hours and really got into it.

David ordered some food. I just looked at it, but I couldn't eat it because I didn't know what it was. It didn't look like food. It didn't smell like food. It wasn't people food—it was hotel food. The environment was completely artificial. I couldn't survive in this fake universe.

Everyone went to sleep, and I shot out the door. It was an incredible feeling of escape. I got back to my cowshed, and it was so nice to feel my girlfriends' soft skin. I could smell them, lie with them, and snuggle them in childlike bliss. Richard Alpert could have the Soalti Hotel. This was paradise!

I cooked myself some dhal, rice, and fried some chapati, some real food. For the first time I really understood how profound food is, and how susceptible it is to the vibrations around it. You're really not eating the food, you're eating the vibrations carried by the food. So it's important to be selective about what you eat and who cooks it. Richard and David were the way they were because of the vibrations they ate.

ॐ

THE NEXT DAY, I was having a wonderful time with my two girls when David's Land Rover pulled up outside the cowshed. Richard, David, and Harish wanted to talk about the LSD trip.

I admitted to them that it was the most incredible thing I'd ever experienced in my life. It was amazing to go that deep that fast. Within a few hours I'd reached a deep *samadhi* (psychic absorption) and still had psychic energy going. I must have done one hundred thousand mantras or more on that trip . . . three days of constant repetition. It was very powerful.

When I was finished describing it, David said, "We're going back to

India and we want you to come with us. You can ride in the Land Rover and we'll pay your way with rupees and LSD."

The American power had come to tempt me—money, drugs, and fast cars. I was really torn. On the one hand, there was the Land Rover, LSD, and hanging out with Richard, who was already famous with Timothy Leary for turning the world onto LSD at Harvard, and on the other was the two girls and my peaceful existence. I wanted to stay with the two girls, but I left.

The Land Rover was a trip in and of itself; it was practically a ship. It had a bathroom, kitchen, shower, and stove, and it slept four people. Double tires on the rear, water containers on the side, enormous gas tanks—this jeep had everything. It was a safari rig!

Richard had hundreds of tapes and musical instruments he was bringing back to the states. He was a museum curator! I'd never seen so much stuff: T-shirts, sweaters, socks, shoes, sleeping bags, and more sleeping bags! It was an American capsule. At Patna, Harish had to go home. David took off, leaving Richard and me with his Land Rover. We planned to meet later.

He let me drive the Land Rover. I was dodging trucks, ox carts and bullocks, people, and bicycles. It was intense, and I was having a great time. I loved it. It was like driving an elephant. Richard was sitting next to me, playing his Indian tapes. He kept asking, "Where are we going?" and I just kept on driving.

We drove to Calcutta and went to the Kali temple at Kalighat. The steps were covered with blood. Richard was absolutely horrified but was willing to go anywhere because he was so devoted to me. It was a tease because he had a bottle of LSD with maybe fifty trips in it. I really wanted the bottle, and he really wanted to have sex with me.

I was a Guru at last. I had a real devotee—a famous American with lots of money. It didn't matter to me that his intentions weren't spiritual. I figured I would show him the path and he would come around.

I had always wanted to visit the Sun Temple at Kanorak in Orissa. So Richard and I set off. It was built like a giant chariot with stone horses in space. Surrounding the temple were intricate, intensely erotic sculptures. I couldn't figure out what they had to do with God.

Richard headed for the tourist bungalow, where he spent all his time lying down. He had gone through thousands of hours of psychotherapy in the states. When Richard would lie down he would be in a very receptive mode—his female mode. When he was up, he would be in his male mode—his compulsive mode. And he loved the bathtub. He was always taking baths by candlelight.

I took off for the temple to explore. I wandered around the sanctum sanctorium. It was like a round dance floor. I realized that it was the control center of the temple and that it was where I needed to be. I had fasted for three days in preparation. I snuck into the temple at about three in the morning. I took two hits of LSD. At the crack of dawn I became Surya, God of the Sun, and drove the solar chariot through the sky. I felt the horses moving; I actually felt the reins in my hands. I started doing my Surya prayer: "Om Sri Savitri Surya Narayana Namaha!" I was riding on rays of light. I stayed in that state as long as I could hold on to the reins.

Then the crowds started arriving. To them the Sun Temple was only a tourist attraction, but it was the control center of the universe to me. It had pulsating energy inside, and I felt like I had the key, LSD.

I felt uneasy because people were coming, but the guards bowed to me and allowed me to continue my meditation. When I finally stepped outside, all the people looked like balls of energy. They were round, glowing balls—disturbed energy moving in different patterns. I then realized what the erotic sculptures were about: We have to get as serious about God as we are about sex.

I went back to the bungalow to talk to Richard about his sexual energy. I wanted to share with him what I'd just realized. As I sat on the leopard skin, with my head in the clouds, he sat at my feet, high on LSD, looking to me with devotion. I jumped right in with my explanation.

"Richard, just as your LSD is soma to take me deeper into my practice, your seed is soma to take you deeper into your practice. What's going on between us is that my sexual energy is focused on your LSD bottle, and yours is focused on me.

"But I thought we were doing a spiritual practice." Richard looked confused.

"We are—but there's all this sexual energy and it's distracting both of us. You think you're attracted to me physically, when in fact you're attracted to my energy. The idea is to worship the sex act as God. The key to realization is transforming the sexual energy. Lust is the last barrier." I had no idea if I was making myself clear.

"But my sexual energy is so intense, Bhagavan Das."

"That's because the only energy you've known is sexual energy. You're locked in your second chakra—the sex chakra. But sexual energy can be the key when you bring it up into the head with the inward breath and down through the body with the mantra, and then let it flow down over the body. You've got to raise the energy and make love to God. This is the real sex.

"If you allow yourself to learn tantric sex, where you hold your seed as you bring your energy up through the chakras, it will become the golden nectar of soma and permeate your body. It will be the best sex you've ever had."

Unfortunately, what started out as a discussion of how sexual energy can be transformed into spiritual energy ended up sounding like a come-on. Why was I having such a hard time teaching this man?

IT WAS TIME for me to get back to my guru's feet, and I was going to take Richard with me. I wanted him to see where I came from, that the qualities he believed he was drawn to were really coming from Neem Karoli Baba. He needed to see the source of the energy he was attracted to.

I was having a hard time dealing with Richard and my homophobia. Only Neem Karoli Baba, Hanuman himself, could deal with this character.

I got in the car. Richard, as usual, was extremely tense. "Where are you taking me?" he asked.

"Get in the car and close the door. We're going now." He was half-crazed because I didn't tell him where we were going. He was really getting on my nerves. I rolled him a joint to calm him down. We drove up to Naini Tal. I spotted some people who knew me and asked where Maharaji was. They told me he was outside of Bhumyadhar, down the mountain a bit.

I drove to Bhumyadhar and saw a huge crowd of people heading toward the local temple. We were in the right place. I parked and ran up the hill, so eager to see my guru. I felt like the prodigal son coming home. In my mind I was calling, "Maharaji, you've got to accept me back! Please help me out! This man has attached himself to me and I don't know what to do with him."

Maharaji was sitting on top of the hill on a blanket someone had laid down, surrounded by devotees. Everyone was laughing and chatting. I was weeping. Tears were soaking my dhoti.

I was so happy to be with Maharaji.

I was so happy to be passing Richard on to Maharaji.

I would be free again!

I considered the Land Rover keys in my hand. I gave Maharaji the keys and said, "Maharaji, this car is yours."

Richard became angry and flustered. His face turned red. "You can't do that! It's David's car!"

I said, "Maharaji, it's yours. Everything is yours." And Richard's yours, too, I was thinking. I wanted to just walk away and go back to my empty room and sit quietly by the river again. I wanted all these entanglements to go away.

Maharaji looked at me and then looked over at Richard. After a moment he pointed to Richard and said to me in Hindi, "He loves you very much."

I sputtered, "Yes Maharaji, I know!"

Maharaji laughed and laughed and laughed.

Maharaji instructed, "Give him a picture of me." One of the other devotees ran up with a photograph and handed it to Richard.

Richard didn't understand the significance of this and thought Maharaji was being arrogant.

Then Maharaji turned back to me and said, "You take care of him. He loves you."

I didn't want the responsibility, but if Maharaji wanted to give him back to me now, that was okay, because whether Richard knew it or not, he'd just received the blessings of one of the greatest saints on the planet. Richard was just sitting there angry, watching the scene. He couldn't fathom any of it.

Chapter I 8

THE NEXT DAY, Maharaji wanted to go for a ride in the Land Rover. Richard was still upset about my giving the car to him. It was a difficult thing for him to understand. A group of us piled in, and I drove to an orchard where we sprawled out over the grass. Maharaji turned to Richard and said, "Spleen." Richard looked confused—he didn't understand Hindi. Someone came over to translate, and Maharaji continued, "You were thinking of your mother last night, while you were looking at the stars. She died of the spleen."

Richard's mother had died recently of an enlarged spleen. The night before, he had been sitting out under the stars, near tears, remembering her. He hadn't mentioned his pain to anyone. But of course Maharaji knew. And so, he opened Richard's heart.

Richard started sobbing. This incident broke him open. It shattered his heart, and then Maharaji put it back together again. He sat with his head on Maharaji's lap, weeping from the innermost part of his soul.

An amazing transformation happened to Richard Alpert that day: he showed his true feelings. The mask dropped. There was no more pretense, and his concern with prestige seemed to fade. Richard didn't share with me how things had internally changed for him, but I could see it and feel it. He had gone from a thinking state to a feeling state. He was not the same person after the day in the orchard.

Our relationship changed, too. After spending time with "the old man," Richard took me seriously—I was no longer some twenty-three-year-old kid he wanted to have sex with. He gave me back my astral space. Maharaji gave us our own rooms in Kanchi and told me to teach Richard. I became his guru.

We would get up at three in the morning, and I would get the fire going and boil water for his bath and make him tea. Then we'd have discourses on the scriptures and I would teach him hatha-yoga. We'd do a couple hours of postures and chant mantras. I would then go back to my room to keep my own practice going and give him a lot of space.

In the middle of all this was Hari Das Baba, who was taking care of us, providing supplies, tea, and food. I was cooking rice and lentils and chapatis and had my own stove going. Hari Das Baba would teach, too—he'd sit and answer questions on his slate board. Richard had a little puja table set up. He had pictures of holy beings like Ramakrishna,

Ramana Maharshi, and of course Maharaji. There were at least twenty different saints on his puja table—he was covering his bases. He spent all his time in devotion. Whatever he saw me do, he did. It was a true teacher-disciple relationship. Richard Alpert was realizing God.

Maharaji was traveling all the time, but he would come back to Kanchi every week or so, and then there was always a party. Sacks of potatoes would arrive, and huge amounts of food would be cooked: lentils, chickpeas, bread, sweets, mangoes, kiwi, papaya, star fruit, and the finest teas. We had ten-course meals. There was always a feast wherever Maharaji touched down. Wherever he went, everyone was lavishly fed. Maharaji used the prasad to give his blessings; his grace would flow through the food.

At one of these feasts, Maharaji initiated Richard to be Ram Dass. When the moment came, Richard wept openly. Saint school had been tough, but he'd made it. Now he was part of Maharaji's team. That was the feeling, and it was a strong brotherhood. There were very few of us—just five sadhus: Bhagavan Das, Ram Dass, Khor Das, Hari Das, and Brahmachari Baba. There were hundreds of devotees, but they weren't yogi renunciates like us.

Ram Dass worked hard during this transformation. He wore only one piece of cloth. He was struggling with austerities; he just couldn't manage the cold bath—that was just too much—so I'd heat water for him. We tried to make the food a little less spicy for him. His heart was really into it, but it was a bit overwhelming. Having been very wealthy and successful back in the United States, he was used to the amenities.

RAM DASS WAS always extremely generous. He gave me the sitar he'd bought in Delhi because he knew I loved music.

A sitar is a very complicated instrument. This one had dozens of strings, and I didn't know how to tune it. I didn't know where to begin, so I left it in the empty room next to Ram Dass's room. Every day I'd bring it flowers and worship it as Sarasvati—the goddess of music, art, and letters. For weeks I sat with it and meditated.

One day, the sitar spoke to me and told me to pick it up. I picked it up very respectfully, as if I was holding a beautiful woman in my arms. Then it said, "Tune me." And I started tuning the strings. For the next couple weeks I spent hours tuning the sitar, never playing it. Finally, something happened and it all came together. I started to play. But it didn't feel like I was playing the sitar—it felt like the sitar was playing me. Sarasvati was playing the sitar by using my fingers. I never had a lesson. I just surrendered to the Goddess. The music was sublime.

Soon after I learned to play, Ram Dass told me he had been sitting in the next room listening to me play the sitar for about an hour. It was the most beautiful melody. Then he happened to look out the window and saw me over at the tea stand across the street. And still, the divine music continued. He turned white and ran next door, and there was the sitar lying by itself on the floor. There was no one in the room.

Ram Dass realized he had tuned in to where music itself comes from. He realized that I was tuned in to where it was coming from when I sat down to play perfectly, never having had a lesson. In India, musicians practice nada yoga, the yoga of sound following the notes back to their source, searching for the original player. It's so arrogant of us to believe we can make music. Only God makes music. The universe is her song.

In the beginning, Ram Dass constantly tried to impress me:

"When I was having dinner with the president of Harvard, Kissinger came and . . ."

"Flying solo over the Grand Canyon alone is something everyone should do. . . ."

He was always spinning off some yarn of famous people he had met, great lectures he'd given, or some amazing trip he had taken. I was uninterested. I was happy living a simple life.

I would tell Richard, "Stop tripping in the past. Stop future-tripping and worrying about what's going to happen to you. Just drop into the now, the present moment, with the breath." I taught him how to watch his breath, how to do simple breathing exercises to still the mind, how to do yoga postures, and how to chant.

Richard did a lot of spiritual practice with great sincerity. He spent a lot of time alone. He re-created himself with Maharaji's blessing.

Ram Dass would go on to become a great soul—teaching, writing, and practicing selfless service for numerous charities. He personally served the sick and dying and helped raise enormous amounts of money to aid the poor and sick throughout the world. It's funny how once he stopped trying to impress people so much he became very impressive indeed.

ONE DAY IN the midst of our austerities, a message arrived that Maharaji wanted to see us. We drove down to Bhumidhar Temple, where he was staying, and sat down close to him. Maharaji asked Richard where the medicine was. Richard didn't know what he meant. Did he need aspirin or an antibiotic, or maybe a laxative? I had heard Maharaji mention the new "yogi medicine that gives psychic powers" and realized immediately what he was talking about. I whispered to Richard, "He means the LSD."

"This is so cool," I was thinking. "Maharaji wants to check it out. We're going to see Maharaji tripping!"

Richard went out to the Land Rover and came back with his travel kit: a bottle full of different tablets—librium, LSD, STP, anything you might need on the road. He took out one 305-microgram pill of Osley White Lightning and dropped it into Maharaji's hand. Maharaji looked at it and held out his hand again toward Richard. Richard was shocked. Maharaji waved his hand. "Another one." So Richard put another hit in his hand. "More." Richard gave him a third one. That was 915 mikes in all, and believe me, just one of those pills was a solid, guaranteed ego-loss trip where the floor dissolves and your hand goes through the wall.

I watched Maharaji lift his palm up, pop all three pills in his mouth, and drink some water. I stayed as close to him as I could for hours, literally hanging on to his leg. Richard was observing him like a scientist, notepad and pen in hand, ready to begin scribbling.

Nothing happened.

We sat there all day, and there was no change in his state. He simply carried on, twinkling at us. He was completely calm—just being there as usual. We had tea, people came and went, and he talked with visitors about different worldly affairs like he always did. Sometimes he'd pause for a moment, turning into Shiva, suddenly sitting up very straight and turning within for a couple seconds, going wherever he went when he checked in like that. Then he'd lie back down and continue to converse with those around him. But he always did that. It wasn't unusual at all.

Maharaji took enough LSD to make an elephant grow wings and fly over Mount Everest. And absolutely nothing happened.

Richard was in a state of disbelief. I was nonchalant. I figured, the state Maharaji was in, he could watch a comet smash into the earth and turn it into a ball of planetary dust and he wouldn't even blink an eye. Maharaji was the reality in which the entire solar system abided. The supreme consciousness is not affected by time or space, by life or death. Why should it be affected by LSD?

Shortly after this experience, we were riding in the Land Rover when Maharaji said to Ram Dass, "You have my blessings for your book."

Ram Dass was confused. "What book?"

Maharaji just smiled. He was planning on coming to America, but he wasn't coming in his body. He would come in the form of a book.

That moment, in the car, Maharaji laid the seed in Ram Dass's mind. He would return to the United States and write a book about his experiences in India and Nepal, about the yoga tradition, about the great master Neem Karoli Baba, and about Bhagavan Das. Over the next twenty-five years, *Be Here Now* would go through nearly forty printings and find its way into every bookstore throughout the world. Ram Dass would describe me as if I were some kind of enlightened, mythical being. But I was just a lost child, trying to find my way home to Mother.

After staying with us for six months, Richard decided to go back to America. I drove him to Delhi and put him on a plane. He gave me all his Indian money—2,000 rupees—and a beautiful Tibetan bell and dorje. He was so grateful to me. Yes, he loved me a lot, but Maharaji had transformed his profane love into something quite profound.

After he left, I headed back up to the mountains. I felt relieved. I hadn't realized what a burden it was to be a teacher. The gurus knew— Kalu Rinpoche and the Karmapa and Maharaji all made it look so effortless. It wasn't that Ram Dass wasn't a good friend or student; on the contrary, he surpassed my expectations in every way. I would never have expected such a neurotic, academic type to completely pull himself together and so sincerely lay his life at God's feet. But taking on another person's karma is an enormous responsibility. At that time I felt that I was still too spiritually immature myself to be anyone else's teacher. Unfortunately, because of my work with Ram Dass and because I was Maharaji's sadhu, many of the Indians were starting to overestimate my powers. I didn't ask for their adoration, but, nonetheless, I also didn't want to disappoint them.

Maharaji gave me a *kutir,* which is a cavelike hut. It was located in the middle of a forest in a place called Jhokyapani, which means "leech water," about ten miles between Kanchi and Naini Tal, outside Bhumyadhar. It was a small medieval building made of rock and mud.

I was fed by a villager who had been told to serve me. At seven o'clock every evening, this skinny man, naked except for a dirty rag around his loins, would show up with a tray heaped with spicy food. He would put the plate before me, prostrate, and then sit there while I ate, waiting to take the tray home. He hadn't eaten all day because he had been ordered to feed me before feeding himself. So he would drool like a dog in front of me, making me feel guilty. I could hear him swallowing saliva.

I knew this would catch up with me soon enough. One day, he brought his son, who was extremely sick, and demanded, "Cure him." I had never healed anyone before. I couldn't even heal myself. But I was a sadhu and was supposed to have spiritual power. I couldn't let my brotherhood of sadhus down. I wanted to show this man I was the real thing, someone worth feeding. So I tried to heal the boy.

I put my faith in my Tibetan trip, which wasn't really authentic for me but was the spiritual practice I was doing at the time. So I prayed and chanted and waved my arms and did the Vajrasattva mantra.

It didn't work.

The man took his son home, and I never saw him again.

I lost my dinner.

I wasn't able to cure the man's son because I forgot my root guru. I forgot Neem Karoli Baba. I should have called out to Maharaji. I should have chanted, "Ram, Ram, Ram." Instead I invoked a deity who wasn't completely real to me, using a mantra that wasn't fully energized. I had come so far, only to fall back. It was a depressing and humiliating failure.

Chapter 19

CLEARLY IT WAS time for me to intensify my spiritual practice. Ram Dass's metamorphosis from Richard Alpert had drained me. And then I had made a mess of it in the forest, trying to heal the sick child. I left for Bhareilly, the town where Harish Johari lived.

Harish took me to the cremation ground outside town.

There was so much shakti. Kali Ma was everywhere, but the cremation grounds were her favorite haunt. There were lots of bodies lying around but no people—just demons. I needed the reality of death in my life because death reminds me to go to God. I vowed to stay there for two weeks.

It was the longest two weeks of my life. After the first day, I saw enough death to last a lifetime—at least four or five bodies during the first hour. And the bodies all came with funeral parties. Everyone was moaning and grieving and miserable.

"Ram nam satyahai satyabol sattyahai!" ("God's name is True, say the truth, it is true.") they chanted as they brought the bodies down on bamboo poles with cloth stretched across. Business was brisk. In those two weeks I must have seen over fifty bodies, a steady stream coming in every day, and I saw the whole drama—the depth of people's attachments and loss.

After being there for three days, I was incredibly alert. Wide awake. There were fifteen funeral pyres on one side of the road and twelve pits dug in the ground on the other side. Outside the cemetery wall at the very back was the baby graveyard—tiny skulls everywhere. They didn't burn infant corpses in India, they just threw them over the walls to be devoured by jackals and wild hyenas.

Howling dogs were always around, which added immensely to the atmosphere. They'd fight over a rib cage and tear arms and legs to pieces. I thought, life is not a test. Life is the real thing. And there's nothing in life more real than death.

Harish introduced me to a householder yogi named Mashani Baba. He looked like any other thin, middle-age Hindu male, though he seemed very inner directed. He was a railway clerk who had been spending every night of the last eleven years at the cremation grounds.

The stench of burning flesh wafted through the air. In the eerie twilight I sensed something very unsettling about Mashani. He glowed like one of the fires in the falling darkness.

Mashani Baba had been traveling by train near Hyderabad in central India eleven years earlier when the train made an emergency stop in the desert far from any village. He climbed off the train and walked into an open field some distance away to relieve himself. Looking up, he found himself staring into the eyes of a naked holy man. Mashani Baba was overcome with emotion and bent down to touch the sadhu's feet. The holy man initiated Mashani in a mantra and told him that if he repeated it in the burning grounds for twelve years, he would attain *siddhi*— spiritual perfection. Mashani returned to the train with the mantra planted in his heart.

In my grass hut on the outskirts of the cremation grounds, I would sit in deep meditation as I watched Mashani Baba come and go. And I watched the bodies carried in, night and day, to feed the roaring fires. The continual sight of stiff and swollen human bodies shriveling into ashes was tremendously motivating for my spiritual practice.

Kali Ma, the goddess of death and rebirth, came alive inside me during those two weeks. I surrendered to the darkness as I let go. And as I let go, the light appeared—Kali Ma!

Kali Ma—Goddess of Birth and Death, of darkness and light. She is the thorn on the rose, getting her taste of blood before releasing the prize. She is the beautiful, thick-coated lamb, and she is the shivering shearling. She is the baby being nursed while the frail old woman decays in the corner.

Barren Indian women worship Kali to get pregnant. Four times a year the priests carry water pots covered in flowers and red cloth to symbolize the Mother. As they chant "Kali Ma," they travel from village to village. The women line up along the path with their chickens and goats. The priests lop off the heads of the animals with a sword and spray the water pot with blood. The women make their request and one month later get pregnant. This is the death-to-give-birth cycle of Kali.

ॐ

AFTER ABOUT TEN days, Mashani Baba asked if I would like to do the ritual worship with him in the main section of the fire pits. I had been avoiding that area; the presence of death was strong enough where I was staying, near the main gate of the compound. On that night, though, I agreed to go with him.

At midnight, Mashani Baba took off his clothes, folded them in a neat pile, and took a cold bath. He came out of the water, still dripping, and opened a sack of ashes, powdering his entire body with them. He motioned me to follow, and I walked behind him in the garden of fires. Some were glowing, some smoking, and others had burned out.

When we reached the hottest fire pits, Mashani knelt down and began to breathe deeply. It was as if he was inhaling the energy of the fire. Then he calmly walked over the burning coals into the middle of the fire and, climbing up into the hottest part, sat down facing me through the flames. My knees were shaking, and sweat was pouring down my body from the intense heat and pure fear.

I sat down on the edge of the pit a few feet from the outermost burning coals and stared at this naked railway clerk sitting on a heap of burning human flesh. The body beneath him was still decomposing in the fierce heat when Mashani Baba assumed a squatting position. I could feel his breath ten feet away. He was filling himself with energy from the fires.

What I saw next made my hair stand on end. Mashani Baba's skin color darkened to black, and his eyes became large and wild like a tiger's. He plunged his dark arms into the flames, pulled up a piece of flesh, and began eating it. At that moment his teeth became fangs, and I was shocked to see that he had large breasts and a vagina. He was transformed into Mother Kali and was feeding on death.

My body was shaking violently. I could feel the kundalini shakti beating in my solar plexus like a drum. My eyes were locked on Goddess Mashani, and I felt an energy streak up my spine like lightning. I could hear "Om" whirling like a tornado in my ears, blowing open my third eye. The bliss I experienced was beyond the beyond, greater than any sexual experience in my life. It was pure communion of flesh and spirit as the Cosmic Mother drank the hot blood of my ego from my skull. My body completely disappeared; I was just a severed head in Kali's hand as I inhaled the pungent incense of burning flesh.

My spirit imploded back into my body like a shock wave. Mashani Baba picked up fire in his bare hands and began throwing burning coals at me. The cloth I was wearing was starting to burn, and I watched with total detachment as a hot coal burned a hole in my thigh. As the smell of my burning flesh filled my nostrils, I came to my senses and was able to push the coal off my leg. I still have deep scars in my thigh to this day.

I bowed before the flames, stood up slowly, and walked out of the realm of death. I couldn't believe what had just happened. My mind was totally blown. Looking down, I saw the burnt hole in my cloth.

I went back to my hut and sat motionlessly, watching the naked man, covered in ashes, come out into the dawn and take his bath. He unfolded his clothes, put them on, and walked over to me. We shared a morning cup of tea before he walked his bicycle out to the main road and headed for the railway station to begin his workday.

ॐ

I'M GOING TO tell you something awful and true. There's something actually thrilling about sitting on the side of a hill overlooking human barbecue pits with flames leaping into the air, feeling demons everywhere. The demons are great because they keep you awake, guaranteed. They're dancing all around you just at the edge of your peripheral vision. And they sneak right behind you. Death makes you absolutely lucid.

ॐ

I COULDN'T SLEEP a wink. Everytime I'd lie down, something lurking in the shadows would tap or pinch me. The place was crawling with spooks. I've never felt so many ghosts in my life. My hair was constantly standing on edge. I could feel the demons shaking me. It takes a lot of presence to hold the energy of that space. You have to have a lot of faith just to be there.

I used to sit with my skull cup in front of me, and it would vibrate and shake from the shakti. Demons were attracted to it because it was human bone. When you are in that atmosphere, you get into the bhava (divine mood) of Lord Shiva.

Lord Shiva did all his spiritual practice in the cremation grounds. The ghouls were his servants. I chanted "Shivo'ham, Shivo'ham. I am Shiva, I am Shiva. This world is a cremation ground. Burn my desires, Mother. Make me free. I love you more than I love my life. Take it. It's yours."

Shiva lies in the burning grounds. He is pallid, and there is no breath as Kali Ma dances over his chest. *Shiva* means "God"; *shaiva* means "corpse." The difference between Shiva and *shaiva* is the touch of the Divine Mother's feet.

This was my emotional state: "Come, Mother, come. I am here, in your place of worship. Take me away. I want to know you, I want to love you, I want to see the beauty of death. I want to make love to death. Show me how alive you are, death. Lead me from the unreal to the real, from darkness to light, from death to immortality."

I would sit on the hill overlooking the play of life and death, naked, covered in ashes of the dead, skull cup in hand, beads in the other hand, back straight, chanting Divine Mother's name. There was something so still about it—so pure and clean and free. There was no con. There were no games. No one was selling anything, and no one was buying anything. It was the first place I felt absolute stillness in India: the hush of fires burning as the last vortex of human life was sucked into the center of the earth, into the mouth of Kali Ma.

I began to feed on the shakti of the corpses myself. I'd look forward to when a corpse would arrive. I'd sit up really straight. I'd feel the shakti rising. It was such a release of bliss, sitting there worshiping her—Mother death, Mother life!

Chapter 2 O

TWO WEEKS LATER I was back at Harish's house.

I had a big pillowcase in the back of the Land Rover with ashes I'd collected from the dead bodies. They over-flowed with shakti and put me in the state of being Shiva.

In India, after you bring a body to be burnt at the cremation grounds, you're considered ritually impure and have to go through elaborate purification rites before you're allowed to go back into your home. The poles you carried the bodies on have to be burned at the cremation grounds. The clothes you wore are taken off when you arrive home and are burned in front of your door before you enter your house. Serious pollution has taken place because you've been in contact with demons and the dead.

The tantric sadhana I'd just done was considered a horrible thing by orthodox Hindus; it placed me outside the veil of society. After I left the cremation grounds, all my social connections evaporated. None of my friends in India liked me anymore because I'd broken the great taboo. I had lived in the cremation grounds and worn the ashes of the dead. I had crossed some kind of line, and now I was a pariah.

I dropped Harish off in Delhi and headed back up to the mountains to process this experience. Something had really shifted. I had stepped into outer space. I was completely alone. The village people used to come up to my hut and do kirtan with me, but no one was coming anymore.

For the first time since being at the Temple of Silence, I felt agonizingly alone. I sat with the loneliness and rejection and realized it was a great blessing. When difficult things come, I have to count them as blessings because they enable me to have insight into the true nature of reality. I saw the fickleness of people's feelings for me. Emotionally, it hurt, but it was an important realization. I put so much stock in the things of the world, like friendship. This stock always depreciates. The only stock that never loses its value is a connection with God. If I don't have God, then when my world's falling apart, I don't have anything.

I was sitting in meditation in my hut when I got a telepathic call from Hari Das Baba. He was afraid and crying out for help.

I called back, "Where are you?"

"I'm at the doctor's house in Lucknow. Lucknow! Lucknow!" Hari Das's voice in my mind was desperate.

Lucknow was a five-hour drive from where I lived, and it would cost

600 rupees for gas. But Hari Das was in trouble; I couldn't delay. I hopped into the Land Rover and raced to Lucknow. I arrived about two in the morning and drove straight to the doctor's place. I went right up to a window and looked through the glass, and there was Hari Das Baba lying in bed with tubes sticking out of his body.

I climbed through the window. I pulled the tubes out of his limbs, picked him up like a baby, and walked out of the house. I laid him in the passenger seat of the Land Rover and drove back to Naini Tal. After carrying him into his room and putting his blanket over him, I went back to my hut.

A couple days later he gave me another call. His voice in my mind pleaded, "Come pick me up." I drove to Naini Tal temple, and there was Hari Das Baba, waiting in the parking lot. He got in the car, picked up his slate, and wrote, "You saved my life." He erased that and wrote, "Maharaji is trying to kill me."

I didn't know what to make of it. Did Hari Das think that being subjected to Western medical techniques was a death sentence? What was going on? I thought Hari Das Baba had gone out of his mind. But things were strange around me, too. Since I'd come back from the city of the dead, I was an outcast.

Things were getting too crazy. I was guided to return to Nepal.

NEPAL HAD CHANGED dramatically. Kathmandu was a hippie haven. A group of people was living outside Bodhanth at the Double Dorje House, a two-story stucco suburban house in the middle of Nepal. It really stood out because all the other houses looked liked they'd been built in the seventh century. Double Dorje was something right out of New Jersey.

Three American guys had rented it. They called themselves the Fuzzies—hair and beards down to their waists, perpetually stoned. I began to hang out with them and smoke.

Walking through the corridors upstairs, I opened a door and there was a beautiful woman sitting on a bed at the far end of the room, with a cat on her lap, staring out the window. I felt like I was walking in on a goddess. I sat with her for half an hour. She was in a beautiful space, on LSD at the time, digging it. Before I left, she offered me some food— the sure way to a man's heart. Her name was Bhavani.

Bhavani was Jewish and from Oklahoma. She grew up riding horses and looked like a Chinese princess with oriental eyes. She was strikingly beautiful. Bhavani was also extraordinarily bright—she had studied Mandarin Chinese at the University of Chicago.

She was very devoted to me. I allowed the love to happen, but I didn't allow myself to completely have it. As much as I liked Bhavani, I was distancing myself from commitments because I was still maintaining a sadhu stance.

I decided to go to Solokumbhu, up near Namshi Bazaar, for a three-month walk in the Himalayas. Bhavani tagged along. I was barefoot, carrying about fifty pounds on my back. She wore boots but also carried some weight. She'd fall behind about four hours on the trail, but by evening she always caught up.

We discovered an old abandoned *gompa* (a Tibetan monastery) off the road and entered the shrine room to drop acid. Although it was completely empty, we heard a puja being celebrated. We heard conch shells and chanting. We sat against the wall for eight hours listening to puja ghosts, experiencing the total ritual simultaneously.

Bhavani hung right in there with me. I was amazed at her toughness, and her devotion continued. She was very cool, always there wanting to serve me and learn from me—she became my disciple. The guru role was once again thrust upon me. But I wasn't owning up to it at all. I wasn't willing to commit to having something to teach.

ॐ

WE LIVED WITH a powerful Nyingma lama in a village of about thirty houses on the side of a mountain. The lama had long matted hair down to his feet. He wore a big turban and had a wispy beard. We'd meditate every morning, and he'd lead us in a great practice. We'd chant "Om Ah Hum," visualizing the colors and chakras and coordinating the breath.

ॐ

OM IS A white light in the forehead. *Ah* is a red light in the throat. And *Hum* is a blue light in the heart. You synchronize the lights together with the breath in whatever sequence comes to you. There is no right way to do it, and the only wrong way is to not do it. It has to be practiced every day.

There's no riding on merit, cruising on good karma. We each need to develop a personal relationship with a personal God, who is a form. Then spiritual practices become real. It takes off when it's fueled with devotion.

It's particularly easy to relate to God as Ma, the most beautiful woman in the universe. We can use the libido to bring us to God. Use everything to bring you to God, and you'll never stumble on anything. There's nowhere to fall except into the arms of the Holy Mother. So every time you slide into lust, it trips you right into God.

You have to use what attracts you. Money trips you up? Money is the energy of Lakshmi Ma. See the Goddess in it, worship her in the money, let money be the expression of Lakshmi—divine abundance in our lives. Money is not a problem. Like the Bible says, it's the love of money that's the problem. Love God instead. Love money only as the flow of God's grace moving through you to help others.

Get with the program. It is not a head trip. Get out of your head. What are you clinging to? The separate identity you're holding is your pain; you're holding your sorrow. Be blissful. Accept the happiness, which is your real identity, Atma Ram, your real Self. Breathe in your heart *Ma,* breathe out of the top of your head *Om,* and you're free. Accept and acknowledge your freedom. Don't settle for birth and death. Settle for limitless blue sky.

It's important to do things out of love. Worship out of love. Love God. God loves love. That love comes back a thousandfold. Pass it on and bring everyone into the picture; let everyone be God. Do we see people or do we see God? The way to see God is to look out and see nothing but divine souls like stars in the night sky.

THE NEPALESE HAD given me a visa for a year and a half, because they could see I was a real sadhu. I could sit up with a straight back in the visa office for five hours, waiting for them to fill out my papers. But finally they said to me, "You can't keep coming here. You must leave."

We made our way back to India. I left Bhavani at Bodh Gaya to do a meditation course, and I went on to see Maharaji. I had to get help with this "Quit India" notice, and I thought that he was the only person who could help me.

It was such a confusing time for me. I knew I was in trouble. I had been running my drama through my mind before I reached the temple. I didn't know what to do. Bhavani and I had developed a serious relationship, and I didn't know whether I should stay with her or break free.

How would I maintain my sadhu lifestyle? I didn't know what was going on with my visa.

I was amazed at the guards and the gates. The temple was enclosed for the first time. There had never been gates. And there were soldiers wearing fatigues, holding guns. When they told Maharaji I was there, they opened the gates. It felt like Maharaji was in jail even though he was running the place.

Gates? Guards? After having had such intimacy with the temple in the past, this was a shock. I had had many visions there. That's where I had met Maharaji. I had done my spiritual practive there.

I walked across the large, empty courtyard of the temple. It was like walking into a steady flame. No one was around. The guard had gone back to the gate. It was just me and Maharaji.

There was incredible stillness as I bowed before Maharaji. Incredible peace—no anxiety, no stress, no worry. Just the light of Ram. Just God. I sat for several minutes in this meditative bliss. There was no time at all.

And then I spoke and told him the problems with my visa.

He answered, "Go to Delhi."

I asked him, "What do I do in Delhi?"

Again, he said, "Go to Delhi."

I knew this was a brush-off. He was sending me back to America. I realized then that I would never see him again. My time had expired on the meter. My seven years were over. He had been everything to me and still is my devotion.

As I stood there, many feelings and memories washed over me. My initiation at the Kumbha Mela: the boats on the water, the thousands of flowers, and the nectar pouring down on me from the sky as I was named Bhagavan Das. I remembered the incredible ride in the Land Rover when Maharaji did his disappearing act—one minute he was next to me and the next minute there was only a blanket.

WITHOUT A DOUBT, the guru is God. He is a ball of love. Nobody owns the ball, because God is the ball of love. God is the guru, the teacher of all teachers. Only God is the guru. Maharaji knew that. It wasn't Maharaji's will doing things. It was God working through him.

The temple is the human body.

The form of God is the breath.

The name of God is the light. The name is the flame.

Again, I was completely surrounded by the flame of Ram. I felt the heart and majesty of my guru. I felt I was sitting in front of a mountain.

Eternity.

I was completely plunged into the now.

I felt as though I was going to be executed in five minutes—all of a sudden, every moment was intensely precious. Bare bones. Ashes to ashes, dust to dust.

I had come to him for help. And he cut me loose. It was time for me to grow up, become a man—a process that continues to this day.

It was our last meeting.

I WENT TO Delhi and nothing happened. I didn't know what to do.

I'd heard some people talking about a miracle baba named Muktananda who had really powerful siddhis. People were going into *kriyas*, which are spontaneous yoga postures that happen suddenly when the Kundalini rises. So I went to Ganeshpuri and ended up at his marble ashram in the middle of a completely medieval village. There was nothing in the vicinity except mud huts, cows, and a giant marble Maharaja palace where Muktananda lived. The contrast was stark. It was amazing. I'd never seen such a structure.

I met Muktananda and touched his feet. He gave me a big hug. He knew my guru. I told him about my visa, but nothing came of it. "You have a visa problem? Okay, okay."

On my third anxious day at his ashram, Muktananda came to me and said, "You need to leave."

I said, "Where will I go?" It was ten o'clock at night.

He said, "Go to the town and stay in the dharmsala."

Ganeshpuri was the town where Muktananda's guru, Nityananda, lived. I knew nothing about Nityananda. The dharmsala was a huge room like a high school gym with bright lights and hundreds of people camped out on the floor. I laid down my bedroll and went to sleep. In the middle of the night I had a vivid dream. Nityananada came to me. He was standing naked in front of me and moved his hand and said, "Go to the *kund*."

I woke up. I knew what a *kund* was (a pool of water), but I didn't know which kund he meant. I went outside and asked around, "Kund kahan Hai?" People pointed me to a hot spring. I settled into the water, and there was a remarkable Shiva lingam in front of me just on the other side of the spring. I ended up sitting in the hot water looking at the Shiva lingam, chanting "Om Namah Shivaya," a mantra that spontaneously started pouring out of me, until dawn. The next morning I learned that Nityananda used to go to that very kund every morning at three o'clock. He would sit in it and meditate. I was completely awestruck at the blessing—Muktananda had sent me to town, and his guru took over, brought me to the kund, and initiated me in the mantra. It's amazing how God works.

But, like Maharaji, Muktananda did nothing about the visa.

I next heard about a very famous guru in South India with millions of followers. His name was Satya Sai Baba, and he did many miracles all the time. He would materialize *vibhuti* (sacred ash worn by Lord Shiva) out of the palms of his hands. When given to you, the vibhuti had the power to cure, heal, and bless. Satya Sai Baba was going to be in Bombay to accommodate twenty thousand people. I'd never seen so many people in one place outside the Kumbha Mela.

I brought a rose to give Sai Baba, thinking I'd be able to talk to him about my visa. But it was a circus, and I realized my chances of actually meeting him were nonexistent. I sat down in a row of people probably a mile from the stage. Sai Baba was so far away, he looked barely a half-inch tall from where I was. The devotees chanted for about three hours, and then Baba whipped the chanting up, really taking it high. Then he started walking into the crowd. He got closer and closer and closer to me. This took quite a while. People were constantly jumping at his feet, and he would kind of dance back and forth, dodging some people, letting others touch his feet. He was giving them vibhuti.

The next thing I knew, he was standing right in front of me. He reached out, and I put the rose in his hands. Then he very daintily lifted up his skirt, and I touched his feet. It was a beautiful, beautiful meeting. I totally forgot about my visa, I got so high.

Meanwhile, I was surrendering to my plight. It was time to move my car. Even the gods are kicked out of heaven when their good karma runs out.

I went to the police station in Bombay and turned myself in. I was on their wanted list—a known fugitive in India. They placed me under house arrest and told me to get a ticket out of India pronto! I called my mother, who was surprised and relieved to hear from me, and I had a ticket in three days.

When I went to the government office to get my exit visa, I ran into an unusual-looking man, quite aged, dressed as a Swami, who was getting a visa to come to America. He had a powerful vibration and loads of shakti. I immediately touched his feet, and he put his hands on my head and blessed me. When I looked up into his eyes he said, "Chant Hare Krishna, Hare Krishna, Krishna, Krishna, Hare, Hare, Hare Rama, Hare Rama, Rama Rama, Hare Hare."

It was 1971. His name was Swami Bhaktivedanta Prabhupada. Within a few months, teenagers in New York would begin chanting "Hare Krishna" on the avenues. He was in his seventies, and he didn't have a dime. He started his movement in the Lower East Side of New York, sitting on a park bench in Thompkins Square, chanting "Hare Krishna, Hare Krishna, Krishna, Krishna, Hare, Hare, Hare Rama, Hare Rama Rama Rama, Hare Hare." People gathered around him and started chanting with him. Allen Ginsberg chanted with him in public. The crowds swelled, and thousands of people joined in. For me to go to India and survive without a cent was one thing, but for Swami to come to America and start a world movement without a penny was something else. The power of God's name was that great.

ॐ

I WAS STILL in touch with Bhavani. She met me in Bombay and decided she would come back to the United States with me. I wasn't sure how I should relate to her. As my girlfriend? As my disciple? As my assistant? But I said okay.

It was very, very hard to leave India. I was particularly upset because I couldn't go back and visit my Guru one last time. I would never see Neem Karoli Baba again. I vowed to keep him alive in my heart forever. Though I was leaving India, I would never leave his feet.

ॐ

INDIA WAS DHARMA BHUMI: the land of religion. America was Karma Bhumi: the land of action. I promised myself that when I returned to a country where doing was more important than being, I would not lose myself. I had one aim in life: to become completely enlightened. I firmly believed that nothing could sweep me off my path.

Part 2

Chapter 22

IT WAS THE winter of 1971. I had been in India for seven years and felt like I was truly an Indian. I had become immersed in the culture. I had grown up there—how could I not be Indian? I spoke good Hindi and spoke English with a perfect Indian accent for ten years after I left.

Visas and passports aside, I didn't understand why I had to go back to America. I was afraid of the way things were there. America represented everything I didn't believe in. I felt that the country had ruined the world. It was a horrible materialistic culture: McDonald's, Denny's, credit cards—everything was plastic. There was no substance in America, especially spiritual substance. In India I was constantly reminded of God—in America I would have no familiar, spiritual support system.

Once when I was on a long retreat in India, I had written a poem to one of my heroes from the beatnik era, Gary Snyder. He wrote a really nice letter back to me, encouraging me to continue my practice and inviting me to Japan. I wanted to meet him and so began tracking him down. I knew he was in Kyoto, so Bhavani and I flew there.

Getting around in Japan was unbelievable—just crossing the street was a miracle, with thousands of people at every light. India had been like this, too, but not with so many cars. The past and the present were all mixed up in Japan. I'd look down one street and see medieval Japan, and then the next block would be filled with highrises.

I never got to meet Gary because he wasn't there. But I became good friends with Dick Baker, who was living in Gary's house. He was the former abbot of the Zen Center in California. He practiced zazen, a type of Buddhist practice done in Japan, which is basically just sitting peacefully. No mindmesh, no concepts—just pure sitting.

I spent my days with Dick, and he often invited me to join him at the Zen Center and told me about his guru, Suzuki Roshi. I felt really close to Suzuki Roshi because I had just read his book *Zen Mind, Beginner's Mind*. Dick had written the introduction and talked a lot about his guru. I felt the same kind of devotion for Maharaji that he was expressing for his teacher.

At the time, Dick was in the middle of very intense Zen training. He was sitting eight to ten hours a day in a temple in Kyoto. He was very open to me and generous—a beautiful, warmhearted person. We had a lot of fun together. He was excited to hear about India and about meeting me. He and Ram Dass were friends, and Ram Dass had told him about me.

When I wasn't with Dick, I was meditating, in retreat, and doing *puja*. Bhavani taught English, made money, and took care of me because I was so freaked out with all the changes. In my heart, I wanted to go back to my hut in India. I wanted to return to the jungle and ride the elephant, once more, into the dawn. But my place, my space, was gone.

Money got really tight, even with Bhavani's teaching, and we didn't know what to do. So during the lean times I put my harmonica to my mouth and tied my guitar around me with a rope. Bhavani and I would walk throughout the nightclub district of Kyoto, go into different clubs, and I would start singing:

"Let the midnight special shine her light on me. . . ." or

"Betty Lou, Betty Lou got a new pair of shoes. . . ."

Bhavani would go around to all the tables and collect money. Working a couple hours like that would take care of our rent and food for another week.

ॐ

I DECIDED I needed to leave the city and see the country. I hitch-hiked to Kyushu, an island south of Japan. (I was surprised that I was picked up, because in Japan people don't usually pick up hitchhikers.)

Bhavani remained behind to continue teaching English. Even though I was closer to her than any other woman I'd ever been with, I was having a hard time staying committed to her and the relationship. She was falling deeply in love with me. But I was still not into permanent relationships. I was starting to feel smothered. I needed to get away for a while.

When I got to Hiroshima I had absolutely no money. I hadn't eaten for days. So I went down to the busiest business district and sat in full lotus position. I meditated for five hours with a little blanket in front of me. I wasn't begging; I was meditating. People laid a lot of money down, so I could travel on.

I went on a retreat to a mystical place called Suwanasai, a tiny volcanic island off the southern tip of Japan in the China Sea. Suwanasai is where Gary Snyder started a commune of Japanese hippies. It was, indeed, a very rustic hippie scene.

The goddess of Japan came to me in the form of Ah. Ah was a hippie and one of the Mas on Suwanasai. Her hair was long, black, and lustrous. She spoke two words, "Come back," but otherwise didn't speak a word of English. Our entire relationship was telepathic. It was absolutely amazing, a fascinating encounter with a Japanese mind . . . and body.

I was in old Japan, and the island was a wonderful ashram. I moved in with Ah. We lived together for one month in a straw house, barefoot, and we slept on tatami mats.

Ah did not express any emotion, so there was no romance of "making love" or even the concept of "making love" for Ah. For her, there was only passionate fucking.

We would meditate together, eat together in complete stillness, and have the most awesome sex. I surrendered to the stillness.

She loved me in an extremely detached way, which I really enjoyed. I had never been loved like that before.

I would go fishing with a little hunchbacked man named Pon. He was only 4′8″. A total earth person. A gnome. He'd dance along the edges of the rocks where the waves crashed, waving his long bamboo fishing pole in his hand. Watching him was like looking at a Chinese brush painting.

During one of our fishing expeditions I decided to take a swim in the China Sea. I wasn't prepared for the rocks and got cut up pretty badly. I came out covered in blood. This was a far cry from the Ganges.

I used to meditate under a huge banyan tree for hours. Ah would come out and call to me, "Bhagavan Das, come back, come back. Bhagavan Das come back." I was like a sailor she could lose to the sea.

Ah would approach me, pull me out of my meditation, and then lie down under the tree. We would begin a slow dance of sex. I pleased the goddess of Japan for hours under the banyan tree as I held my seed, using the tantric skills that Gay had taught me.

Chapter 2 3

WHEN I RETURNED to Kyoto a month later, Bhavani was two months pregnant. She didn't want to have the baby. I begged her to keep it, and she finally gave in. Since we didn't have any money left, it was time to go back to America. So I flew back to Los Angeles with my pregnant girlfriend.

I got off the plane wearing sandals and long maroon robes. My hair was roped and I wore it up in a big bun. I had earrings and a long beard. Bhavani wore long, flowing robes made of beautiful Chinese silk. We were both in medieval robe mode.

I had arranged for my mother and father to meet us at the airport. We were going to stay with them for a while as we got settled. When they saw us, they just stood there, faces frozen. I was very formal with my parents, and I touched their feet. I said:

"Hello mother."

"Hello father."

They were so shocked that all they wanted to do was get us out of the airport and into the Cadillac. They thought we'd joined a cult and wanted to take us home and deprogram us. We were quite a sight, I guess.

I never felt like I was "going back" to them. I felt like I was just passing through because of my high state of consciousness. I didn't react to feelings and thoughts the way most people do. I was living in a realm where I was doing eight hours of mantra a day—my beads were going continuously, regardless of where I was. Regardless of what was going on, I was introverted into the word and the breath. My feelings and my thoughts were different than those around me. I didn't feel like I was going back anywhere. I felt like I was passing through America, just like I had passed through India, had passed through Japan, and was passing through existence while continuing my practice.

I had worn glasses before going to India. I could see really well there because I had no stress. Shortly after coming home, I was sitting in the living room with my dad and he said, "Mike, did you have your glasses in India?"

"No Dad, I didn't."

Horrified, he said, "Oh gosh, you missed everything!"

My parents gave us a room to sleep in with a nice comfy bed. I chose the floor. After all those cement slabs and wooden cots, I couldn't sleep in a real bed.

Everybody wanted to see me. *Be Here Now* had been published a few months before I came home and had created a stir. It became clear to me that Ram Dass had created quite a mystique about me. People had never read anything like it before. It was completely new information, and people were curious about me. They wanted to meet me and know who I was. When Bhavani and I arrived in L.A., we didn't even know that Ram Dass had published a book. It was a complete surprise. I didn't understand what all the fuss was about, but people were coming out of the woodwork to see me.

It was strange being a sadhu in America, truly strange. I went back to Laguna Beach, where I had grown up, and went swimming and surfing. But everything had changed. It had become a big city. I was already freaked out as a kid, and it was mostly rural then. I knew the city was coming—I could see it down the road even when I was little.

My mother was distressed because Bhavani was pregnant and we weren't married. We didn't care one way or the other. But I thought, if they wanted it so much we should just do it! There were no Hindu churches around, so I wanted to get married in a Buddhist church. We found one and got married in it. We had a nice civil ceremony, which pleased the parents. Her parents were in Tulsa, Oklahoma, and even though we hadn't gone to see them, they were happy to hear their daughter was married.

We stayed with my parents for a week and then an Egyptologist and his wife I had befriended in Pondicherry by the name of Andre and Goldian Vandenbrook invited us to their beautiful Sadhana Farm in upstate New York. I needed to get away from my parents, so we went.

I was concerned about my health. I had amoebas and animals inside me, and they were eating me alive. I went to an oriental specialist at Syracuse University who did extensive testing on me. He said I had over thirty-five different parasites and that he didn't know what half of them were. He decided to treat me with medicine used to deworm horses. It was very strong, and he didn't know what kind of reaction I would have. Death was a possible side effect.

I went back to the farm and lay under the tree for three days with my blanket. If I was going to die, it was going to be outside. I was quite sick for a while, but I was eventually cured. We remained at Sadhana Farm for a while before we decided to go back to New York City.

We saw *Be Here Now* for the first time in Manhattan, and the swell of the energy was starting to move toward me. I stayed with David Padwa, who had brought Ram Dass to India. (He was the man who had given us the Land Rover and had become my patron.)

David put us up in his beautiful, narrow, seven-story townhouse on East 77th Street, between Madison and Park. We had a Japanese houseman who lived on the seventh floor. An international lawyer, David was in and out a lot because he traveled all over the world.

The townhouse was amazing. A beautiful dining room on the second floor, rich carpeting, oriental rugs, a magnificent kitchen, special lighting, original masterpieces on the walls. The study was filled with rich, embossed books. And it was so peaceful and quiet.

It was like a deluxe cave with a revolving door—someone was always coming to visit. When I got to David's I decided to call Allen Ginsberg and see if we could meet. He hopped on a train and came right over. He was a guru hunter, and I was the new guru in town. I was Ram Dass's teacher, and he had great respect for Ram Dass. So he was eager to meet this "golden guru."

When I answered the door, Allen came right into my face and gave me a big, wet kiss on the mouth. I was amazed at his candor and the glow in his eyes. He looked just like an Indian holy man. I felt completely at home with him—we were sitting by the Ganges in India in David's New York townhouse. We talked nonstop for four hours about everyone we knew and about India and the different teachers we knew, the practices, the deities. I told him all about Neem Karoli Baba. I saw Allen as a God man, a holy man. He was at one with his soul.

His shakti was unbelievable. He took out his harmonium, a little Indian accordion, and we sang and chanted together. Then we went downstairs and I made him tea. It was like we were all over the universe together, as though we were old bosom, heartfelt buddies. With him I felt the most amazing warmth and openness. It was real love. I was feeling God's love. I was with a real holy man, and I was so happy because they are so few and far between. No one would have ever guessed that this was our first real meeting.

Allen and I had actually connected even before I met him. At seventeen I read his work *Howl,* his most famous poem, published by City Lights on Balboa Island in California. I had gone once to City Lights and saw Allen, black hair flowing down his back, and I just couldn't approach him because the aura around him was so intense. I couldn't believe I was seeing him. He was my hero; he was like a prophet.

In 1963 I had gone to listen to Joan Baez and Bob Dylan in Carmel. Afterward I went over to the Carmel library. I picked up a copy of *Esquire,* and there was a picture of Allen, naked with his black hair down his back, standing in the Ganges with water buffalo. I felt this strange familiarity with who he was. I realize now that Allen was a holy man and that I was drawn to the God energy that he was manifesting.

Another frequent visitor at David's was Alan Watts—a famous writer, a Zen Buddhist, a brilliant man, *the* counterculture guru of the time, and an alcoholic who was dead drunk most of the time. There was always a girl with him, propping him up. He began his day with a glass of vodka and ended his day with a glass of vodka. I had never met anyone who could function in that state. I was shocked by the behavior—it was so intense! I loved him, though, and was a real fan of his writing. He planted a lot of spiritual ideas in my mind.

Then there was Hilda Charlton, a very famous guru who taught in New York. She was a spiritual teacher who had lived in India for twenty-six years. Hilda was amazing. She wore a giant blue cape over her shoulder and incredible flowing gowns. She looked like the good witch from the Wizard of Oz.

I went to Hilda's classes and sang for her. When I finished singing, a huge line of people was waiting to hug me. I couldn't get away, so I had to hug everybody. I found this really difficult. There were so many people clamoring to see me that I began withdrawing, trying to protect myself. I couldn't figure it out. What was going on? What did all these people want?

I was supposed to be this enlightened being; I had the answers for everybody; people wanted this really heavy hit from me, this special blessing I was supposed to give them. I retreated and kept pulling in more, feeling very lost and alone. I chanted a lot during this time.

I was in shock—culture shock. I felt totally out of touch with spiritual support. I continued to retreat into my practice, spending most of my time in the corner of the room facing the wall doing my beads, repeating "Om Mani Padme Hum." I didn't know what else to do. I was really confused.

When I first saw Be Here Now, I thought, "Why did Ram Dass do this? I don't want all this attention." And now there were thousands of people going to India hunting for Maharaji. It had snowballed, and I had unleashed all these hordes of hippies on the trail to Maharaji.

Ram Dass and I were reunited in New York, and he was with me a lot of the time, bringing all these people to meet me. I remember going out for a chiropractic appointment, and he and I decided to walk down the street. We were standing on the sidewalk and suddenly we had a crowd of fifty people standing around, looking at me—just like in India. One of the princes of Bhutan came by and invited me to his country.

We'd go to the post office and there would be a huge crowd of people staring at me. I had on my robes and was wearing my bun. People had never seen anyone like me before.

I started hiding out in the townhouse and seeing just a few people. I had the ultimate pad—this little castle in Manhattan. Ram Dass would come over all the time; Peter Max, the artist, was always around; Alan Watts was there. Allen Ginsberg would make his appearances. We became a tight little circle.

During this time, Bhavani was sewing, doing her beads, cooking, and taking care of me as her pregnancy progressed. We got along great. She was so loving and devoted—I just was incapable of receiving the love. I still held on to my old ideas of women at this point—I still didn't trust them. I hadn't learned yet that all women are the embodiment of the Divine Mother. I wouldn't learn this until much later and would suffer, and cause suffering, because of it.

A friend of David, Sam Clapp, offered us his mansion on Paradise Island in the Bahamas to have our baby. We agreed to go there and found ourselves surrounded by crystal blue water and blankets of white sand as far as the eye could see. There were two servants from England to look after our needs, a Criss Craft motorboat, and a Mercedes to drive around in. I spent all my time on the beach praying and meditating, and I was thankful that at last there were no people!

Even though we had an experienced Bahamian midwife, I basically guided the whole birth. The midwife sat in the corner and watched me. Our daughter came out with her eyes wide open, looking directly at me with eternity in her newborn eyes. I was so shocked and transformed and initiated by that first meeting. It was awe-inspiring to be looking down at God's head in the yoni. It was the most amazing experience of my life—right up there with being with Maharaji. It was the absolute meeting with the Divine Mother.

With the next contraction she came out. I had on my white dhoti and was covered in blood. I wrapped her up and placed her on Bhavani's breast. Then I took the placenta and made a soup out of it. There was so much light coming off it. Bhavani and I ate it together and it was really good. My time with the Tibetans cured me of the queasiness about this sort of thing.

We named her Soma because that's the first word Bhavani spoke as Soma came out. *Soma* means "nectar." It also means "the moon."

Bhavani and I spent the next couple months worshiping Baby Soma every moment of every day. I'd walk on the beach with her, this miracle in my arms, celebrating the beauty of her space. I'd cover her in flowers and sing to her. She was beautiful, and this was the most precious time of my life.

We spent six blissful months in the Bahamas. I would float in the water and feel like I was Lord Vishnu sleeping in the milky ocean. It was so warm and beautiful—heaven on earth.

And then we had to get back to hell.

Chapter 24

WHEN WE RETURNED to David's house in New York, all the fame really started exploding around me. *Be Here Now* had built the momentum. People were just dying to get their hands on me. People were diving at my feet. I was going out and having dinner with twenty or thirty people a night. Everyone wanted to be in my presence.

I didn't know exactly what I wanted to do, but I knew I wanted to sing, and my chanting became my offering.

Peter Max set up a recording session in Manhattan at the Electric Lady Land studio, founded by Jimi Hendrix. I recorded an album called "AH" with Bhavani singing backup. It became very successful.

At this time Ram Dass introduced me to Michael Jeffries, who had been Hendrix's manager until he died. He saw the commercial potential in me. Michael and I really mixed well, and he wanted to make me into a big star. And he knew how to do it.

Two weeks after I met him, Michael died in a private plane crash in Woodstock. That was it. Everything evaporated on that level.

I still had hordes of people all over me. I didn't feel that I had any control in my life. It was a disconcerting experience. I was being shipped all around like a power object by wealthy people. I was their salon guest, and they would call their friends over. "He's here! He's arrived! Bhagavan Das will be here for a week. You've got to come by and see him!" I felt like an animal that people were gawking at, talking to, and looking at for answers, which I didn't have. At one point Ram Dass said to me, "I'm amazed at your lack of ambition." But I was living a very deep internal life and I just couldn't get into the program with all the people. I found fame annoying.

I felt trapped by the fame. At the time, I couldn't really use it. I didn't know what to teach. I knew everyone wanted me to teach and open up an ashram, or temple, or something—but I had no idea what to do.

I missed India so much. Often I would sit alone in a room and listen to Indian music on headphones.

I was still a student. I couldn't assume a teacher role. I refused to assume the guru role because I realized I was too young. I didn't know anything. I was in the middle of my spiritual practice. My pot hadn't been fired yet, so I avoided the dangerous role of guru. Yet it was hunting me down.

Baba Ram Dass had been running around for a year promoting me and telling everyone that "I knew," that I had mystical knowledge, was one of the highest beings on the planet, and on and on. I was a living myth, the hero returning home. I couldn't avoid it. So I just stepped into it.

I had amazing experiences with real devotees in America who just came out of the woods with tears in their eyes, just to get a blessing from me. They wanted me to name their babies. People brought me things to bless: paintings, beads, images of gods and goddesses. They really wanted to be with me. They wanted to know me. It was very powerful. I did thousands and thousands of "Manis." I chanted "Om Mani Padme Hum" fifteen hours a day. I was constantly praying for everyone's liberation, that everyone would get a blessing. That was my prayer. I didn't do a lot of things, just one simple practice for twelve years. I chanted and put all my devotion into Ma, bowing and keeping it simple. I combined the Mani practice with the visualization and breathing every day—I did tens of thousands of those.

I wore out a whole mala of beads in three years; I wore the beads down to the disks.

I didn't hang out to talk and visit that much. I was on the beads. I was a bead fanatic, mantra man, doing the mantra. This was my reality. I was a living prayer wheel. Wherever I went the atmosphere became still and sacred because I didn't have anything to say except "Om Mani Padme Hum."

But I was floundering. I needed to put myself in the hands of an enlightened being.

Once, when Ram Dass and I had been in a Bombay hotel, he had shown me a photograph of a Tibetan lama who really struck me. His name was Chogyam Trungpa, the 11th incarnation of the Trungpa Tulku. He had come to America in 1970 to set up Tail of the Tiger meditation center in Barnet, Vermont. Trungpa had a center in Scotland, and he'd been asked to come teach in the United States. Many students wanted to hear his style of teaching Buddhism. He was Allen Ginsberg's guru, and I thought he could help me.

I met him in 1971 when Andre and Goldian Vandenbrook took me to his farmhouse in Vermont. I was looking for a spiritual community so that I could balance my life in the West. When I met Trungpa I was taken by his sincerity and boyish quality of innocence. He was very bright and made himself very accessible to all his students, which was unusual considering he was such a high-level lama. In the Tibetan tradition, lamas of his stature are usually difficult to connect with. They're very guarded, with huge entourages, and it's difficult to get close to them. But this was not Trungpa's style.

The left side of Trungpa's body was paralyzed. He had gotten into a car accident in England a year earlier. Driving drunk he smashed into a novelty joke shop. But being slightly crippled didn't seem to bother him.

I liked him. I liked his presence and what he was doing in the West. And he liked me. I asked him if he would be my teacher. He said he would. I felt I had my anchor. So I stayed with him in his commune, and Bhavani and Soma stayed with me.

Trungpa Rinpoche was kicked back and casual with his students. It was obvious to me that he was one of the first-string lamas. He was in the front row, right up there with the major rinpoches I had met in India—hanging out in blue jeans, chain smoking Marlboros, getting into the American mood.

He would sit outside on sunny days with everybody, totally open to discussing anything. He spoke fluent English, which was remarkable. He was attempting to demystify the Tibetan teachings. Trungpa was very attractive in that he had a lot of very strong male energy around him, and yet he was very gentle and soft at the same time. There was a lot of "ooze" around him—he was very juicy.

And Trungpa was becoming very Americanized. He drank sake non-stop, smoked nonstop, and was sleeping with all the girls. But he was crippled on one side. No problem for him—he just limped a bit, smiled at you, and fell down the stairs.

The community felt good. We were one big family of a few hundred people. I became Trungpa's tea person, so I was constantly around him and the others, pouring his tea, which was good for me. He gave me special teachings of Vajra Dakini, which I continued doing for fifteen years. He encouraged my devotion. I was with him for a week, the beginning of a very deep friendship.

I did a lot of retreats during this time because I was doing one hundred thousand prostrations for purification . . . over and over again. Then there was my ongoing meditation and solitude. I kept retreating from the world. I was overwhelmed, and this was the only way I could deal with it.

🕉

DAVID PADWA HAD another beautiful, posh house outside of Santa Fe in a place called Sierra Gordo. Bhavani and I were invited to stay there, and so I began my New Mexico adventure. Soma was still a baby. I was up with her every morning at three. I would take her into the living room and worship her until nine. Every morning I would do *kumari puja* for six hours, do all my rituals, and cover her in flowers. I had a live murti—a live image of God.

Soma would be on her back laughing and rolling around, so aware. She'd look at me the whole time. I was looking in her eyes while worshiping her. It was a profound experience to have a live murti of the Divine Mother to worship and chant to.

While in New Mexico, Bhavani, Soma, and I spent the winter in a small wooden yurt at the Lama Foundation, a spiritual community founded by Steve Durkee and Asha Greer in the late '60s. Baba Ram Dass was part of the Lama spiritual family. All of his talks were collected, and, with editing help from his friends, he wrote *Be Here Now*.

Lama was about twenty miles north of Taos, located 8,400 feet in the San Cristobal Mountains. Being there was like being back in the foothills of the Himalayas. At the Lama's temple, the American Indian vibes were so strong that I would chant under the huge dome into the dawn. But the rustic scene was hard on Bhavani and Soma, so they stayed most of the time at David's home in Santa Fe, leaving me alone to do my spiritual practice. Now that I was back in the mountains it was so easy to Be Here Now.

Chapter **25**

I MET LITTLE JOE in the Safeway in Taos. I remember standing in the aisle seeing this little Indian man, looking like a bubble of light, come floating toward me about two inches off the ground. It was all I could do not to fall at his feet and worship him in the store. I had found my next guru in America: Little Joe Gomez, with whom I would study and stay for a year. He was a completely liberated saint and one of the grandpas of the tribe. The first thing he did was adopt me and say, "You're my grandson." In a sense, this was like Neem Karoli Baba making me his son.

Little Joe was about 4'8". He was an old Indian man with extremely wrinkled skin. Little Joe looked like the earth itself. Without a doubt, he was a total earth man. He had a little corn patch that he hoed, and he talked to everybody. He had a couple mules and lived in a hogan, an eight-sided house that the Navajo Indians live in. It was outside of Taos-Pueblo.

Little Joe was one of the elder shamans of the tribe. A shaman is the spiritual magic man that communes with the spirits for the tribe and helps the collective people of the tribe understand what's going on. He is the man of wisdom and understanding and the powerful medicine man for the tribe. He also works with the weather and gives people counseling. Little Joe was known to be a bit radical compared with the other leaders. He would have peyote meetings and let all the hippies come. Peyote meetings are religious rituals that originated in Mexico from the Huichole Indians and then brought to the Comanche people by Quanna Parker, who was a Kiowa chief. The peyote cult moved from the plains and into the pueblos. The Gomez brothers, Little Joe and his brother John, were very famous for spreading the peyote cult.

PEYOTE IS A cactus that grows in the high desert near Mexico. The root is deep like a carrot. The mushroomlike top, called a button, is cut off and dried or eaten fresh. The Indians call it the flesh of God. They eat it to talk to God and become one with God. It's a powerful healing plant that gives visions. Peyote contains many alkaloids, mescaline being the predominant one.

Peyote meetings are held for a specific purpose. For instance, if you are sick, your friends get together and sit up all night to pray for you. First they erect a tepee in a good spot with the entrance facing east. They brush the earth to make a smooth surface and then use clay to sculpt a low altar in the shape of a crescent moon, with the horns of the moon facing the entrance. The fire is then made on the ground within the crescent of the moon.

There are four officers at a peyote meeting: the chief, the carrier of the drum, the cedar man, and the fire man. When the chief sits down behind the moon facing the door, he takes out a great grandpa peyote button and puts it in the center of the moon. The peyote is the real chief who runs the meeting.

ॐ

MY FIRST MEETING was outside of Little Joe's hogan. It was just getting dark when we started to go inside the tepee, which glowed like a temple of light against the high desert sky. We sat in a tight circle around the moon and fire. The woman next to me said, "Eat as much medicine as you can." Then the fire man took a glowing staff out of the fire and passed it around so that everybody could light their tobacco prayer smokes rolled with corn husks. All at once, we started to pray out loud.

The cedar man blessed the peyote and offered it to the creator. It was passed around the tepee clockwise. When it came to me, I looked down into the wooden bowl of fresh green peyote buttons. I took a handful and washed them down with a strong peyote tea. It was like eating the earth, it was so alive. A water drum was passed around with a staff and a gourd rattle. Each person sang four songs and then gave the instruments to the next person—this went on all night. About two hours after eating the peyote, waves of bliss came over me, and the fire started talking.

"Keep your eye on the Chief," it said. I looked over at Little Joe, and blue light was shining forth from the eagle feather he was holding.

At one point during the night, the fire swallowed me. It was so hot, I fainted. When I finally awoke, Little Joe came over and told me to stand up. I followed him to the center of the moon. As I stood there looking down at the moon and flames, I knew I was the holy Mother. Little Joe threw cedar on the fire and smudged the smoke all over me with his eagle feather. I was born again at that moment.

At midnight, sacred water was brought in by the Holy Mother, an Indian woman dressed for the part in all her feathered finery. She returned again at dawn with another big bucket of sacred water. The Holy Mother prayed over this water for a very long time while she cried. She always cries over the water—it is a symbol of new life. Then she smokes the holy tobacco.

Little Joe once told me that tobacco was the most powerful drug he knew of. I didn't understand. He told me, "If you don't think it's so, look at how many people It's smoking." Little Joe insisted you prayed "with" the tobacco. You couldn't just smoke it. It was too powerful and dangerous.

The Holy Mother prayed with the tobacco. Then the water was offered to the earth and the fire. The water was passed around and everybody drank the blessings in that water. People were cured, healed—new life from the nectar of the water. It is the sweetest water on earth.

Then closing songs were sung. The women and children came into the tepee and enjoyed the radiance and spiritual energy that was built up the previous night. They sat in the vibration for an hour, and then they brought the breakfast in—which consisted of four things: corn meal, dried deer meat, fruit, and the water. All of it was prayed upon with tobacco before being passed around.

After the food was eaten, the instruments were taken apart. The water drum, which is like an iron kettle that has been tied with a sheathe of wet hide, was taken apart. All the prayers were in the drum. It was passed around and everyone squeezed it and touched it to bless themselves. This was deep shakti worship—worship of the Mother Earth.

Little Joe was very much into taking peyote, but not for the religious aspects. He'd walk out alone into the mountains and take peyote a lot. He was against the religious aspect of the native American Indian Church. He was into the ritual without the church. He used to say, "This is all my church. That tree is a holy tree. That rock is a holy rock." He saw all creation as holy, completely sacred, and filled with God.

The earth was his Bible. He'd say, "We don't need a bible. We have our bible right here. Nature is the bible. Read nature and you can see." Little Joe talked to nature, and nature talked back.

There were many parallels between what I learned from Little Joe and what I learned from Neem Karoli Baba. If I had met Little Joe when I was eighteen, before I went to Asia, I wouldn't have gone to India at all. I didn't know that such a being existed. The knowledge that I thought was unique to Indians on the other side of the ocean was actually here in the American Indian tradition all along. This ancient, sacred knowledge has been preserved in the reservations on our own continent.

Little Joe went to church one day and took communion and got the body of Jesus. He was filled with the Holy Ghost from that moment on and was totally in love with Jesus. I could tell he saw Jesus and spoke to him—he had a real relationship with Jesus.

I was pretty anti-Jesus at the time, but I tried to be open. I liked little Joe's Jesus. He gave Jesus a good recommendation.

Joe was the most childlike person I knew. He would smile and beam love. And he could be totally invisible. I would walk by him and think he was a crumpled-up piece of clothing, covered in the dust of the earth. He wore his hair in two little braids. He was such a simple person, a beautiful soul. He was my grandpa. In the Indian tradition, elders are everyone's grandparents because they believe we are all related.

I went out one day to his house in the wintertime. I wanted him to initiate me. This was very important to me. He was living in a tepee then, as his hogan was still being built. I was really cold, and snow was everywhere. It looked like a scene from the 1880s. We were out in the middle of nowhere—a little truck, a mule and its shed, and an outhouse.

I had brought Grandpa a white silk scarf and a couple packs of Pall Mall cigarettes as an offering. The tepee was sort of a mess, and Grandpa was sitting in front of the fire. We sat together as he smoked and prayed, for a long time. Total silence.

Then he said, "Come here."

I moved closer.

"Look in my eyes."

I looked in his eyes, and all of a sudden his whole face turned into a skull. All the skin was gone. I was staring directly at death. His eyes were like burning light, and I could barely look at them. I was swooning from the light coming out of his eyes. I was just about to faint when he grabbed my hand and said, "Keep going, look, look!"

I opened my eyes really wide, and the light dissolved into this black sky. I went into the sky through his eyes. It was an incredible sensation of bliss. And then I came back.

I had many experiences with Grandpa. He would keep his eagle feather fan wrapped up in a silk American flag. He always prayed for the president, the chief of the country. It was an important ritual to him.

Little Joe was eighty-four when I knew him, and he had been to Hollywood and in some movies. He was really proud of this. He was on four or five postcards. I lived and breathed to be around Grandpa Joe. I'd bring him Kentucky Fried Chicken—one of his favorite foods.

We would just sit together and be quiet all the time. He was so in the presence of God. There was this incredible stillness and silence around him. It had the same feeling as being with Maharaji, only the setting was completely different.

One evening I was sitting in front of the fire, and the fire was so hot—everything was fire. I looked over at Little Joe and said, "Grandpa, take me to Blue Lake."

Blue Lake is the sacred lake that the Taos-Pueblo Indians come from. They come out of the lake and go back into the lake when they die. It's a holy lake on top of a mountain.

The next thing I knew, I had turned into a light body and was standing in front of the lake. Grandpa was next to me. The breeze was coming off the lake; it was cool and blue and beautiful. The trees were temples. Grandpa had a little cedar fire at my feet, and he was cedaring me off with his eagle fan.

That morning I came out of the tepee and felt like I was Jesus. I walked way out from the tepee because I didn't want to be around any people—I was too high on peyote. I walked miles to the river, along a thorny path, barefoot. Each step was painful. When I got to the river I pulled out the thorns and washed my bloody feet.

I sat by the river and then suddenly heard thunder. The sound was so intense that there was a rumbling in my body. I looked up and saw that the clouds were billowing toward me, and out of the clouds came Little Joe on a horse. The horse had lightning coming out of its nostrils, and its eyes were glowing with light. Little Joe was covered in eagle feathers. In his hand he held a gourd as a shaker, and he was yelling. Then out of the gourd came lightning. It was the most dazzling vision I'd ever seen.

Little Joe taught me all about devotion and the presence of the moment, the time of the moment. He taught me that everything was holy and that everywhere was sacred. He lived in this light world.

He told me, "Everyday I make mistakes and everyday I ask for forgiveness. And I learn something new."

When Little Joe sang and prayed, it was awesome. He'd start to shake his gourd and sing, sounding like the old man he was. Then the second song would come, and it would be stronger. By the third song he would start to bark and yelp like a dog. The fourth song was something from another world, and the whole tepee would start to shake and spin. It would leave the ground and shoot off into space. Everyone would be completely transported to God.

DURING THIS TIME in my life I had many girlfriends—I was busy all the time. Bhavani was in the background, in Santa Fe, and I had strings and strings of girlfriends. I had groupies I had "to do"—it was my duty. My American Indian friends loved this. They loved sex, and they loved the young girls I brought around.

Then I came down with the mumps. They hit my left testicle—it was karmic retribution. I was staying on the outskirts of town and was violently ill. I had a fever of 108. My whole body was burning up, and my testicle was as big as a grapefruit.

Someone found out "Ropehead" was really sick (the Indians called me this because of my hair), and they put up a meeting for me. They prayed for me all night. As I was in that fever, all of a sudden I was standing in the tepee in my light body. Little Joe was smudging me off with cedar, waving his eagle fan, and I was standing in front of the moon looking down at the fire. When I woke up from that vision, the fever had broken, and my whole body was soaked in sweat.

PRAYERS WORK. IT'S very important to pray for people. It's really powerful. You can seal the prayer with the God of your choice. God doesn't care what name you call him. He's still God whether you call him Mary or Jesus or Allah or Buddha or Kali or Ram. It doesn't make any difference—God is God. What's behind it is the love and sincerity. The love carries the prayer to its fruition when you really care about people.

ॐ

ONE DAY AT Blue Lake, Little Joe was sitting with an anthropologist who had come to study him. The anthropologist said, "Oh yeah, we know where you people come from. You're like Mongolian people, and you come from over there."

Little Joe said, "Nope. I'm from here. I came from right here." He was really into the place. He came from Blue Lake. That was where he would go when he died.

He told us, "You think we worship the eagle as a symbol of God. That's not the way it is. The eagle *is* God.

"See that tree over there? That's a holy tree. It's Jesus. You white people lost your way. You've got to find your own way. We'll help you find it, but don't take our way."

One time an Orthodox rabbi, Zalman Schachter, came into the tepee. I sat next to him. Everyone was singing peyote songs, and he was eating a lot of peyote. The gourd came around to the rabbi. He had his prayer shawl over his head, the box on his forehead—full dress—and he took the gourd and started shaking that rattle and wailing in Hebrew. It was the most intense Hebrew chant. It was fabulous. The whole tepee turned into the tents of Abraham. The Indians sat up board straight. That rabbi really brought God in.

I learned only four peyote songs. I was just into being with Grandpa. I'd go to meetings only with him. With Grandpa I saw an entirely different world. The earth opened up. He taught me how to listen and how to respect feelings.

I became close to other elders as well: Little Joe's brother John, Frankie Zamorra, Tell Us Good Morning, and Geronimo's grandson, Joe Sandabal.

Joe Sandabal was called Sun Hawk, and he gave me a special blessing. He took the energy from the sun and put it in my heart. We were standing on top of a mountain at dawn. I saw this liquid come out of the sun and into his hand. Then he put it in my heart.

I brought Trungpa to see Little Joe. He said that Little Joe was the highest being he'd ever met in the West and that he was completely enlightened.

He was so deceivingly ordinary, just a little old Indian man, and yet so special.

We went to a last graduation meeting together in Colorado before he died. I was sitting next to his wife, Adrianne, when she leaned over and said to me, "Why do you bad boys sing so good?" Grandpa gently lifted a beautiful golden eagle feather out of his peyote box and gave it to me.

"I'm giving you this one feather because there is only one."

GRANDPA WOULD COME up to you and look you in the eye, get all your attention, and he would say, "God bless you." When he said "you" he'd lean into it and get close to you. You would feel a light mist of golden rain fall over you. It was like the anointing of the Holy Spirit.

ॐ

I LEARNED SO much about devotion during this period in my life. We are here to give. Our life is an offering. We're not here for ourselves—we're here for everybody. "There's no way. . . . There's only *Way,*" said Grandpa.

Chapter 26

AFTER MY TIME spent with Little Joe, life got crazier. I was touring on this jet-set trip, patronized by different people who'd give me blank checks. I could do whatever I wanted, go wherever I wanted—no questions asked. After all, I was Bhagavan Das, the "golden guru" boy. And I wasn't alone. It was the early '70s, and there was a great influx of spiritual teachers coming to the United States from the East.

Transcendental Meditation was the rage. Almost everybody had a mantra. The different Eastern religions were becoming very popular with people from all walks of life because they had lost their faith in Western thinking. Kennedy's death and the Vietnam War had pushed most Westerners over the edge. And so, if you hadn't already turned on to drugs, now was the time as you also tapped into Eastern thinking.

White-turbaned Indian Sikhs were everywhere, as popular as the Hare Krishnas. People were eating their spiritual food in alternative restaurants. Yoga, vegetarianism, organic foods, and communes were in vogue. Basically, it was the nirvana racket, and it was all very lucrative.

But a lot of it was a turnoff to me because I didn't like the feel of it. Much of it didn't feel genuine. It felt more like a fashion statement. I wanted to get out of my uniform and disappear from what I perceived to be phoney. But I didn't do it just yet.

The Naropa Institute had just opened up in Colorado. It was the first tantric university in America. Naropa was a mahasiddha (enlightened being) of the Kagyu lineage. The grand opening of the institute was one big party. With Ram Dass and Chogyam Trungpa, I was one of the first instructors. Ram Dass was flirting with Buddhism and taught a course in the *Bhagavad-Gita*. Allen Ginsberg started the Kerouac School of Disembodied Poetics at Naropa and took up permanent residence there, along with the whole beatnik camp. I taught Indian music with Jai Gopal. Naropa was a complete alternative to American study and brought the East to the United States. There were courses in tai chi, twenty kinds of meditation—the works.

On a personal level, there was a kind of war going on between Ram Dass and Chogyam Trungpa—between the Hindus and the Buddhists. I bridged it. I was in both worlds.

I sided more with Trungpa in those days. I was looking for the freedom that he promised. The party energy around him was compelling. In fact, that's basically what Naropa was: a huge blowout party, twenty-four hours a day—different parties all over town. It was school all day, party all night. I got very wrapped up in it.

I was in a very crazed space and very lost. One day, after having sex with three different women, I couldn't get out of bed. I was trauma-tized. It was all too much. I was disgusted with myself and stopped my promiscuous behavior for a while after that. It was a good wake-up call. I had been going deeper and deeper into my shadow.

We had an incredible blues concert at Naropa. I played the electric guitar and had a huge backup band behind me. A thousand rowdy people were throwing beer bottles at me. In the middle of a Blind Willy Johnson song that I was singing about Jesus, I saw a huge blue cross over the audience. During the whole concert I was completely beamed in on this blue cross. (Little did I know that Jesus would soon be coming into my life in a big way.)

I lasted three months at Naropa; then I went back to San Francisco. Almost as soon as I arrived I received a phone call from Trungpa. He told me he was going to be revealing secret vajrayana teachings, which are tantric teachings, for the first time in America and wanted me to come and be a part of this retreat. It was to be held in Jackson Hole, Wyoming.

Trungpa took over a hotel in Jackson Hole and a restaurant called the Mangey Moose and did a three-month meditation retreat with about two hundred of his students. I shared a room with Allen Ginsberg, and he and I became close friends.

Our room had a loft, which Allen took, and I took the ground floor. Allen wanted to be able to watch me have sex with all the girls, which didn't bother me one bit. I was constantly bringing women home. I didn't want to get into a group sex thing with him, although there was a slim chance that it could have happened because I loved him so much. I had never felt such emotional intimacy for a man in my life.

In my part of the room, I built a Kali temple that had a huge Kali face. It was very scary. Allen was up in his loft, with his little poetry desk and light set against one corner of the room, and that's where he did a lot of his work. Writing with a fountain pen, he spent hours composing letters, poetry, and entries in his journal. The process of creating his art was an art in and of itself.

Trungpa's retreat consisted of eight hours of sitting a day and learning about the secret tantric teachings. He was sharing with us his version of these teachings.

The camp split into two: the rowdy camp—including me, Allen Ginsberg, and Peter Orlovsky, which partied all night—and the serious Buddhists and the devoted, straight crowd—the monks and the nuns of the retreat who were there at 7:00 every morning on the cushions.

During the retreat I wore full Tibetan robes and did a lot of Tibetan puja. I still had all the garb: my long hair, earrings, everything. I was worshiping Kali Ma a lot, very deeply at the meditation retreat. I was feeling in neither one world nor the other. I was so disoriented that I didn't know where or what I was. The retreat brought up a lot of old issues for me—just sitting that long and then partying at night and nowhere to go, being surrounded by one group of people all the time.

I flew to Boston to do the "Dharma Festival." It was my debut. There were about five thousand people there. I came out on stage with Ram Dass and Allen Ginsberg, who presented me to the public. I did a long ecstatic Krishna chant with Allen and Ram Dass helping me. But inside I felt lost and alone. It was so confusing, with the groupies, Bhavani, and Baby Soma all pulling me in different directions. The whole scene was really difficult and mixed up. Bhavani didn't mind my one-nighters as long as there were no emotional attachments.

I flew back to Jackson Hole from Boston. Trungpa was hosting a big party that night at his house. On the way, I met an old New Mexico friend, Zim, whom I hadn't seen in a long time. There was six feet of snow everywhere, it was freezing cold, and he possessed one of the finest bottles of cognac I'd ever tasted. We'd finished the bottle by the time we reached Trungpa's house.

It was a wild, intense party. After drinking ouzo on top of the cognac, I passed out with my face in the soup. I was carried into the other room and plopped down onto the floor. A few hours later, Trungpa came in the room with a sharp knife and ceremoniously sawed off my rope hair. It was too thick to cut, so he sawed it, clump by clump. He was saying mantras the whole time. As he sawed each lock off, he handed it to a student. By the time he'd finished, his students were dancing around the room, naked, having an orgy, while waving my locks of hair like flags. He didn't touch my beard.

The next day I woke up at home. Allen was brushing his teeth at the sink and I was standing in the bathroom peeing. I was so used to having this huge ponytail that went all the way down my back. Standing there, I realized my head was really light—there was no weight behind it. I put my hand on the back of my head and felt that all my hair was gone.

"Allen, my hair is gone."

Allen screamed, "What?!" and toothpaste went all over the mirror. He was horrified. I realized he was more attached to my hair than I was. I cut the rest of it off because it was all just like string. And then I went to see Trungpa.

Everyone was expecting some kind of confrontation. But it was really nice to have a light head, so I was very grateful to Trungpa and thanked him for it. That kind of surprised people. But he was my teacher, and this was his next teaching: Join the world! (My dad had once said the same thing to me, "Mike, why don't you just join the world?")

The following day, I cut my beard off. I went from having all this hair and robes and earrings (truckers would almost crash their trucks to get a look at me on the streets of Jackson Hole) to wearing blue jeans, a moustache, and short hair—and no one seemed to notice me. Yet I was the same person.

I thought, "This is great. I'm so grateful to Divine Mother and Trungpa for relieving me of that burden, enlightening me up." They had cut through my spiritual materialism. Now I was here; more here than ever before.

I left on my new adventure—my new life. I was an American again, in a way. It had taken me four years to shed my costume. I was back in the world.

Allen asked me to do a six-week national tour with him. He said I reminded him of Neal Cassady, who was the mentor of Jack Kerouac and Ken Kesey—the whole beatnik trip. Neal had a Pentacostal thing going. He drove all night long for days on end rapping and carrying on. He's in all Ginsberg's and Kerouac's work.

Coming out without my hair and robes was a big deal for me. Many towns we went to had pictures of me with long hair and robes. And people had drawn artwork of me and Allen. It was an incredible experience to be with Allen. He was immensely strong and focused, like a deity, a real baba, a Ganesh baba—he was here on the earth.

Allen glowed with a lot of heart and presence. He was a very kind person, a real love. He had a brilliant mind and was generous in sharing himself.

We had a good time on the tour. We would write poetry flying over the mountains and different parts of America. He got me into a first thought, best thought view of seeing things. He always carried a little notebook and a fountain pen in his top pocket, and he wrote constantly. He was always jotting things down. This was how he worked. He wrote a poem about me in his little notebook. I still remember the sound of the sheet being torn out before he handed it to me.

After our time in Jackson Hole, Allen wasn't into the party aspect of it that much. He was more focused on his work. Of course, I was in a completely different place from him; I was having sex with every pretty groupie who came around. After the concert was more important than before the concert to me. There were a lot of wild parties on the trip. We traveled to all the universities. I was living like a spiritual rock star.

The attendance was really good, and we gave a hot show. Allen would come out first and read his poetry, which included "Cocksucker Blues." All these radically political fans would go crazy and cheer him on.

Then there would be my fans waiting for Allen to finish. As I began, they'd really get into the chanting. Allen would chant with me. He would really get behind me, definitely wanting to cap the energy. He never let it get wild, although I was always going for chaos and total breakthrough. Just as people would start dancing and taking off their clothes during "Om Namah Shivaya," Allen would stop it. He was afraid of the energy getting out of hand.

We ended up in Zellerbach in Berkeley, and who should be in the back of the room but Ram Dass. I went and sat with him. I hadn't seen him for a while.

He said, "You really did it. I'm really jealous—you really put one up on me this time." Touring with Ginsberg was the high point of my career.

Ram Dass always thought I had no ambition, and he was surprised at what he considered my success. But I wasn't ambitious—I was just going along for the ride, doing what I enjoyed.

When I went back to chant, the stage was besieged by streakers. It was during the streaker fad, and people were running naked in front of me. Ginsberg and Ram Dass jumped on stage, too, and we all threw ourselves into the frenzy—it was a great show!

Chapter 27

I⊤ WAS 1976 when we had gone back to California. Ram Dass had a group of about fifty people around him in Berkeley. He'd rented a big house up in the hills. A group of musicians with Jai Gopal—they were all friends from India—had a band called Amazing Grace. They were in the process of making a record called "SWAHA."

I was to be part of it. That was the plan: Amazing Grace and Bhagavan Das.

I was still on that wild party trip of Trungpa's. I would terrorize Ram Dass's house when I went over. He wasn't into that kind of energy. In fact, whenever I went over he insisted that someone be with me at all times. I had to be monitored. But I'd always seduce the monitors into having a party.

In the kitchen of the Berkeley house I met Usha. She was a beautiful strawberry-blonde, curly-haired girl, exciting and energetic. Real sex appeal—I was taken with her. She was juicy, juicy!

Usha was a weaver and always had a loom up in the house. She was Jewish, and very bright. She was enchanting, with an aura of mystery about her. She also had a lot of devotion for Maharaji.

Though I was still married to Bhavani, Usha would eventually become my common-law wife. At the time we first met, she was with Krishna Das—a member of the Ram Dass family. They were obviously boyfriend and girlfriend.

Ram Dass rented out a rock and roll hall called Winterland, and we did a special performance there. It was actually the first huge thing we did: Bhagavan Das, Ram Dass, and Amazing Grace. It was an all-night party, the Grateful Dead were on stage, and lots of people were tripping. There were actually two parties going on: one backstage and onstage and one in the audience. A huge puja table was set up with the Grateful Dead flag on one side and the flag of the Rolling Stones on the other side (even though they weren't there), so it was Shiva and Kali. On one side was the skull and the rose, and on the other side was the tongue of Kali Ma.

We had large slide projections of Neem Karoli Baba running throughout the whole evening. Sitting on the edge of the stage singing, I would look out and see thousands of eyes looking back at me. It was like Kali Ma was everywhere as the energy was spilling out.

Usha and I connected during this concert, and we really fell in love. I took her on tour with me to Canada. When we came back she got pregnant. I wasn't divorced from Bhavani, and yet I already had "wife" number two and another family on the way. Bhavani was furious, and I only felt emotionally numb.

I wanted us to live together as a big family. But Bhavani and Usha didn't get along that well. There was a lot of jealousy, and I was in a lot of emotional pain. And there was a big spinout from it all: I was getting a terrible reputation as a womanizer and party animal.

I didn't know what to do. Usha decided to have the baby. Years later, after Bhavani and I divorced, I lived with Usha. But I never married Usha, which really upset her—it would be a constant source of contention in our relationship.

Our son Mikyo's birth was very difficult. Usha had to have a cesarean section. Mikyo hadn't had a very peaceful time in the womb. Bhavani was bad-vibing Usha, while Usha was trying to stay in a peaceful place. But she was in a very difficult situation considering that I was already married and had a child. So Mikyo had a rough ride. His birth was nothing like Soma's gentle entry into this world. But despite all our troubles his birth was a miracle, and I was thrilled when he was born. I had always wanted a son, and now I had one.

Usha and I were living in Berkeley with a patroness by the name of Deachen. She had a beautiful house with a pool and a waterfall in the backyard. We slept in the master bedroom. Deachen had bought me a huge Bengali tiger skin with claws on it. I would sit on it and chant and do my thing.

One day when Baby Mikyo was just barely a month old, I was peacefully holding and walking him in the bedroom when the phone rang. The caller was a woman named Joya from Brooklyn.

Ram Dass and his group were in Brooklyn hanging out with this Joya person. I was just not into it—I wanted nothing to do with Joya or Ram

Dass or the trip. I was spending time with Usha and my son. Joya was pulling on me: "You need to come." It ended up in psychic warfare (like whose curses were the biggest?). Joya was really working on me on the other end.

Joya was a middle-class Jewish housewife whose husband, Sal, was a Coca-Cola truckdriver. She had grown up in Coney Island. She wore big, black false eyelashes, large acrylic nails, and enough makeup to carve your initials in. Joya wore fifty gold bangles on each arm, giving her about twenty more pounds of power. She was a real home-grown saint.

One day she decided to go to a Jack LaLanne class to lose weight. The teachers had a yoga course and taught the breath of fire, *bhastrika*. They told her that if she did this ten to fifteen minutes a day she'd lose a lot of weight. Joya wanted to get in shape for Sal. She was crazy about him. She'd always say: "There's nobody like my Sal."

Joya was losing weight with the breathing exercises. She decided that if fifteen minutes would have a strong effect, she'd do it for hours to lose weight faster. So she would lock herself in her bathroom and breathe the breath of fire for hours on end.

Her first vision took place when she was doing the breathing in the bathroom. All of a sudden, Swami Nityananda appeared sitting on her toilet. She screamed, "Who are you?!" He started grunting at her, which was just the type of thing he did.

Joya continued the breath, and then Jesus came to her with his cross on his shoulder. She began going into different states. She was like someone possessed. She started shrieking and running around her house with enormous energy. Then she took all her children, got them into her bed, and pulled the covers over her head, screaming. Finally, Neem Karoli Baba, this little fat man with a blanket on, showed up. Joya knew nothing about him.

Someone called Hilda Charlton because she was very experienced in altered states and had been in India for twenty-six years, living with Sai

Baba. Hilda had been an exotic dancer and was an incredible incarnation of the Divine Mother. Hilda came over and knew exactly what was going on.

Joya started channeling all these different beings. Different energies were coming into her body. She would go from being this harsh, screaming woman to having the most exquisite voice—hour after hour, poetry would come from her mouth. It took my breath away. The energy in the room would shift. Joya was definitely capable of moving lots of energy.

Hilda started working with her, teaching her how to work the energy. Ram Dass came to town one day and Hilda said, "You've got to meet this woman. It's so rare to see someone who's really in Samadhi. She's even talking to Neem Karoli Baba.

Ram Dass went to her house in Brooklyn, and Joya started screaming at him, "Do you know this old man—this old man in the blanket?!" She continued talking about things that had happened between Neem Karoli Baba and Ram Dass, things that only Ram Dass knew. It blew his mind. He was really shocked. Hilda reeled Ram Dass in and got him to bow down to the Divine Mother. There was this jealousy between him and me because of my spiritual relationship with the Divine Mother. He could never do Divine Mother because, being bisexual, he was sexually conflicted. But he felt now that he was going to get the real, secret, super-duper tantric teachings that I hadn't given him. Hari Das Baba and I had given him only the kindergarten stuff. Now he was in graduate school, and he was excited!

Ram Dass became a believer, and the triangle was formed. Ram Dass was Jesus Christ, Hilda was Mother Mary, and Joya was Mary Magdalene. The group of believers mushroomed, getting bigger and bigger and bigger.

Joya would spend hours in samadhi; her whole body would get stiff like a board while energy pulsated through her. People would get transmissions of shakti from her. An exhilarating life force would just flow throughout the room when she was around.

Her group grew to include about three hundred people who would get together all the time. She had about ten to twelve houses rented out for her disciples. Ten to fifteen people in each house were constantly practicing the breath of fire. Joya was always calling the houses on the telephone. Whenever she would call a house, everyone there would go into deep meditation for as long as she was on the phone, which could be for two to three hours. She transmitted her shakti through the telephone.

Once she got on the phone, she would do her thing. She was constantly transforming people's lives. She was Kali Ma. Would she transform lives in a good way or a bad way? Who's to say? The pendulum swings both ways. She was incredibly dynamic.

So Ram Dass, Hilda, and Joya had a real scene going. They were grooming Ram Dass to be the next world teacher. They had a room in her house called the Lazuma Room where Joya held her court. It was the inner sanctum. The three of them would stay up all night screaming God's name. Joya would go into trances and then meditate for an hour. Hilda would sit next to her repeating God's name over and over again. She was always invoking God's name.

They were determined to get me to come to Queens. They wouldn't give up. Joya had a picture of me, and she and Hilda would tap the glass every day. I would get phone calls from Hilda, phone calls from Ram Dass, and phone calls from Joya. I felt that the whole thing was a power trip and that Ram Dass was deluded. I knew Hilda, and I felt she was very genuine—but she was a witch.

Joya wouldn't let up. She would call me all the time. When she called, I definitely went into altered states of consciousness. She had so much shakti. Many times I would want to hang up on her, but I couldn't because her energy was so compelling. It was hard, too, being a Mother worshiper and having the Divine Mother pulling on me. This warfare went on for a couple weeks. I had my newborn son and didn't want to leave. And we were sharing Deachen's beautiful house.

Finally we decided to go to New York. Joya was the hottest thing happening, and we had to be part of it.

Chapter 28

So WE ALL moved: my wife, Bhavani, and our daughter, Soma; Usha and our son, Mikyo; Deachen; and myself. We were put up in one of Joya's houses. When the phone would ring, we'd answer, "Hi Ma." It could be four o'clock in the morning. This would be the signal for everyone to go into meditation and start "pulling," the idea being that Joya was always going into samadhi. Our job was to pull her down by drawing off her shakti, and then we'd get to use the shakti to go up on.

Sometimes we would all go to her house. Of course, I'd have to sit in the very front, in front of her, which was always extremely embarrassing for me. I'd walk into the room and there would be hundreds of people there, and I'd have to walk over everyone to get to the front. The powerful had to draw the shakti off. There was Krishna Das, me, and four or five other people in the front.

When Joya went into samadhi, Hilda would say, "Draw, kids, draw! Draw! She's going up. Quick! Draw. Pull!" And everyone, three hundred people, would start to breathe noisily. Hilda was trying to get Joya to integrate the shakti and get grounded enough. But it was tough because Joya would get high on the spiritual energy.

She was an incredible force of nature—a very powerful being. She was a souped-up car, and Hilda was driving. Ram Dass was going along for the ride. He would just sit there with an expression of awe.

So many dramas went down in Queens. Supposedly, the Tibetans were coming to capture Joya because she was the incarnation of Tara, so we had to hide her from them. We ran all over town looking for Tibetans. People were watching her house twenty-four hours a day. We had to walk around the house and take patrols in the freezing wintertime. We'd be sitting in cars watching for Tibetans. Finally the attempted Tibetan takeover petered out.

Joya rented different churches in Manhattan, and we'd all go. She would really work the room. She'd call someone's name, and they'd stand up, and she would totally strip them emotionally. She'd call them on all their stuff, ridicule them, and really make them freak out.

She separated me immediately from my wives. She proclaimed, "Oh, Bhagavan Das, you have two wives! Oh great! We'll take care of that!"

Her nickname for me was Bhagavan Dick. She split us all up, putting us in different houses.

The first thing she said to me when I came to see her was "Oh! So you're the great Bhagavan Das! Okay, are you ready, Hilda? Here it goes!" I was sitting right in front of her. She leaned back and slapped me across the face as hard as she could, twice, in front of three hundred people. She hit me so hard that I think she threw my neck out. Then I cried—my face hurt so much.

I basically surrendered and went for it. Being a Mother worshiper, I thought, "Okay, she seems to fit the bill. She's certainly a Kali Ma." She looked the part: black hair down to her waist, the jewelry, the white teeth, the eyes—she had the look.

Joya channeled everyone from Neem Karoli Baba to American Indians. She could put you into an altered state just by touching you. It was like a light acid trip, like 150 mikes, where everything would get real fluidy and the light would change and you'd feel really intoxicated. She could do all that just by touching you.

David Manangi, a 110-year-old blind Hopi leader, came to see her. The Hopi were delivering their message to the U.N., and David came with Rolling Thunder, who wore a big hat. It was quite a trip. David sat in front of Joya, who did her American Indian channeling. David would go out, leaning forward like he was leaving his body periodically. Rolling Thunder stood behind him with his eagle feather. Every time David would start to nod, he would whip the eagle feather in the air and David would perk up.

I lived in the basement in Queens in this little house off Woodhaven Boulevard, a ten-lane street with massive traffic going to the Triboro Bridge into Manhattan. My wives and children had been placed in other houses.

The subway station was close by, and when the trains would pass, the whole house would rumble. My diet consisted of two greasy slices of pizza a day and Coca-Cola. All the pipes were exposed above me, and I could see just a little bit of light. It was a cell. Joya put me on a real strict regime of the Mahadavananda breath. I did this breathing ten hours a day.

I had my own phone, and Joya would call me up all the time. She was always breaking up my sleep patterns. Her system was to destroy you, then work you. After I got shakti from her phone call I would go into these different states of samadhi with the breath. My life consisted of doing her breathing, worshiping Maharaji and Kali Ma, and going to all her functions. I lived for a year and a half doing sadhana, living in Queens, with my room rumbling.

I lived close to the airport, so planes were flying over all the time. And my house was right in front of the largest graveyard in New York; it went on for miles and miles. At least once a week, people would steal cars, park them near our house, and torch them. The cars would be burning and the whole street would be littered with powdered glass. That was the scene—it was even rougher than Calcutta, as gangs of hoods roamed the streets.

Deachen had bought me a beautiful black Mercedes. People would walk down the street, pull out their keys, and run them along the side of the car. The car ended up totally trashed. This put me through a lot of pain.

Joya wanted me to do sadhana (spiritual practice) and didn't want me to be distracted by my children. Bhavani and Usha were wondering, "Who's going to be the one? Whom will Joya choose for him to be with?"

Joya was playing me off with the women. Everyone there was celibate, so you'd have a huge room of incredibly horny people, which she played upon, because all she talked about was sex. She'd say to the girls, "Oh, so you've got a juicy tomato today? How're you feeling? This guy is really a hunk." On and on she'd talk. It was one sexual innuendo after another. There was always incredible sexual tension in the room. Her girls were sexed up as much as possible, so it was in your face all the time. There was a real tantric flavor to it all.

Joya came into my room once and jumped in my bed. Of course, there were fifty other people there, too. There was so much energy. I took it at face value: All right, you're the Divine Mother and I want to be free and I want to be liberated. Joya said, "Okay, Bhagavan Das. I'm going to give it to you. Close your eyes." We didn't have sex, but I made love to her heart. She put her knuckle in my mouth, and I felt her energy come into me, like mother's milk from the breast.

There were rumors that she and Ram Dass were having sex. Joya totally denied it.

The finale for me was Christmas Day. We were having a huge meeting and Joya said, "Bhagavan Das, stand up!" I stood up and she said, "Shivaya stand up! Shivaya, take Bhagavan Das to a whorehouse right now!" The next thing I knew I was in a whorehouse in Manhattan on Christmas Day. I was there to worship the whores as Divine Mother.

I was lying down in bed with a whore and just started laughing in ecstasy. She was laughing and playing with me and trying to get me going. I couldn't get a hard-on. There was nothing sexy about it. I felt like I was on an operating table. I just wasn't getting turned on. I was actually leaving my body in ecstasy, saying, "Om Kali, Om Kali!" Finally, after a lot of work, she got me hard, put on a rubber, and sat on top of me. I was laughing deliriously.

The ego-loss part of this experience was deeply humiliating. But it was great because it was such a confrontation, considering everything and being celibate for a year and a half. This was my big cosmic fuck.

Joya's school was the school of detachment and ego loss. She'd have couples stand up in the room and she'd say, "Does he beat you? What's going on with you two? Do you love him? Do you want to leave him? Then get out now!" She'd separate people all the time, as she had with me and my wives, and she would marry people. She would tell people to have babies.

After this last encounter, I decided that I'd had enough and was ready to leave town. I pulled out of her group—a lot of people did eventually. Joya sent several people, including a close friend of mine, to confront me about leaving the group. Things got heated and my friend started punching me. Then all these other people start hitting me, and as I'm getting beaten I'm saying, "Om Kali, jai Ma!" I didn't hit anyone back. I was beaten until I was bruised and bleeding. Fortunately, they didn't break any bones.

I gazed out over the graveyard and thought, "We have given Joya the power of God. It's time to leave."

Chapter 29

How to get out of Queens?

Buy a school bus.

I sold Deachen back her Bengali tiger skin for $2,500
and bought a school bus in Coney Island to drive back to
California. It had a governor on it, so it went only 45 miles
per hour. Imagine traveling three thousand miles at 45.

My passengers were Usha, son Mikyo, and Usha's friend Kiki. Bhavani and Soma flew back. During the trip, Usha and I took a break and went to Paradise Island in the Bahamas. It was there that my daughter Lalita was conceived.

When we finally reached Berkeley months later, we parked on the streets in front of friends' houses and used their kitchen and bathroom facilities. Then, wanting to be in the country, we drove to Santa Cruz, where we could park on friends' lawns and use their facilities.

Later we went back to Berkeley and rented a house in Bonnie Dune. Usha, pregnant, craved the comforts of a home, carpeting, and a backyard. I went to Esalen at Big Sur, home of the New Age and where almost all U.S. human potential movements began. Through a friend from India I met a man named Prem Das, who introduced me to a very powerful Huichole shaman named Don José.

A shaman takes each moment as an eternity. He is seen usually as the medicine man for a group of people because he personally encounters the collective; he intervenes for the village in the spiritual realm. The shaman is the expert—the focal point of the village. He's like the whole village combined into one being. What people think of as shamanism today has nothing to do with this. Most of the New Age shamanism is minor occultism.

Don José had ten wives—he had sired practically the whole village himself. Everyone was related to him. When I met him, he was over one hundred years old and had crinkled skin like a mummy. One arm was gone—just an old stump was left—and he was missing two fingers on his other hand. Don José and I became very close and spent a lot of time together.

Prem Das talked me into going to Mexico to visit Don José's village. Usha was very upset because Mikyo was so young and she was pregnant with another baby. She couldn't believe I was going off on a drug trip.

We traveled in a tiny Pinto. Don José was stuffed in the back seat with two huge gunnysacks of peyote (about five hundred peyote buttons) and all kinds of feathers.

Don José lived in a village near Nayarit in the Sierra Madres mountains. Once again, I was in another intense Indian situation.

After driving to the area, we walked five miles because no roads led to his village. It was wild—cacti twelve feet high and Mexican guys with guns in their belts. Prem Das had a gun. The moment we got to Mexico he laid it across the dashboard of the car.

I was having a great time. We ate peyote continually as we walked to the village, which was neolithic. I'd never seen such poverty in India, though it was a close second. People, pigs, chickens, dogs, cats—all lived in one-room houses. There were only one or two pots. The men would be out all day in the corn fields working with machetes, and the women would be home alone in the village making food and embroidering and sewing. These Indian women did incredible embroidery work.

It was a total peyote culture. They worshiped the peyote as God. They even went on pilgrimages to find the peyote because they believe God is at the root of the cactus, and they look on peyote and mushrooms as the flesh of God that has fallen from heaven. It's a bit of God's growth, a seed of God. It's the sun seed.

ॐ

IF WE TAKE this sun seed into our body, then our body bears fruit, and pretty soon, soma is flowing in the atmosphere. So the growth soma is the psychedelic substance that opens up access to the spiritual body, and your spiritual practice produces the higher octave of soma, which opens up another spiritual body. Each soma at each level opens up the body to the soma at the next level.

Soma is a seed as well as a fruit. It opens up and you eat of it. It has this dual nature. It's an initiator—and all initiation opens up potential. Spiritual practice carries you through that potential to realization. It was with this idea in mind that Bhavani and I named our daughter.

If you eat peyote (or another soma, like LSD) but don't dance, chant, and pray, then nothing spiritual will happen. This is why the '60s dead-ended. Everybody was eating soma but didn't do anything with it. They just celebrated the ego—"Let's go out and eat breakfast while we're high. Let's have an orgy!" If we had sat down and worked it together, like the American Indians do, then many things would have been possible—especially tremendous spiritual growth. The earthly and the spiritual would have had a chance to bridge.

I WAS TOTALLY wrung out, what with Usha and another baby due, and Bhavani, and what I had been through with Joya. So I just went out on this shamanic drug trip with the peyote and *Amanita mascaria,* which are the red and white mushrooms.

Don José was the real thing, a real shaman. He reminded me very much of the old yogis in India. He had incredible power. I saw him do amazing things. He had so much energy in his body that when he came to our house in Bonnie Dune the lights would flicker and the motor in the refrigerator would change pitch.

I knew he was Ma. He was so one with the Mother—he *was* the Mother. He was facing death, and yet he had the kind of energy that a teenage kid didn't even have—particularly when he would do ceremonies. Don José had all this juice even though his body looked like the return of the mummy.

We'd sit up all night with him, Prem Das on one side and me on the other, drumming. Don José would be chanting to the fire, "Tatuwari (Great Grandfather Fire)." We would each eat as much peyote as we could. I would eat thirty to forty buttons, really getting into it, whereas Don José would take one teeny peyote button the size of a thumb. He'd hold it and look at it for ten minutes. Then he'd blow on it, pray on it, eat it, and be flying as high as an eagle. Here we were, trying to keep up with him, eating these massive amounts of peyote to keep drumming with him all night. Others would do the deer dance counterclockwise around the campfire, shaking their rattles.

Inevitably, every time we'd do a ceremony, it would rain the next morning. Don José said that it meant the gods were happy. It rained after every single ceremony I did with him.

We'd go to Toltec power spots in Mexico. Prem Das and I would go out at two o'clock in the morning and do an anesthetic type of soma called *ketamine*. We'd leave our bodies and connect with the spirits of the shamans who had done ceremonies in those spots. Psychically this was very risky. It was strong magic, and I got into some very dangerous places.

One night I started speaking a language I didn't know. I became completely possessed by a Toltec spirit (the Toltec Indians predate the Huichole and the Aztec). The Huichole language comes from Toltec. They were the ancestors of Don José. I was caught up in this whole Toltec shamanic world of Mexico.

Prem Das and I went to find the peyote fields of Mexico at a holy place called Zakutekus. We got out in the desert and searched for hours and couldn't find any peyote. There was nothing—it was just desert. So we sat down, prayed, and started singing some songs. Then we walked and found one peyote button. We created a whole ceremony around it. We got our feathers out and put them around it. We prayed to the peyote, carefully wiping the dust off it. And then we dug it out of the ground (it has a long root like a carrot) and shared it sacramentally. Within five minutes we stood up and everywhere we looked were peyote buttons. They were like little lights coming out of the earth—

bright green lights shooting up. There were thousands everywhere, and we were thrilled!

We were at 10,000 feet in the mountains of Mexico eating peyote buttons like apples—but nothing happened. We didn't think about the altitude. After we had our fill, we took a bunch with us. By the time we got down to the lower altitude and hit this little town, we were so high we couldn't even get out of the car to eat.

I went on two or three trips with Prem Das to Mexico. We brought Don José back to Marin County with us in a car filled with gunnysacks of macaw feathers and peyote.

We drove into San Diego in a Pinto. There we were: two hippies, gunnysacks of peyote and feathers, and an old Indian man. Five minutes before we got to the border, Prem Das stopped the car and Don José took out a feather and said a prayer. We literally just drove through. If I had been the border patrol and had taken one look at us, I would have had the car X-rayed. But they just waved us on like we were ordinary people. Don José had incredible power.

We'd bring Don José to someone's house and do a ceremony for a group of yuppies in the backyard. Prem Das would bring artwork to sell—Huichole beadwork and embroidery. Don José was quite a star. People were very taken with him and paid to see him. He performed blessings with his feathers for people, and he did a lot of healings.

Prem Das was paying me to sing and drum at the ceremonies, so I had money to give Usha when I'd come home. We went to Anadarko, Oklahoma, to visit some of the peyote Indians. What was to be a two-week trip turned into a six-week trip. We visited Nelson Big Bow, and I ended up trading him some macaw feathers. His wife made me a real peyote fan, so I had all my own peyote gear.

I had run away for as long as I could from Usha's pregnancy. I lost myself in the shamanic world. It came time to go home to Bonnie Dune and the impending birth of our daughter.

On a full-moon night we drove to the Berkeley hospital where my daughter Lalita was born. I took the placenta home from the hospital to cook it for Usha. You should have seen the look on the nurses' faces when I asked for it! They gave it to me in a shoe box.

I put the placenta on the cutting board. With knife in hand, I looked down at it, and it turned to pure light. I was hit by this shakti, fell backward, and went out of my body into ecstasy. My whole body was shaking.

I came back to myself and was able to chop it up and get the soup going. When I brought it to the hospital, Usha was lying ghost-white in bed with an IV in her arm. I took all my feathers out, lit some cedar incense, smudged her off, and then put the feathers on the IV and around her bed. I fed her the placenta soup, and within minutes, red color came into her face. The shakti was coming back into her strongly. It was absolutely amazing.

I was shamanizing up a storm and was really into my feathers. I basically left everything but the feathers at that time. Now I had two children with Usha, and I started doing a few music events because we needed money. I went to the college in Santa Cruz and did a weekly kirtan. At times I'd have a group of a hundred people, and at other times there would be only twenty or thirty and I'd just pass the hat. Sometimes I'd make a few hundred dollars. We were living on that, and welfare.

Our lives were very difficult. The money problems were really intense, and the children were very intense. We had two babies less than a year apart. I was walking one; Usha was taking care of the other. Then we'd trade off. I'd wake up at four o'clock and take the baby while she was nursing the other and changing diapers.

I had to get something "real" going for money. I was driving in town when a friend, Ajatin, called out to me, "Hey, Bhagavan Das! Hi, how are you?!" I stopped and talked to him. He was standing in front of a car dealership.

"What are you doing?" I asked.

"I'm selling cars. It's great. I'm making so much money. You should try it!"

Ajatin introduced me to the owner of the company. Wolfgang Thrun was his name, and the place was Thrun Dodge. He was a German guy and he liked me.

He looked at me and said, "Get a haircut and a shave and come to work."

I was thrilled.

Chapter 30

I WENT HOME, cut and shaved my beard off, got all my hair cut off, and bought some new clothes. I went back and stood out on the line at the Dodge dealership, with a suit on, looking for my first sale. I'd never sold anything or done anything like this in my life. And I absolutely loved it! I made almost $3,000 the first month.

We'd been living on $400 a month. What a change. I made $500 in commission on just one car. I began taking all my shakti, and all the shamanism I'd been practicing, and put it into cars. I became the top salesman at the place.

I was moving eight to thirteen cars a month. The average salesman would sell three to four cars a month. Five to eight cars, and you'd really be successful—you could make a good living. I was good. I got really excited making all the money.

Two months later I had a brand new car to drive. Three months later we moved out of hippie hovel and into suburbia.

But my relationship with Usha was getting strained. I was spending all my time working because I couldn't deal with my home environment. I didn't like the suburban house, the carpet, the backyard. But I did it for Usha. I kept myself occupied selling up a storm and just making lots of money.

I also started selling different kinds of oil for cars, pushing many different products, building a customer base. And I was into fixing cars because I was really good at mechanics. I rebuilt engines, put in clutches, tuned up cars—all on the side. I had my jumpsuit and tools. I was happy under cars.

Someone came by the car lot one day from the San Jose *Mercury News*. They did a huge article on me using a picture of me naked, covered in ashes, in India. The headline said: Would You Buy a Used Car from This Man? This brought me even more customers. People drove all the way from San Jose to buy cars from me. I would stop people in the street and bring them into the dealership and get them jazzed for a car they liked. I would give them some ridiculous price and then ask them to give me some money. I was into the whole trip: production, accomplishment, and sales. That's what I was getting pats on the back for. And, of course, the money. And I kept getting bigger, more expensive cars for myself.

There was another hippie guru in town named John Panama, whom I knew from Telegraph Avenue in Berkeley. He had a huge following. He was always coming by the car dealership and making fun of me, putting me down. One day he came by and started sticking hundred-dollar bills in my suit pockets.

He would say: "Oh you're just into money. Let me give you some money. Who are you? You're selling out!"

It eventually got to me. I took a break and went to Esalen. I needed to sing. Mike Nesmith from the Monkees was there and flipped out over me. He decided he was going to put out my record "AH" through his company. On the back of the record jacket was a picture of the car dealership with me in a suit. On the front I was in India. I was in all the record stores for a while. It was neat to walk up the street, look in the store window, and see the record.

When I went back to work, business was better than ever. Then this chain letter came along called the Circle of Gold. Rather than throw it out, I did exactly what it instructed. I got Ram Dass into it, and he made $42,000. Everyone I directed it to made at least $20,000. Usha and I made $30,000 on the letter, all cash, within two weeks, and it all came in the mailbox. In 1977–1978, it hit everywhere, all over Marin.

So I was making all this money, business at the dealership was booming, and I was even looking into buying a house. In other words, I was really getting into the family way of life. I was excited and having a good time. It was much more fun than the spiritual trip I'd been through in America. There was plenty of money for entertainment and really good restaurants.

But Usha was unhappy. She felt our relationship was stressed out, which it always was because I never married her. She thought we needed a change to move to Hawaii because it was really romantic there and would help our relationship. So we took all our chain letter money, packed up everything we owned, put our car on a boat, jumped on a plane, and landed on the big island of Hawaii.

We were in Hilo, where we didn't know a soul. It was like being in another country. Everyone spoke pidgin English, so we couldn't understand anybody. We'd just pull our car off to the side of the road and cry for half an hour—me included. And then we'd move on and camp out.

Finally, we moved to Maui because some friends who'd been with Joya were there. Bhavani and Soma remained in California. Bhavani was going to medical school, determined to become a doctor.

It was warm and friendly in Maui, but it was hard on me. I had been loving my new life, all the money I was making, and here I was a hippie again. Our savings were dwindling, I had a beard, and we were back to fighting in paradise. Nothing had really changed. (How it starts is how it ends.)

I started going off and doing month-long retreats in Maui. I'd go up in the mountains with a tent and a stove, pitching my tent secretly in the national forest so nobody could find me. I'd stay at my campsight for a month of meditation, doing my Tibetan mantra on Vajra Dakini.

During this period I realized that the reason my female relationships had been unsuccessful was because I was first and foremost married to Kali Ma. The Divine Mother was my wife. Because the women in my life wouldn't acknowledge her as the first, jealousy erupted and relationships were destroyed. Kali Ma was my spirit wife, my demon lover.

So actually, Bhavani would have been wife number two, and Usha, wife number three. But neither could accept this. They both wanted to be the only one. Kali wouldn't have it. She's numero uno, so she destroyed the relationships.

I went back after one retreat and started doing Hawaiian shamanism. I went to the crater in Kilauea and prayed to the goddess Pele. I brought gin to her (she loves gin) and special red berries. I made a package and prayed to her to bless us in Hawaii and take care of us.

Divine Mother took good care of us, except for the relationship with Usha. We fought all the time. It was fight and fuck for eleven years. That's all we did. It got to be really hard on the children. The only way we could live was to have thirty or forty people around us all the time. We had a huge scene. I had a Big Daddy persona, so people gravitated to us. People came and went. Huge feasts were made. That's how we dealt with our relationship.

Usha had her female friends, and I had my male friends. The moment I was with Usha, I had no energy for womanizing. I completely gave it up. No flirtation or kisses. I didn't hold hands with any woman besides Usha. I really gave her the energy and showed her as much respect as I could.

But as I've said, my love was Vajra Dakini, Divine Mother. Usha got very upset when I went off on retreats to be with my inner wife, but I had to get away. The retreats saved my sanity. I couldn't take the energy of all the anger and fighting.

My money was running out on Maui when we met this guy called C.O.G.—Child of God. He said, "Come to work with me. I grow magic mushrooms. I'll pay you $25 an hour to cultivate the mushrooms."

So I started working in a mushroom factory with thousands and thousands of chambers of mushrooms—a shamanic world. We were growing a lot of mushrooms, we had a huge laboratory, everything was going great, and I was making a lot of money—some of which we were able to save.

Our house in Maui was great, and we had a huge Maui family of seventy-five to one hundred people who would get together once a week. I was able to do kirtans again. Word got out, and many people would come. We were the center of activity on the island.

We did this for eleven years. No peaceful nights, no TV, no books—just an ongoing party of high-energy chanting, lots of singing, lots of devotion, and lots of kids. Everyone was welcome.

SOME OF OUR buyers got busted for cocaine use, and our mushroom packages happened to be in their house. Major panic hit, and the mushroom business dried up.

We had to leave Maui in the middle of the night because paranoia rose in the mushroom underworld, and nobody wanted to go to work anymore. The laboratory was disassembled, and within forty-eight hours none of it existed.

I went to Oahu with $20,000 in cash, looking for a new life for us. We had been living an extreme hippie lifestyle in Maui, very rural, and now we were in the big city. Honolulu is similar to L.A., with very intense energy and horrible traffic.

It was jarring; it set my nerves on edge. I rented a house, and then Usha came—things were still not going well between us. Our money was vanishing, and I didn't know what to do in Oahu. We decided to make a move to a house on the ocean. It was nice and cost a lot of money.

I ran into a man who was very successful selling *Encyclopaedia Britannica*. He was a former Hare Krishna person. His whole practice was Krishna, and he was really good at Britannica. He convinced me that I could sell *Britannica*.

He worked at the Kaneohe marine corps station on Windward Oahu. He initiated me into selling *Britannica,* and then I took over his post as his disciple. The company is structured like a lineage.

I became the world champion three months in a row. I outsold every person in the nation—that's tens of thousands of salespeople.

I broke a company record—I became Rookie of the Month and Salesperson of the Month at the same time. No rookie has ever done that. I sold thirty-four sets of books a month, three or four months in a row. Most salespeople sold four or five and could live quite nicely on that. The president of Britannica was so impressed that he had a special breakfast set up so he could meet me, sent Usha two dozen gorgeous long-stem red roses, and had a Rolls Royce pick us up for a night on the town and dinner.

It was easy to control the military personnel. They were used to taking orders. So I would simply tell everyone what to do. And I did everything my Britannica guru told me to do. He said, "You stand here.

Learn this presentation word for word. Then really put your heart into it. Then watch the people." He taught me how to look at people's body language and how to watch their eyes. I had lessons in how to lower my voice and then create silence—and then how to start again and close the sale.

This man turned me into a closing machine. I sold and I sold. Each day, I sold at least two sets, and many days I sold four. I spiritually invoked the Divine Mother to help me. Not knowing it, not meaning it, I was really calling on God to help me.

I got very excited by it, and so did Usha. All the money made her happy—and we were in Hawaii. I continued to work with the marines for a year on Oahu. Then I was completely in the armed services: I worked the navy base, Pearl Harbor, and the Kaneohe station, where there must have been about twenty thousand people.

I tapped out my base, selling to everyone—probably three hundred sets of books. Then I moved on to some of the smaller stations. I liked the armed forces—it was good shakti.

I was having a lot of fun, enjoying the city energy, the different people, and the accomplishment of being able to make so much money. I knew I could sell—but as I said, I had pretty well tapped out all potential customers. Money problems reared their ugly head once again, and Usha and I started fighting more than ever.

I needed more money, and I knew I could sell, so I started selling solar energy. I was selling the sun. Remember my teachings from Surya, in India? It came back around. I could sell the sun. I could talk about the sun with so much conviction. I sold a lot of solar on Oahu. I was doing presentations, and the sales were pouring in. I had nothing to do with Bhagavan Das on Oahu. I was Michael Riggs, salesman of the year.

But I was slowly sinking. I missed my retreats, my spiritual connections. I carried a skull-bone mala in my pocket. It was old, with 108 beads made from different human skulls, and I spent a lot of time working the beads and invoking my Kali mantra, which brought me some peace.

I also started running every day along the ocean and spent lots of time with my kids, doing family life. Then I became the top solar salesman in this company and won a lot of rewards. So I was having lots of success in the external world. But I missed being in those long flights of ecstasy and solitude I had on Maui. There was nowhere to do a retreat now.

Usha started doing astrology work. She got into a real feminist kick with *New Woman* magazine and worked her astrology career. She was making a lot of money, so she was feeling really good about herself. Many of her clients came to our home.

ॐ

ONE DAY, IN 1982, I came home and the energy was really strange in the house. Usha told me Bhavani was dead. I sobbed and howled.

I was mad at Bhavani for dying on me. And I felt tremendous guilt. I was her teacher and hadn't taken care of her or even been a good friend because of Usha. I had a vivid dream of her flying through the sky with stars in her hair, and she had on this dark blue gown.

She had died of a cocaine overdose in Berkeley. The funeral was very painful and difficult. Dick Baker did the ceremony at Green Gulch, where her ashes are buried.

Soma was only nine years old when Bhavani died. She found her mother's body in the morning when she got up for school. She had tried to wake her and had made the call to the police. She watched them put her mother in a body bag. The trauma was unbelievable.

I assumed she would join my other family, but Usha would not take her. She thought two kids was already too much. She said that I was never any help and that she just couldn't do it. It broke my heart. It also ended our relationship. We'd fought so long that my organs were sore. I couldn't engage with her anymore. I couldn't battle anymore—it was just too much.

ॐ

I MOVED OUT, and a friend who was going to be gone for a month gave me his house to live in. It was the time of Wesak, the Buddha's enlightenment, and I started meditating again. All my puja gear was under the bed in a suitcase.

One night I had a dream vision that I was walking in a very dark, huge Tibetan temple. Monks were chanting, and light was coming in through tall windows, twenty feet up. As I walked down a hall I saw an icon of Milarepa at eye level. It was glowing with light. The next thing I knew I was inside the icon sitting at Milarepa's feet, and he was alive. As I looked up at him he turned into Jamgon Kontrul, a Tibetan tulku I'd known very well since he was a young monk and with whom I'd always felt this incredible connection.

I said, "Jamgon Kontrul, it's you! You're Milarepa!" I had an incredible feeling of ecstasy being in the icon. The light was coming off him, beaming me with his love.

Next I was standing outside the icon looking at it, and then it rolled off the wall and crumbled on the floor. I picked it up, and on the back of it were two handprints in blood. The blood was flowing off the hands and dripping on me. Then I woke up.

I started fasting and running every day. It was how I was dealing with not dealing with Usha—the pain of the separation and the inevitable loss of my family. I was very attached to my children and extremely affectionate with them—lots of hugging, holding, kissing, and telling bedtime stories before I tucked them in. I could feel the hole in my heart.

When my friend returned, he said, "You should return to the mainland and reconnect with your old friends." He was trying to support my spiritual side, not the good provider and money-making side. He gave me some money, and I returned to San Francisco.

At this time, 1981, Kalu Rinpoche was doing a Kalachakra in San Francisco. I went there and then ended up in Boulder, Colorado, because I wanted to see Chogyam Trungpa again. In effect, I had had to cross the ocean to see the great man.

In Boulder I stayed with Allen Ginsberg and Peter Orlovsky, Allen's lover of thirty years. Anne Waldman and Gregory Corso, teachers at Naropa's Kerouac School of Disembodied Poetics, were also around.

We went to see Trungpa for darshan at about 1:30 in the morning, when he would wake up. He had his first glass of sake at about 2:00 A.M. The salon was full of poets. It was like a Hotel California—dark, scorpio, castle-type energy, with this underworld Godfather. Many people were at Naropa by this time—many had waited for years to spend just five minutes with Trungpa. I was ushered in as a VIP and had my five minutes. I drank sake with him, one-on-one for the five minutes.

He was on a Japanese warlord trip. He had armor behind him, and he was shrouded in a dark, demonic, underworld kind of energy. I'd never seen him so wrathful and dark. Something had totally changed in him since the last time I'd seen him. I think he'd progressed to a level of alcoholism. It was a big booze party every night until six in the morning, with Trungpa carrying on spontaneous poetry and giving darshan for the salon.

He was his normal Kaliesque self. Should I divorce Usha? Yes, I think that's a great idea. Whatever I said, it was a great idea. Should I kill myself? Yes, very good idea. He was constantly drawing me over the edge. But this time he looked like he'd gone over the edge as well.

People started leaving around 7 A.M. It had been a very depressing darshan for me.

I WENT BACK to Hawaii deeply depressed and went out in the ocean for the first time since Bhavani had died. I started crying and yelled out, "Help me God!" The next thing I knew, it was raining. A little cloud had come right over my head and started raining on me. The sky was clear everywhere else.

Before Bhavani died I had gone to see her to resolve things between us—but she couldn't do it with me. She wouldn't allow us to close the circle. Things were going crazy with her; there was so much cocaine around. This was when everyone was doing cocaine. It was still trailing off from the '70s, and people were freebasing. It's a very, very expensive habit. A person can freebase $5,000 a month in coke. The only way to do it is to deal it. And because you feel so tremendously guilty spending that much money on cocaine, you completely deny doing it. That is what happened to her.

WITHIN A YEAR I got a call from my mother and sister that my father was dying. He had had a heart attack while playing the piano and was in a coma. I went home to deal with his death. My parents had moved from California to Sandpoint, Idaho, the previous year.

When I entered his hospital room, he came out of the coma briefly—as if to say goodbye—and when I left the room he went back into the coma and soon afterward died. I was comforting my sister and mother in the lounge when he died.

I spent an hour alone with his corpse. It was so beautiful to be with him then. I had a vision of him as a king on a barge in Egypt. I was a priest doing mantras and invocations, the incense was going, and the barge was moving down the Nile. Dad was in a sarcophagus on the barge. I was doing the prayers, and he was the king.

Still, his death had been an incredible shock to me. It was like someone punched me in the stomach and knocked me down completely. My grief was intense.

I went to bed for two weeks and cried, going through every single memory of my dad. I took his clothes out of the dresser and hugged them. I let myself have that sorrow. I spent a lot of time outside taking long walks, really grieving. I replayed every experience I had ever had with him. It was like I died with him someplace as well.

ॐ

YOU HAVE TO allow your heart to open to let the pain through. Allow the genuine heartache.

Chapter 32

I WAS FORTY years old, single, and in so much pain. I'd been married for fifteen years, had three kids, and now I was supposed to hang out and date. It wasn't what I wanted to do at all.

Still, I started partying with some of my old friends in Santa Cruz and continued selling solar. I met a woman at a party and ended up having an affair with her. Her name was April, she was twenty-six, and we had a lot of fun together. I went to her house, we went to bed, and before falling asleep I remember looking at her and thinking, "God, I don't even know her. She's a total stranger. I really miss my wife." I let that feeling slide me into sleep.

I woke up with a shock to a very loud male voice saying, "Michael!" I looked around and no one was there. I went back to sleep and just a little before dawn it was, "Michael!" I woke up again. By this time I was totally awake and shaken up.

"What's going on? Who is it?"

I got my clothes on and walked outside to a hill. A wave of emotion came over me. The dawn was coming up, and the birds were merging into the sky. My knees started to shake. The tears started in my gut, like they did when Bhavani died and when my father died. Then I had an awful, gut-wrenching sob. I got down on my knees and started sobbing to the earth.

"God help me! God help me! I can't go on! Please help me!"

I opened my eyes. In front of me, like a technicolor movie, was Jesus on the cross. It was the crucifixion with two Marys standing underneath the cross, with light coming off it, in vivid detail. I was amazed and shocked. Then I was staring up at Jesus' feet under the cross. A stream of blood flowed from his feet onto me. It went from red to a milky-white stream of light washing over me.

I shuddered in ecstasy. And then the vision was gone. I started sobbing again. When I came back into my body I stood up and felt as light as a feather, like I had just shed a hundred pounds. I walked to my car with a kind of buoyant happiness I hadn't felt in years.

I was born again. I felt like a new baby. Nothing mattered anymore. Everything was okay. I felt completely detached from the divorce, from all the death, and from the sales world.

I drove back to Marin in ecstasy. I absolutely could not put it to-

gether. I didn't even try. I went to Usha's house. She was away with one
of her boyfriends. About twenty minutes later, out of the blue, my
friend Surya Bhakta walked in the door.

"Surya, I'm saved!"

He was thrilled because he, too, was saved and had been praying for
me. "I know, I can see it. I was driving home and when I got to
Tiburon, God turned the wheel and I drove here. I've been praying for
this for two years!"

I told him, "You've got to give me the sinner's prayer."

He replied, "No, no, no, you've got to come to church and have the
pastor do that."

I demanded, "No, you do it right now!"

We got down on our knees, and I made him give me the sinner's
prayer. I said it and felt confirmed with him as a witness. He still insisted
I go to church.

So we went to the Assemblies of God church in Novato. The altar call
came. "Who wants to give witness?" I went up and publicly confessed
Jesus Christ as my Savior. Everyone came up and put their hands on me.
They all started talking in tongues and praising God while the piano
played.

I started to cry. I left my body, shuddering in ecstasy and swooning in
the energy of it. The next thing I knew, I was the trophy of the church. I
was in the front row. James, who had played with Van Morrison, was the
piano player. Donna Godchaux, the only woman who'd ever sang with
the Grateful Dead, was also in the pew. So I had support from my kind
of people.

The pastor was very charismatic, a brow beater—like Mad Daddy. All
the sermons were slightly mad. He was a little angry at everyone—we
couldn't be quite good enough. But I often didn't hear what he said
because I was completely focused on Jesus.

I would stand in front of a huge wooden cross and look at its center the whole time the service was going on. And I'd say, "I love you Jesus, I love you Jesus." I would go through the cross right into the center of it, this black dot, and I would go into ecstasy.

I was having this amazing love affair with Jesus. He was so great. I was free, and I felt so happy. Never in my life had I imagined I'd hang out with these kind of people—beehive hairdos, lime-green polyester suits, women in checked polyester. It was the most bizarre scene I could have ever imagined myself in.

I started to dress just like them, and I spent all my time at church. People were constantly working on me. And it was quite a food feast. They'd have tables with twenty-five different pies and sweets and tons of chocolate and coffee and soft drinks, so everyone was totally jacked up on sugar to the max. I was happy. I was now officially in Bible college, and I was going to be a pastor. I was so in love with Jesus. It was a whole new life.

At one of the evening services they all took me behind the pulpit, where they had a small room. All the elders came and put their hands on my head and started speaking in tongues. Within five minutes I started shuddering and talking in tongues with them. They got really loud, and it went on for an hour. Everyone was walking around the room, turning in circles. These straight people were pretty wild in the back room! It was a strange scene. I went to church four to five times a week. I was completely surrounded by Jesus people.

I got rid of everything but my Bible, which I worshiped. I'd go to bed with my Bible, I'd sleep with it, and I'd hug it. And God woke me up at all different times of the night. It was like in India.

I was living in a one-man trailer in Novato underneath the freeway. My trailer would vibrate most of the night, and it was totally okay. I had no money, I didn't know how I was going to pay for the Mercedes, everything was falling apart in my life—but I was happy. I would wake up and start to pray to God and feel Jesus' presence. I'd see this light in my trailer and I'd start to read the Bible. As I read, the words spoke to me. Once I looked down at the Bible and all the English words turned into Hebrew letters. Then the Hebrew letters turned into snakes, and the snakes turned into fire.

This lifestyle continued for about a year. I would go into Denny's restaurant with my Bible, constantly looking for souls to save. I did nothing but read the Bible and pray.

Once, I was sick in bed for a week, and my whole past was being taken away from me. I was talking in tongues. I was experiencing all kinds of minor miracles. I was falling down in ecstasy at every service in the church, rolling all over the carpet, always falling down at the altar call and sobbing. Tears were always streaming down my face. I was completely blissed out with Jesus.

But I would hide under the pews so the pastor wouldn't see me. Still, he would call out, "Michael Riggs, the Lord has a word for you!" I'd go down the aisle and the pastor would turn into an angel as I walked toward him. He'd put his hand out to bless me and before his hand would even reach my forehead I would fall backward and be caught by two professional catchers just before my head hit the floor. This happened every day.

I was sitting in the church one day, and Donna Godchaux turned around. As she looked at me I saw these two beams of blue light come out of her eyes. It was complete supernatural. She smiled and said, "To really come into the fullness of Christ, get rid of anything that is not of the Lord."

I thought of my Tibetan skull cup, which was my most prized possession. It was the skull of a young girl who had died naturally. It had been given to me by Lama Kalu. I ate all my meals out of it and drank out of it. It had been my begging bowl for six years in India, so it had a lot of energy.

I had a magic dagger, a Tibetan *purba,* that was made of meteorite iron that had fallen from the sky. This purba had so much shakti. When it would rain and storm I would hold the purba and invoke the deity—it would glow with a green light. It had a power of its own. I had slain a lot of demons with it when I was living in Tibet. It was very charged.

I had an old Maha Kala, too, with six arms. It would speak to me. I also had a very powerful Tibetan Ganesh, urine from the Karmapa, and hair from Dudjon Rinpoche. I had enough relics in my bag to start a monastery. I had a small *damaru,* which is a Shiva hand drum made of a male skull and a female skull (it was very, very old), and a bell and dorje that Ram Dass had given me in India.

I put them all in a Kermit the Frog lunch pail and drove across the Richmond Bridge. I stopped in the middle of the bridge and threw them off; just as they hit the water, two rainbows appeared. It felt great not to need magic anymore because I had Jesus Christ as my Lord and Savior. All I needed was to be closer to Jesus. (Looking back on it, I think the entire San Francisco Bay area must have been sanctified by those relics.)

I terrorized Usha. I was really on it. I told her she was a whore and a witch and was going to hell—that astrology was total witchcraft. She would scream and sob. I had become a fundamentalist Christian poster boy—a fallen guru saved by Jesus. All my previous beliefs had been obliterated and replaced.

Chapter 33

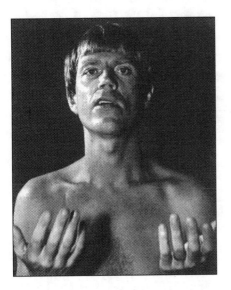

ONE EVENING I was standing up at the altar call when I saw a really sexy blonde next to me with tight blue jeans. A wave of lust came over me. I hadn't had sex in about a year because all my energy was in the cross and Bible college. I had learned that I was a bad man: a devil-worshiping guru, a horrible black magician, and a sex addict. My sins went on and on and on. But now I was saved! And I shouldn't be having lustful thoughts.

But I couldn't resist putting the make on her. She was very young—eighteen or nineteen—but she told me she was twenty-three. She was one of the choir girls. We started romancing each other. It was a long courtship. We went out for two months like we were in high school: three dates holding hands and the first good-night kiss four weeks later. I couldn't believe I was doing this, but she had an incredible magnetism about her.

And then it happened. I came over one day and she opened the door in an incredibly sexy outfit. She was really into teasing me with it. We ended up in bed, and the moment I started having sex with her I was standing in front of the cross. I was going into these waves of ecstasy and feeling Jesus' presence. The whole room was covered in light. She was glowing in light. She was the Divine Mother, she was Mary—she was so beautiful.

I started talking in tongues while I was making love to her and calling out Jesus' name. She was a total Christian. Christian music was playing, and I could see how it was doing a trip on her. I felt exactly in the same space as when I saw Jesus on the hill. But it didn't match the conceptual mind.

This was sin!

This was fornication!

But my heart, my soul, was filled. It was beyond the beyond. It was the most tantric ecstatic state I had ever been in. The room was filled with light. I couldn't stop praising God. She got into it with me, and we were both sitting up praising God.

News of our affair reached the ears of the congregation. The elders warned me. Everybody knew. We were the talk of the church. You could feel it. She'd be on one side of the church and I'd be on the other, and you could feel the energy.

I was sitting in Bible college a few days later. The pastor walked up to the door and said to me, "You're guilty of fornication. We're throwing you out of the church." I almost started laughing when he said I was guilty of fornication. I felt happy. He said I was a sex addict, I had this problem, and I should go to counseling. Oh lord! I was molesting young girls, I was a sorcerer, I was evil and going to hell.

I started going to counseling with one of the pastors. I was buying into it as if I had a problem. "Help me. I've got all this pain from the divorce and I don't want to date and I've got all this sexual energy. What do I do?" I thought, I have a problem and they'll help me.

So the pastor would browbeat me with the Bible and talk at me. I could never get a dialogue going. It was always a monologue. I got very depressed.

One day a couple weeks later I was sitting in the back of the church, which was a bad place for me because I'd start to people watch. Suddenly I was getting into what they were dressing like, what their dramas were—like people watching at the airport. It was difficult for me to keep the focus on the cross.

I heard a voice inside me speak, and I knew it was Jesus. And Jesus said to me, "Leave the church and worship me as Shiva." I couldn't believe it. I said, "What?" He answered, "I know you love me. You don't need all this head stuff." I was sitting there in my polyester clothes, short hair, all the time thinking, "It's the devil talking to me."

Devil or not, I went with the voice I heard and left the church.

I wandered into every other church in Marin trying to find a body of believers, but I just couldn't vibe with anyone. I had gone from having this rich experience to bouncing in the empty halls of "Churchianity." It was very frustrating because I couldn't get back on the ride and be in that ecstasy.

I ended up opening the Good Guys store in Corte Madera, selling car stereos, telephones, and TVs. I was missing Jesus. "Worship me as Shiva," I was thinking. Did Jesus really say that, or was it the devil? I still felt that all the other stuff was not of God. We don't worship people. We worship God. I had been well indoctrinated. But the thing that always struck me as strange was that I knew I was saved. I felt completely saved and totally free. The freedom I had felt in that tantric sexual experience with the choir girl was like being with Mary and Jesus. It was so real, and yet it didn't jive at all with the doctrine.

You're saved! You're saved! And yet the church would teach that there was always more. It said I didn't really have enough yet. I didn't have all that God had in store for me.

There were more confessions, more altar calls, more tithing, more prayer warriors, more meetings. I would go to meetings at three o'clock in the morning. I'd go to meetings all night and walk up and down the church praying for the pastor who was in India converting the heathens. We'd walk around, we'd stamp our feet, we'd cry out to the Lord—this was half the night. Ten or fifteen men would get together in small circles and pray.

I really liked it. I loved the satsang, which is really important, coming together with people who love God and praying together. God really uses us as that main tool to awaken us. We need to see God in each other: human, intimate, eye to eye. Yeah, feel the love.

That was my problem—I had no satsang. I just bounced around and couldn't find any church to join. I was floundering, missing God. I had a few more girlfriends, and I was drinking wine and smoking pot every night.

Then I met someone who convinced me that I was an alcoholic and that I had a real problem.

I started going to AA meetings. I found satsang there. It was very spiritual, and I felt close to God. AA meetings became my new church.

Then it got to be too AA, too intense, so I stopped going. But it had been a place where I could definitely feel the spirit, where people warmheartedly cared for one another and were real.

I was working at Good Guys and being close to my children, taking them out all the time, living in Marin. But no church—just completely lost.

I saw an ad in the paper for an insurance salesman. It paid $2,500 a month to start. I thought, "Whoopee!" I went down and met the boss, Fred. He liked me and hired me.

Fred said, "There's so much money in insurance, it will make your head swim."

My first day on the job, I made $1,000. I was so excited. I closed one policy after another. I went out and bought a gold watch with it. I was feeling really good. I was on the phones. I was an insurance salesman. I did this for three years, 1986–1989, in Marin County across from the Strawberry shopping center. My office was right on the water.

It was great because it was all telemarketing. I had a big moustache again, I was growing my hair out, and I would put my feet up on my desk and sell up a storm over the phone. I realized just how great the telephone was—I didn't have to get dressed up, get in the car, and do the whole trip. I was in the retail car business, servicing car dealerships. I knew cars—I knew every kind of car and the years and how much they cost. It was fun, and the money was good.

So my living situation was improving (I was living in Mill Valley), and the insurance office started growing, becoming really prosperous. A job opened up in Colma at the Serramonte Auto Plaza. I became an agent in the retail car business. I had to go out and buy five suits and three pairs of shoes. I had to get rid of my old clunker and drive a Mercedes with a car phone to Colma from Mill Valley every day.

I opened the office at twelve in the afternoon, and I would leave about midnight. I'd go to Marin Joe's and have dinner at two in the morning. This was my life.

I would sit there in the cubicle at the top of the insurance office, surrounded by glass, and I could look down and see the car floor. Most people buying cars and coming to me for policies were from Third World countries—the Philippines, China, Southeast Asia, and so forth. I sold substandard auto insurance, which is auto insurance that people with really bad driving records have to get. The average yearly premium was about $1,500, and some were as high as $4,000 dollars. These were people with DUIs and tickets. When they bought a new car, they couldn't take it out of the place without insurance, so they'd have to go upstairs and see Mr. Kermit (my real first name—Michael is my middle name). After they'd been beaten up for hours by the salespeople, I got to finish them off. I'd get their last $500, or however much cash I could get out of them, and sell them a policy.

I averaged $7,000 a month for three years. I'd never consistently had so much money in my life. I had $1,500 a month of play money that I could blow on anything I wanted. I became restaurant rich. I could go out to any restaurant at any time and eat anything I wanted without ever looking at the price. It was a certain level of attainment I'd always wanted to have—a true Taurus's heavenly bliss.

I had two massages a week. I thought nothing of paying $50 for a shirt or $200 for a pair of shoes. I became a professional shopper. And I had my Mercedes.

I lived in a very humble abode about the size of a closet so that I could spend all my spare cash on luxuries. Besides, working six and seven days a week, I was barely home.

I went to work one day and walked right into a brunette standing by the Coke machine. We eyeballed each other with intense energy.

She said, "Oh, you're the insurance guy. I've called you before. My name's Kelly. I just got a car. What would it cost to insure it?"

I answered, "I don't know. Give me a call." I was feeling, mmmmmm, she's really cute, but I instantly put her out of my mind. A few days later she showed up at my office. She was about 5'9" and had jet-black hair. She wore a halter top and a very short, black miniskirt. She had long, long legs, and she sat down across from me.

I didn't have a chance.

Chapter 34

I ENDED UP taking Kelly out to dinner. Afterward she said, "Where do you live? I want to see your place."

I took her back to my room. She took off all her clothes, jumped in my bed, and said, "I'm going to sleep." That was the beginning of my relationship with Kelly.

The truth was that she was eighteen, had just graduated from high school, and had recently moved to California. She was on her own, was on the club scene, and was just a kid.

We were having fun but didn't have much time to spend with each other. I was selling and coming home. I was taking care of her, supporting my concubine. It was a great arrangement for both of us. She really liked to smoke pot, so I started to smoke it again. Whenever I got stoned, waves of devotion started coming over me again. I was thinking of God. I'd be stoned on the rooftop of my Mill Valley apartment, looking at the stars, thinking, "I remember." I was getting into that root chakra muladhar memory bank.

We went to Santa Cruz to see a friend of mine, Shankar, a person I'd taken *Amanita mascaria* with. Although he wasn't qualified, he had "married" Usha and me on Oahu. It wasn't a legal marriage, but it was a spiritual ceremony that made Usha happy.

He had mushrooms all over his room and posters of Jesus as the mushroom and the mushroom on the cross. So we went on the mushroom hunt again. We went out to the side of the mountain and they were all over the place. It was a deep spiritual experience for me, being with the *Amanita* again. I started connecting to God again, through the mushrooms. They're like *Amanita* girls—goddesses. They sing and are like messengers of light.

We dried the mushrooms before we ate them because they're very toxic. They're not a type of recreational drug; they're a serious shamanic tool. We'd eat the dried mushrooms, and then we'd drink our urine about three or four hours later. The psychotropic alkaloids were in the urine.

Kelly took a lot and nothing really happened to her. She ate ten, fifteen mushrooms. I ate the same amount and had an incredible journey on them.

We came back and I went to work.

I had this American Indian peyote box that I kept all my feathers in.

That night, when I came home, Kelly was dancing around the room naked with my feathers out all over the place. She was full of wild energy. I'd never seen her like that—it wasn't like her. Kelly was a reserved Scandinavian girl. And now she had gone wild!

We had a passionate night after I put all my beautiful feathers away. Then she started talking about God. The next day she was calling me at work still talking about God. She said, "I know who you are! I've found out!" I was trying to ignore her, not knowing what to do.

I had invested $10,000 in a company with people in Los Angeles. They were having a party at their house and told me it was important to come to do some networking. So Kelly and I went. I bought her a beautiful new silk dress, and it cost $120 to get into the party. It was a huge banquet on a hill in Beverly Hills.

When we got to the party, Kelly went totally mad. She took off all her clothes and ran around terrorizing everyone. The mushrooms had kicked in again a week later. She was a deity—a naked goddess whom nobody could contain.

She was running and jumping. She'd run up to people and say, "You're full of shit. You're a phony! You're a liar!" She was confronting people on all kinds of stuff.

People were coming up to me saying, "You've got to get rid of your girlfriend. Gag her and get her out of here!"

The men were freaking out because here was this nineteen-year-old naked girl. These were sophisticated people, with security agents. Tibetan lamas and famous celebrities were there. I was totally embarrassed.

Kelly was flaming with energy. Every time I'd get near her she'd yell, "Get away from me! You're not real! You don't even know who you are!" Then she'd laugh this cackling laugh and run off across the lawn. I had to get out of there. Everyone was furious with me.

At two in the morning she was in the pool room and wouldn't come home with me. She fought me and screamed at me. So I left her there. I went back to Topanga Canyon. The security guards brought her home at five o'clock. I was so angry I could have strangled her. Her expensive silk dress was ripped and her hair was a mess.

I was elbowing her to go away when she threw the covers off me and started passionately making love to me. It was the most passionate, intense sex she and I had ever had. She had always been a little on the cool side. This shocked me. We continued for another two hours into the dawn.

I paid dearly for those two hours for the rest of the day. Just as Kali Ma had embodied Joya, she now embodied Kelly.

After we made love, Kelly got off me and proceeded to run around terrorizing my friend's house. She ran outside naked, spouting out poetry.

My friend said, "You've got to get rid of her. She's like a wild cat. Drop her in a lake—drop her off on a street corner somewhere."

All day long she went on like this! She'd go on about Jesus, Revelations, and God. "God is all that is real," and "There's nothing in this world that's real," and "I know who you are; you don't know who you are. You must come back now!"

She went out in the backyard. She stood on top of a rock and started invoking Jesus. This went on all day.

With the help of my friend I got her clothes on—she was completely mad and powerfully strong—and got her into the Mercedes, put her seatbelt on, locked the door, and took off down to the valley.

As I turned a corner driving about ten miles an hour, she threw the door open and jumped out of the car. She had no shoes on, no underwear, just this ripped silk dress, and she was running down the sidewalk as fast as she could.

I parked the car and ran after her. I got her back in the car and she did the whole thing all over again. I desperately tried to keep her in the car, but she was saying, "I have to go to the party! We must go back to the party! I was talking to the cat and the cat knows!" Talk about out there. I was holding her down and trying to make it to the freeway.

When I got to the next corner, she jumped out of the car and went running down the block again. I made a U-turn and drove after her. She cut across a lawn and ended up on the lawn of a Beverly Hills mansion. She leapt into the pool and started bathing in the cold water at five o'clock in the afternoon.

I cautiously approached her. "Kelly?"

She looked up at me and said, "This is the water of eternal life. This is the fountain of God's grace. You must come drink it with me!" I did drink the water, my mind began to float, and then I snapped back into reality.

I went to grab her and she fought me. She was so strong I couldn't hold her. I was finally able to pull her down the hill to the car, but I couldn't get her into it. She was kicking me and biting me and scratching me and beating me and making me bleed. I realized the only way I'd get her under control would be to knock her unconscious, tie her hands, and throw her in the back seat.

But I couldn't do it.

I chickened out.

And I let her go.

She ran to the top of the hill screaming, "You don't own me! God owns me!"

I yelled back as I drove away, "Then God will take care of you!"

Eight hours later I finally got back to Mill Valley. It was seven o'clock in the morning. The moment I walked in the door the police called and asked if I knew her. They'd found her.

"I do know her. This is the name of her mother and here's her mother's phone number. Goodbye!"

After I had left her, she had run all over Beverly Hills terrorizing people, ending up in another swimming pool. Then she started talking to a cat, and the cat told her numbers 4, 7, 9, 3. So she walked up to the door of the mansion and punched into the security alarm 4-7-9-3 and the door opened.

Kelly picked up the cat and walked into the master bedroom. The occupants sat up in bed to see a soaking-wet, naked girl holding their cat.

She ended up in a mental institution. They gave her Thorazine and made her sign her life away. Then they tied her on a gurney and strapped her in. She broke the straps in the middle of the night and wandered around the hospital. They tied her down again.

She called me every day at my insurance office from the nut house for two weeks. She was trying to come back into reality, but it was a very slow process. I tried to shut her out.

I couldn't believe this had happened. Everything was different in my mind; something was being churned up.

Kelly got out of the institution, came back, and I fell in love with her all over again because I felt so guilty for leaving her stranded by the roadside. I bought her clothes and jewelry and took her out to dinner.

A week later she drove to my insurance office in my other car at eleven o'clock at night. There were people around because the dealership was open late. She came in my office and threw my computer off my desk onto the floor, threw all my papers off the desk, screaming and lividly angry, "You're a phony! This is not who you are! You're Bhagavan Das! You must come back to God! You cannot live this lie! You're only in it for the money!! There's going to be an earthquake and everything is going to be destroyed! We have to leave now! You must get in the car with me!"

She was so forceful. I ended up leaving the insurance office the way it was. I knew my job was finished. She'd ripped out lines in the walls.

Everyone in the place was freaked out. I tried to hush her up. I let her drive my Mercedes. She drove all night to L.A. with this superhuman energy. I was so mad when we got there that I left her and drove back to San Francisco.

The next day was October 9, 1989. The San Francisco earthquake hit. I was in my insurance office selling a policy to a woman, and all of a sudden my desk started moving and the woman started screaming. Kelly had been on to something, and I should have paid attention. But I hadn't.

A few days after this, I talked to my boss. I had worked for him for three years, and I said, "Fred, half the business I write is referral business, and the other half is new business. Since people are coming just to see me, I want one percent more commission on the deals I'm getting from these people."

I was basically asking for a $500–$1,000-a-month raise, which he refused to give me. He said, "You're making so much money now, how can you ask for more?" I was hurt and disheartened. That's when I quit.

I ended up going to Hawaii for a week to try to chill out from Kelly. I had just a few thousand dollars left and I had a lot of bills. Then I went back to California and started another insurance company with two other guys as equal partners. About two weeks into starting it they cut me out. I went to work one day and they had all my stuff in a little cardboard box. " 'Bye Kermit, it's been great! We'd rather have a two-way split than a three-way split."

I drove back to Marin crying. I knew it was all gone. I watched the Mercedes being towed away as it was repossessed. Now I was driving a $200 beater car that barely ran, with the muffler falling off and a banged-up door. And I was still trying to get rid of Kelly. Just before we split up she got pregnant. She had an abortion and we finally ended it.

I tried to go back to selling *Britannica,* but it was slipping through my fingers. I couldn't do it anymore. I had one run in Santa Cruz where I sold thirteen sets in one week and I made $5,000. I paid my bills and got a better car, but I still couldn't do it. All the money pressure pushed me into a hole of anxiety and worry. I did all types of odd sales jobs. I worked on the telephone, I sold this, and I sold that. . . .

But I was going down very fast.

Chapter 35

S̲RIDHAR, A FRIEND of mine with whom I'd done a lot
of business, told me he'd just met a new Indian saint and
that she was "one of the highest beings on the planet."
Her name was Ammachi, and she was from southern India. He told me I had to see her; she would change my

life. I said, "Sridhar, get off that guru crap. I'm just not into it." Besides, I didn't want to change my life.

"Guru, shmuru," I said. "Good luck, Sridhar."

"She has more shakti than Muktananda," Sridhar added. My ears picked up. More spiritual energy than Muktananda? It might be amusing to check out the new guru on the block. Sridhar sent me her tour schedule for the Bay area. It reminded me of an Amway ad.

I showed up at Berkeley Church in the hills at 8:30 P.M. The street was full of New Age types. Deadheads and businesspeople—a curious mix. I didn't feel out of place as I walked in the door. The walls were plastered with images of the guru's face like, Mao Tse-tung posters in Nepal. I was repelled by the bazaarlike selling of plastic rings and clothes Ammachi had worn or touched. "This is a full-on cult," I thought. As a born-again Christian, I had worked for some time with the Spiritual Counterfeit Project in Berkeley and was on the alert for this kind of thing.

But there was a good feeling in the air: a warm, homey, Indian feeling. The church was as packed as an Indian train station. The energy was focused on a small, dark woman seated on a throne with an umbrella over her head. What struck me most was the light coming off her head. I looked closer—it was a silver crown encrusted with jewels.

Funny, standing there looking at that glittering crown, my brain unexpectedly changed channels. I started feeling how much I loved God. I found myself swept up in the tide of devotion surging through the hall. The line of devotees waiting to meet Ammachi was the longest queue I had stood in since I saw the movie *Gandhi* in Honolulu. The movie's theme song, "Raghupati Raghava Raja Ram," started playing in my head, and I remembered Ram. "Ram, Ram, Ram, Ram," the eternal mantra of Mother India, had been grunted from the mouth of every ricksha wallah and chai vendor. "Ram, Ram, Ram." I started crying as the line got closer to Ammachi's chair. She was hugging everyone, which I had never seen a holy person do before. Her fifteen-piece band of Hindu renunciates was wailing southern Indian *bhajans* of Kali and Krishna, the two dark lords of the Hindu jungle.

I felt a sudden wave of fear. This guru had shakti, no doubt, but who was she? My mind advised, "Protect yourself." The "Rams" were flowing like a stream over my breath. I couldn't take my eyes off her.

When I finally got into close range, I caught the light off her eyes and saw a black face with a red tongue sticking out. Kali Ma! "She is Kali, the goddess of death," my ego started to scream. The "Rams" were spinning out of my heart like a rosary. "Ram, Ram, help me, Maharaji!"

When I closed my eyes I saw blue-violet light. My knees were shaking so badly I sank down and inched closer in prayer position. I felt like a goat waiting to get my head cut off at the Kalighat temple in Calcutta. Memories of hundreds of severed goat heads with butter lamps balancing between their horns appeared vividly before my mind's eye.

Waves of shakti were pulsating out from Ammachi as the fragrance of flowers filled the air. "Ram!" I called as Ammachi reached out, seeming to recognize me, and grabbed my hair. I reached up to hug her like I had seen others do, but she pushed my head down. I was shocked and, face pressed against her lap, I couldn't breathe. It was black and I was all alone, dropping like a stone to the bottom of a well. Suffocating, I freaked and struggled with my 6'5" frame and 240 pounds of strength to raise my head. I managed to lift my nose a few inches and caught a deep breath, then felt her hand come down on my head like a great wave drowning me in the Pacific. I felt Kali shift her body and push her elbow down on my back, pinning me like a wrestler. I couldn't breathe. My mind started doing flashbacks: I saw a young sadhu worshiping Kali on the banks of the Ganges, singing to the Divine with his whole heart, his arms raised in ecstatic propitiation, his long blonde locks streaming down his naked torso. I recognized him: he was someone I had been once.

I knew I was going to die. But I was going to die in the lap of the Divine Mother. I let go!

I was hurtling down a black tunnel at lightning speed, shooting toward a bright white light.

The Goddess lifted my head and I looked up into Kali's eyes. Love flowed into my heart as Ammachi kissed and hugged me. She gave me candy and a flower, and someone helped me move my body a few feet away from her. I closed my eyes and felt peace and bliss wash over me for hours.

Sridhar was right: the little woman from southern India changed my life. I was alive again. I could breathe again.

A few days later I awoke suddenly in the early morning. An old man stood twinkling before me in a tattered plaid blanket. My guru, Neem Karoli Baba, came to me and reminded me that I am not Michael Riggs, that years ago he gave me another name: Bhagavan Das.

Chapter 36

Aғтеr мy мeeтıng with Ammachi, I had several days of inner peace. I replayed in my mind, over and over again, the meeting and the bliss. Inwardly I knew I was Bhagavan Das, but still I was fighting the demands and desires of the outer world.

I went to a party in Marin County at the house of an

old friend, Ramana Das. There was a beautiful, sexy girl in the back room who had a lot of charisma, Taressa. I started talking to her and she was very friendly, but she wanted me to meet her friend, Jay. She thought it was important for us to meet. I agreed to meet him because I wanted to impress her, but it turned out that meeting Jay was one of the pivotal moments in my life. Jay would help me bring out Bhagavan Das.

Jay was a young beatnik, an intellectual, artistic guy in the navy. He was eighteen in 1968. He ended up on leave in San Francisco, went to a Grateful Dead concert, got into the energy of the Haight-Ashbury days, and ended up in some apartment in San Francisco taking STP, which is like really strong LSD. He realized while he was on the hallucinogenic that he was God. He couldn't handle the blasphemy of it and jumped out a window. He took a swan dive and ended up in Kali's lap—his blood-splattered skull on the pavement, a broken neck, lying in excruciating pain. He's written great poetry describing this. He was extremely psychedelicized in this incredible state of awareness while they were cutting his skull open and stitching him up; he was really there. It's a perfect analogy of really not dealing with the Divine Mother and then really dealing with her in a very, very stark way. He had many visions while he was in this state in the hospital. Finally, the only thing he could cling to was Mary, and he started doing Hail Marys. She got him out of the pain.

So he spent years wandering out of his body with Jesus and Mary, having incredible experiences with them. He got religious real fast. He clung to that cross, so Jesus and Mary really brought him through. When I met him he was despondent and bummed out and wanted to die. He was a quadriplegic, confined to a wheelchair. He could move his arms and hands a little but had no feeling from the waist down.

Spiritually, Jay and I had a lot in common. We both had the Jesus thing going strong, so the first thing we did was start talking about Jesus. We would get together and get stoned and have prayer meetings together. We'd play John Coltrane and talk about poetry, but it would always end up as a devotional trip in which we'd pray together. We'd get as high as we could on pot and then go into long prayer sessions. He'd tell me about his experiences with Mother Mary and Jesus.

Jay had hurt himself on the side of his hip, and this left him with a bad wound. It was infecting his whole body and heading toward his brain, but he was neglecting it because he felt that it would be a way to get out of his body—he really wanted to die. He'd already tried to kill himself several times before we met. He was so unhappy with his life. Finally, one day, he said to me, "We should take communion together."

Jay was with Father Paul in the Holy Order of Mans in San Francisco for three years. He got all his communion things together. We got stoned, took communion, and praised God for three hours. We started doing this on a regular basis. I'd never shared the Mass with anyone before. I felt like I was having satsang again. Jay was really there with me.

I was still financially strapped, and Jay was helping me out with money. He tried to help me out in all areas of my life.

"Michael, what do you want?"

I said, "I want money and sex. That's what I want."

He said, "Michael, you've got to sing."

I said, "What?"

He said, "You've got to sing."

I thought, "What is he talking about?" I'd go back to try to make another sale, get beaten down, and end up at Jay's house. Finally, Jay said, "You've just got to ask the old man. Talk to the old man."

"What are you talking about?"

"You know, the old guy in the blanket."

"But I'm a Christian!" Maharaji hardly ever came into my consciousness anymore; when he did, he would come in and roll out. But I had told Jay about him, and Jay had read *Be Here Now*.

It was almost like Jay wanted me to reconnect so I could give him something. Neem Karoli Baba started coming through me, and Jay was blessed by him. An initiation took place between Jay and me. The initiation completely changed Jay's life—he was touched profoundly by Maharaji.

I watched Neem Karoli get inside Jay and change him. Jay finally ended up going to the Vet hospital and getting his side sewn up. There was a huge scar on the side of his hip about ten inches long. But there was a problem. Even with all the sutures, they couldn't get the skin to close. It kept opening up.

I got a call from Jay at three o'clock one morning from the hospital. He said, "You need to come down immediately and put your hands on me and heal me. You're the only one who can do it. I know Maharaji wants this to happen."

I immediately left for the hospital. No one was in the room. I put my hands on the gash, not believing it myself, just doing what I was told. His faith was so strong in me. I said Maharaji's name, and it began to close up and heal. The doctors came back that night and were surprised that the wound was finally closing.

Jay started roaring back to life again. He accepted the blessing of the wheelchair and the blessing of Kali Ma. Our love and friendship grew.

His love for Maharaji became a part of his practice. He felt his grace and power in his life; he was seeing him and laughing with him. Jay was completely in love with Maharaji. He talked to him all the time. He went to sleep at night with his picture in his lap. He played a video of Maharaji over and over again, for hours and hours.

My experience in healing Jay, and our friendship, brought Maharaji back into my life. One morning, I prayed to Maharaji again and really felt him. I put his picture up and made a temple in my house. Someone had given me a little pamphlet about an Indian saint named Shree Maa. I put it in the temple. I was thinking, "I wish I had something of

Maharaji. I wish I had a relic. I wish I had some ashes, some beard hairs, some fingernails." I wanted something—anything—to hold onto.

And then the dreams and visions started: all of a sudden I was in Maharaji's office, sitting right in front of him. He was sitting on a low wooden platform with his blanket around him. He spoke to me in perfect English, saying, "You did such and such, you sold insurance, you did this, you did that, you've been going to Grateful Dead shows." He talked to me about all the things I'd been doing, like he used to. I was completely ecstatic sitting in front of him. Then he leaned back and gave me two thin Indian blankets and said, "Here." I looked at them and felt them and said, "No, I don't want these, Maharaji—I want this." I felt *his* blanket. "I want a thick blanket like yours." And so he put the two blankets to the side, looked at me, cocked his head, and then took my hand and stood up. He opened this dark room and we walked out into the bright sunlight holding hands. Then he dropped my hand. I followed him on this sunlit path in a country setting over to an opening where there was this big old Pontiac from 1960, with a huge hood. Maharaji sat on the hood. I went to the car, and the hood was still warm. His blanket had opened up, and he was naked underneath. He beckoned me to come to him. He kept saying, "Come on, come on."

I got up on the fender of the car and moved over to hug him. He pulled me into his stomach and I dissolved into it. I went into this completely, utterly blissful, ecstatic, awesome state in the dream—the ultimate orgasm. It was complete fulfillment and happiness.

The next thing I knew, I came out of that space and was sitting on the hood of the car. Maharaji was gone, and I was wearing his blanket around my shoulder. Then the phone rang and I woke up! It was Kelly. And it was dawn. I spoke to her for a second, hung up, and wrote the dream down.

Maharaji had also said, "Sing!! Go!"

When I came out of the dream I was Bhagavan Das.

I surrendered.

I started doing a kirtan once a week at Jay's house for a year and a half. People would be spilling out into the streets. Jay and I would do Mass at the beginning of the kirtan and give everyone the Eucharist and pass around the wine. It was Mass of the Holy Order of Mans. After Mass I would start the kirtan and we'd sing for two, three hours.

I was starting to have visions of Maharaji in the daytime. Once, Jay and I were sitting in his van listening to "Mr. Tambourine Man" by Bob Dylan, and we were breathing together. We would breathe in "Ram" and breathe out "Ma." I saw a huge crowd of people, and Maharaji was a hurdy-gurdy man, cranking on his hurdy-gurdy. With him was a little monkey with a little red uniform and a little cup. Other Maharaji devotees were there, chanting, "Maharaji's here! Maharaji's here!" But Maharaji said, "No, no, no, don't look at me! Look at the monkey!" I wasn't asleep when this happened. I was awake, and it was broad daylight.

Another time, I saw a train that snaked out for eternity—Maharaji was the driver. He was wearing an engineer's hat and bib overalls. He was looking out the window and twinkling at me. On the side of the train were silver letters like in the Pontiac insignia from the 1940s. It said: NEEM KAROLI CHRISTOS. The cars went on for infinity.

Chapter 37

I STARTED WORSHIPING the Divine Mother as Mary and brought Maharaji back into my life again. I prayed a lot. Energy started to gather immediately in the temple. It happened so fast, I was amazed. I felt that I was finally surrendering to being Bhagavan Das. I'd constantly bring my prayers to my guru and say, "I can't do it, I can't do it. Please help me. Make it okay. Bring me close." I had incredible faith in my guru after that first vision. And it wasn't my imagination.

I didn't miss the fast lifestyle too much. I was just concerned about paying the rent and keeping it together on a very simple basis. But that came to $1,500 a month, and without a steady job I felt a lot of pressure. I was very insecure about losing my apartment; I had had it for six years. It was my place. I'd paid the first and the last. I knew the landlord well. And it held my vibrations. And yet I was also feeling, very sincerely, "Thy will be done." I kept asking for help, and it seemed to come.

I did two or three tours. I went to New York and had a huge response at the Jivamukti Yoga Center in Manhattan. The response was so strong, it really got me fired up. I did nada yoga workshops and it seemed I could pull it together—but I needed a big enough fan base to support myself. I also had my first concert in Marin County at a church. It was a very powerful evening. I could see the people feel the music. I felt strongly connected to Bhagavan Das, and I was in a place of letting whatever come down. And if I had to leave, I would leave.

I told Maharaji I couldn't worry about money anymore. Slowly the anxiety started to diminish. I also got a lot of support from my friends, the satsang with like-minded people. "When two or more are gathered in my name, I am there." I truly experienced this—the simple love between two people and the friendship and merging of the soul with God, loving God together. Experiencing that form of devotion is very, very powerful. That's all the church you need—one other soul to align with your prayers. Then the spirit will come.

ॐ

THERE ARE NO phases. You're either asleep or awake. Like Ramakrishna said, the water is either boiled or not boiled. It's not hot, getting hot, getting hotter. This is the mistake people make. We must bring about the awakening, which is realizing the depth of our inner journey. The way to become aware of it is to begin engaging the devotional practice. Maybe on a daily basis you connect with a form you can see through, form that light can go through—it's like the lens of the divine. In Kali yoga, the worship of images is the way because faith is little. The image gives focus to the mind. One can then begin to concentrate.

THAT'S EXACTLY WHAT I was doing. I had my guru. I was worshiping a beautiful picture of Mary. I had the Virgin of Guadalupe, which I'd had for many, many years and still have. My American Indian stuff didn't go over the bridge with the Tibetan stuff, so I had my feathers and my gourd. I had the hair of my children from when they were babies and their umbilical cords so that I could pray for them and keep them close to me.

Through prayer, the burden was lifted off me. I was merging Christianity with Hinduism. I was worshiping Jesus as Shiva in an ecstatic way—not overtly because of the problems of the emotional response Christians have about Jesus. But reality is reality, and this was a deep reality in my heart.

The way I pray, the way that works for me, is that I just talk to God like we're talking to each other in real, straightforward terms. If you don't believe in God, tell him you don't. Ask him to show you his face. But when he looks at you, you must look back. It's just like when you fall in love and flirt. You need to flirt with God, get into a relationship with him. It's like a date. It's the deepest romance of the soul, and the soul is the love of our life.

Then, everything began to peel away. My roommate was a very

yuppie Marinite guy, with the "cool" music, gourmet cooking, fine bottles of wine—you know the trip. I saw the intense struggle he was going through; it was the same kind of struggle I'd been through over the previous fifteen years with money, jobs, children, former wife. That samsaric drama was fading in my consciousness, and God was becoming more real. I was doing what Jesus said to do, "Seek ye first the kingdom of heaven and all else shall be added unto you." I was taking him at his word, in faith. And it all came about.

I wasn't into the teacher role. I had a lot of faith in the mantra, in God's name, and I felt the chanting of the kirtan was enough to awaken people. Nothing needed to be said, since it's all beyond words anyway.

ॐ

WE DON'T NEED more concepts. We need to see through the mindmesh and make it lighter. We need to make holes and gaps so we can see the light of Kali—see into reality, into ourselves, and into who we are. Creation is divine, and when we can go back into a childlike state of awareness we open up and are one with all creation. There's no way to process this intellectually. It just happens.

ॐ

I STARTED WORSHIPING a photograph of Kali Ma. The moment I did, things started speeding up. Mother was calling me in to worship her at three and four in the morning. I'd be completely awake and could hear the temple calling me. I'd go to the temple and there would be this light breeze and golden energy. I would sit in front of the altar, look at Mother's eyes, repeat her names, and go into really blissful states. This was happening on a regular basis, so I was really excited about it.

And then it was happening again. The grace was flowing. It was like being back in India—yet I was in Marin!

At about this time I met a beautiful eighteen-year-old girl at kirtan at Jay's house. She loved to dance. I nicknamed her Little Egypt because she would wear costumes and a crown, but her real name was Terra. She was a Deadhead Rainbow Family kind of hippie who always hitchhiked to the kirtan with a backpack and always was alone. Something was very strange about her.

Terra was very artistic, but she was definitely being taken over by the drug. She'd been tripping for three years. A real demonic energy was trying to destroy her. The moment I met her I started praying for her. I felt really concerned about her.

I went to New York and did a concert. When I came back, Terra seemed to have vanished. She was no longer coming to kirtan. Then she called me up and told me she was with the Hare Krishnas. She had gotten off drugs and was really into devotion and Krishna. I told her, "They're brainwashing you! Don't be with the Hare Krishnas! Watch out for them!" She just laughed.

I got another call from her. She was back in Oklahoma with her mother. She had left the Hare Krishnas. We talked and wrote many long letters, and I started falling in love with her. Actually, I was falling in love with my projection of her—a total romantic projection because I barely knew her.

I jumped right into it. It was fulfilling to write love letters to someone again. Then I sent her some of my tapes, and five days before Christmas her mother called me, "I'm sending her to you. She plays your tapes twenty-four hours a day. I'm sick of hearing your voice. I'm putting her on the Greyhound bus to San Francisco." When I went to pick Terra up, she had a ring in her nose, bells on her toes, and tattered clothes. I didn't know what to think.

I became her teacher, and she became my first real student who did what I said and got results from it. She loved Kali Ma and really worshiped her.

At the time, she was smoking a pack of cigarettes a day. I would buy her cartons of cigarettes and would offer them to Kali and ask, "Mother, please help. Every time she smokes one of these cigarettes let her think of you." And I'd stack all the packs in front of Kali Ma so when she wanted one she'd go in the temple to get a new pack. Three cartons later, she quit.

I watched her, within an incredibly short period of time, become illuminated with devotion and love. I could see that she was going through me—I was just a door. She was totally connecting with Neem Karoli's love, not knowing it, and thinking it was me. Terra started singing with me and dancing. We'd spend a lot of time praising God together while we were making love. She could see the tantric vision. I renamed her Uma, which means "Goddess of Light."

Living by the street in Marin, with all the noise and traffic, was really getting to me. I needed to be closer to nature. I prayed to Mother to help me. I couldn't take it anymore and needed to find a new place to live.

Uma and I took a trip two hours north to Harbin Hot Springs to enjoy the baths. While we were there, I ran into Wavy Gravy—the 1960s political activist clown icon, famous for being a famous person. I wondered whether Wavy had to pay to go to the springs. He told me he had a complimentary ticket. I thought there could be some way I could either get a discount or not have to pay at the gate by doing something for them—a trade.

So I went into the office and Ishwara, the founder of Harbin, was there. He knew me and was excited to meet me. He said, "Let's sit down and talk." I was thinking I could bring up the idea. He was getting all worked up and said, "Would you like to live here?" I said, "Yes!" And he picked up the phone and dialed his wife, Jane. She came in, and the next thing I knew, I was living at Harbin. Giving kirtan sessions would take care of my rent.

Harbin is a resort community that gives all kinds of workshops. There were a lot of difficulties when we moved there. I was the new kid in school. This went on for six months. It was a long haul and very, very hard. People were jealous that we had started at the top—most had worked there for ten years to gain their position in the community.

We were staying in a house with other people, and it wasn't working out. It was very confining. Uma and one of the other women in the house got into a hysterical screaming trip, and it brought the heat down. Before we knew it, we were out of the house and staying in a hotel.

At this time I wanted to meet Shree Maa. I had heard that this woman had been on a retreat for five years, didn't talk, and was a real saint. So Uma and I went to Devi Mandir and met Shree Maa. It was like being back in India. It was great.

Shree Maa walked into the temple. She was a very beautiful goddess with dark skin and a shining light around her body. She smiled at me and said, "Bhagavan." We looked at each other. I came close to her and she said, "Bhagavan Das." I got down on my knees, and she touched my heart. I felt her light enter me and illuminate my soul.

I brought Uma to meet her. I wanted her to see a real saint. She really took to Shree Maa, and Maa took Uma in and started working with her. I was so happy to see the connection between the two of them.

WE STARTED DOING Durga Puja (a spiritual practice to remove difficulties) every day.

As we continued to live at the hotel, we were having a hard time, thinking the community just wasn't for us. We couldn't live in a communal situation—I was too old, Uma was too young, and we weren't those kind of people. We liked to get up at three o'clock and chant and burn incense. There was no housing at Harbin, so we were going to have to leave.

We went back to Devi Mandir and talked to Shree Maa. She told us, "No, you can't live that way. You have to have your own temple."

"But where?" There was no answer.

We went back to Harbin and suddenly a beautiful cabin opened up on top of the mountain for us. The shiva devotee who'd been living there got into a fight the day before, while we were at the temple with Shree Maa, and left the community overnight. Just like that, this beautiful temple opened up for us.

We gave the cabin to Kali Ma and named it Kailash (The Eternal Abode of Shiva and Shakti). We praised and thanked Her for it. Her picture went next to Maharaji's. I put the Hanuman flag up and started transforming the demons—there were lots of heavy demons, and I turned them around with lots of prayer and worship and puja.

Things began to lighten up. The leaves on the trees sparkled in the sunlight. In fact, light was everywhere. We were so grateful and happy to be there. Uma and I still live there today.

Miracles happen all the time. Things are thought of, and things happen in the external world continually, giving me confirmation that Divine Mother has come. She's come to take her children home.

Part 3

Chapter 3 8

ॐ

THE PEACE THAT comes from letting go and surrendering is incredible. Again and again it keeps coming back to
letting go of our own will to have a plan about where
we're going and a goal. It seems that we spontaneously
align with the Plan of God for us. I think that's the whole

"follow your bliss" thing. It's really Thy will be done, not mine. Jesus said it all. Love the Lord with all your heart and soul, and your neighbor as yourself. That's it. There is no one out there but us. And if we can just put God first, Om first—offer the food up, offer the day up, become conscious the first moment you wake up, think of God—then there is peace.

Om Kali. Kiss the palms of your hands. Notice which nostril you're breathing out of, right or left. If you're breathing out of the left nostril, then get out of bed with the left foot. If you're breathing out of your right nostril, then get out of bed with the right foot. Start the day right. Start it with God. Give it to God. God seems to take it. An ordinary life turns into an incredible, delightful adventure. You don't bump into any edges anymore.

Surrender to yourself as being God. Go through the great Christian blasphemy—I am God. Who's helping whom? In manifesting what I love to do—which is worship God and chant God's name and do the music—I love my voice, and so I love singing and it comes naturally, and I enjoy listening to it like an audience listens. By just doing that, every-thing else manifests. It's not a passive letting go. Say you lose something. You start cleaning the house, and you find it. What we've lost is our-selves. During the process of doing what needs to be done in the moment, each thing becomes a stepping stone to the next thing. But there needs to be courage because it's a creative process. You can sit there with your paints looking at the white piece of paper forever to get a good idea. Or you can just let your hand sweep into the paint and start to feel what's going to come forth.

Initiation is necessary. It is necessary to have a Guru in the form of a human being whom you can see and feel. There is a certain sense of feeling that's important to be aware of and trust. The music really captures the heart in devotion and brings the mind into a one-pointed space for me. I experience the bindu—the blue dot or the blue ball. Jay told me that Jerry Garcia would see a blue ball when he was on stage and out of the blue ball would come the songs, the riffs that he was playing. The blue ball was singing the notes for him amidst all the chaos. That was the bindu, the blue pearl, he was experiencing. And Robert Hunter, who wrote all the lyrics for the Grateful Dead, also says that his muse is a blue ball, and out of the blue ball comes the poetry. It's a download from the causal plan to the gross plane—not the other way around. Once you've really got it, it's going to manifest—so worry less about the physical and more about the inner space.

When I'm chanting, I'm singing to my guru. I see him sitting in front of me and start worshiping him. I go on different flights of ecstasy. Sometimes it doesn't take long at all—the mind gets extremely still and thoughts seem to fly away like birds, or they seem to go on and my consciousness is numinous. So I'm not really paying attention to the mind, I'm just letting it do its thing. And I'm going out on the sound. I use the sound of my own voice to return to where the sound comes from, which is the bindu. The sound originates in *muladhara* chakra, the earth center at the base of the spine, but it's inaudible. The sound is actually heard in the heart and then becomes audible in the throat. What I do is invoke the bindu in muladhara. It pulls all my energy into that point of concentration. As the sound through the breath rises out of muladhara into the heart and the throat, I feel the heart. My heart is singing and my mouth is in my heart singing. It feels like a stream of water flowing.

The emotion created by the chanting of the names with devotion creates a state of half-swoon. I go into a state called bhava samadhi. I stay in a swoon space for hours, so I'm just on the feather of consciousness, just enough in my body so I'm not going to fall over on the stage; but I'm out of my body enough so that I can feel that I'm a flute and feel this breath come flowing through me. Many times when I start kirtans I have no energy at all. The devotion is doing it. I start doing it with devotion to the name, and I watch the name start on fire and start to burn a hole in the mindmesh of my mind. Once there's a hole, the light of God starts flowing through it, starts coming out, and amazing energy comes upon me. The more I chant, the more I can chant.

My voice is shot. I've gone on stage with a completely hoarse voice, but I sing as clear as a bell. It's all miraculous to me.

The grace of God is being able to remember God.

Chapter 39

THE BIRTH EXPERIENCE is profoundly spiritual, coming from the womb of the mother and connecting with her. As we are on that nipple looking up into the luminosity of our mother's eyes, that is God. We are part of the circle of devotion. It sets the feeling tone for the spiritual journey in our lives.

For me it's important to come back to the feeling tone. To trust intuition. If I can focus more on what's *behind* the feeling, and stop continuously processing information on the mental level through concepts, then I can experience things rather than being there only symbolically. I can actually feel the freshness of the senses and the aliveness and newness of each moment as it appears before me.

We need to enter the stream of awareness, the stream of our eternity, through spiritual practice. We need to humble ourselves. We all tend to think that we create our own reality. We need to remember that we were created, and we need to connect with our creator. We have to stop living with "would-could-should" and let our originality come forth.

I notice that when things come before my consciousness and get the appropriate response, it's always a spontaneous response. This is because until something comes into my view, I feel as if I'm in a blue-sky space, just enjoying the fresh air on the hillside. I'm seeing the art in life. I'm enjoying the sense impressions, not worrying and not overthinking, just simply relaxing in what is happening in the moment because it's here now.

This is how to have more life in our life. It's meditation in action. It's the devotion, and it really is the feeling, the hum of the nada of the sound. To really go into the nada we need to be able to hear the silence. The sound of silence is within us—it's the buzz of creation. We need to hear that tone. Our purified mind becomes our guru, and our own awareness needs to become the universal awareness. The idea behind spiritual practice is to get rid of neurotic mind and discover purified mind. We have to custom design our own spiritual practice to help us purify our mind. That's the transformation that happens.

We are our desires, and we live in a world created by our desires. Our view of the world is where our desire is. We let the desires of the world eat us and motivate us; ultimately they take away our life force and consume it. We always feel that we need more—we climb the corporate ladder, we want a larger house, we want a new spouse or lover. We're never satisfied; we always want more. How do we find some peace in our lives? We need to find eternity. And we can do that by starting to let go—let go of all the stuff, both the material stuff and the stuff that clutters our minds.

Time is eating us. Everyday we fight against time, and time works against us. There is a big difference between time and eternity. Time is what stresses us out—we feel we don't have enough time, we worry about being late, we rush to catch the train. Little Joe said, "Worrying is praying for what you don't want." We have to learn to drop into eternity—and the best way we can do that is through our breath and through the words of the mantra. It can be meditating or praying or saying a mantra while waiting for the train or doing the dishes, or it can be spending time giving unconditional love to a child or a pet. All this is a way to connect to God. We can find God in the everyday—it doesn't have to be so formal. It can be an informal encounter. Only through spiritual practice can we experience eternity so that we are devouring the world and devouring time rather than the other way around.

Realize that every moment is it and that we can live in eternity and time simultaneously. We can move back and forth between them. We're able to go from what the Tibetans call relative truth to absolute truth. Compassion means being able to speak to all people, wherever their consciousness is, with no judgments about them; simply be there with them. That's compassion. No judgment. Just being there. That's being a real spiritual friend to the world.

But there is a place for focused energy as far as doing some form of external practice, but we've got to take it into the subtle and internalize it. Somehow, it has to become part of us. I think all the spiritual trips in the West have ended up in too much of a material trip; they've been too externalized—living in ashrams, being around teachers, all the politics, all the sexual escapades, all the good and bad of these imported religions.

I think Tim Leary was right: Everyone must create his own religion. You must start your own religion. I have my own religion. Every sadhu has his own religion in India. They say every lama has his own religion in Tibet. Find the way you can genuinely be you. What do you like to do? Find God there. Find out what your special gift is and where you find that connection, what really makes you happy, and follow that way.

Personally, I don't really like the New Age movement. I feel it's a conglomeration of surface skimming of so many different lesser mysteries, like astrology, tarot, and occult practices. They're okay until we decide to make a huge leap of faith and go into the eternal deeply, where it turns from the occult to the mystical. This is a big problem that's unacknowledged. I find the New Age and its practices a bit too light for people—I don't see it as a real spiritual trip. Although it's a start, I see it as a more materially minded way of collecting stuff, of distracting ourselves, of finding something else to turn our attention to. The problem is that the energy we can get going with some of this occult and psychic stuff can keep us from really experiencing a breakthrough into a real mystical path.

We need to break through the money, sex, and power trips we're on and find our way back to our hearts. The heart is the real destination. The important thing is how much we love, not what we have. We all want love, but the love of God, of the Divine Mother, is the only true love that never disappoints. Once we reach the heart, we can hear the Nada and we can then begin to merge with the inner sound in the heart, which is the Self, the Atman, the drop, the bindu. Instead of falling down and being burnt up by the fire, the nectar that drips from the brain (the moon in the skull) of power starts to collect as little drops in the heart. The heart is now activated and so it catches the moon drops, and then the nectar starts to nourish the body. This is the alchemical transformation. This is the inner transformation of the breath, the word, and the light. We start circulating the energy because the heart has been touched.

Feel it and see this energy in human beings. The Divine Mother will manifest herself to us through our devotion. The bird will sit on our windowsill at the right mind moment and sing us the right song. It works that way, with the Mother. All the other Gods have abodes. Vishnu has Vaikuntha, Shiva lives in Kailash, but the Divine Mother has no abode. Her abode is the world; she dwells within the heart. She is here, and we're here, so let's take the obvious, which is name and form, and name it. Let's get really courageous and name it. Once we name it, we can go through it into the bindu. We can go into a direct experience of nonduality and, therefore, peace.

Without the juice, the *rasa,* or the bhava of devotion, our spiritual practice is meaningless. It's a dry bone. There's no juice in it. We're not excited to do it. I can hardly wait to get back to my temple so I can be in the presence of the Divine Mother. It's my presence—my love for her that made the temple. I made her a seat, I gave her a form, I gave her a name, I invoked her in the earth, I gave her the spot, and she came.

My desire was to have a temple to Kali Ma. So we have a temple up on the mountain. We've been worshiping, we do Durga Puja every day to Kali Ma because Durga—the lion she rides on—is her aspect of protector. A week after establishing the Kali temple, at midnight on the night of Kali, which is Tuesday night, while I was sitting doing puja, a mountain lion came and ate our rooster. I knew it was Ma. This mountain lion has been at Harbin since we've been there. It's a female mountain lion. She's been eating all the deer, and no one can catch her.

Do you want to surrender to the divine plan, or are you going to try to force your own plan? There's a real problem when you have a plan. When you have a plan, Mother breaks into your room and steals your money. I planned on becoming rich and famous, so Ram Dass introduced me to Jimi Hendrix's manager, Michael Jeffries. He loved my voice, loved my art. He was going to make me a star, yet two weeks after we had made our plan Michael died in an airplane crash. Mother was the pilot. She's always at the controls. If I'd become a star, I'd probably be dead from drugs by now and never would have come back to the Mother. If you keep falling into her arms, you'll become tired of all your external desires. She alone can fulfill your desires.

The kindgom is of the child. It is our child, it is that freshness and openness and spontaneity and glow of the child. All the great saints that I've been with are children—Dudjon Rinpoche, the Karmpa, Lama Kalu, my Guru Neem Karoli Baba—completely spontaneously childlike in every sense, but not childish.

It's really time that we took Jesus off the cross and got into the true meaning of the resurrection. The resurrection is our own consciousness within our hearts, here and now. The divine dwells within us, it is us. It is closer to us than our eyeball, which we can't even see because we're seeing out of it. We can't see it with the mind, it's just a big hide-and-seek game that ends up in total frustration. There is no satisfaction in the mirror image; we're just seeing our own desire. But because of the grace of the Mother, Kali Ma will come to us through our desire. This is the weave of the tantra, because the divine is woven into the profane. We have to keep switching back, making a figure eight. We create solemn stillness, the profound touch of the divine, when we're really in that space, and then we have the laughter and the children and the celebration. This is the curtain of Maya moving back and forth.

In the kirtan, people sit completely still, being Shiva, and other people dance and love Krishna. That's shakti. That's the point. One moment we're Krishna, and Krishna loves Shiva. Krishna is Shiva's greatest devotee. And vice versa. We have to stop this polarity. Tantra brings it together, which is the bindu. The female is within the male, and the male energy is in the female, and we project them outward and constantly become in a state of craziness. Everyone is mad and crazy, pretending they're not. Like Ramakrishna said, "You're mad for the world, you're mad over lust and money and power and stuff. Or are you mad for God?" Pick your madness.

Which is going to take you all the way through? The idea of tantra is we have sensual enjoyment, which is *bhoga,* and yoga, which is union with God. We get to just be here and let this be enough. Why isn't this enough? Why isn't existence enough? What's the problem with existence? The truth is lived when we surrender to existence. By living my truth, it's really the Truth. What I say is that it's all Ma. I worship the ground as Ma. As I walk along the ground, I thank Ma. I start to cry when I walk on her body, and then I look around everywhere and I see triangle rocks, wherever I go, triangles everywhere, yonis everywhere. So I worship her yoni. Mother, this yoni has gotten us into all these problems! Please get me out! I'm going to worship you, not use you. I'll really adore this yoni, the gateway to heaven and earth, the door of desire. Come to her with an open heart and drop it in her lap. "Mother, I don't know. I can't do it." That's a great prayer. It's got to be sincere, and it's got to have a feeling tone behind it. Then we're really excited to dance with her in this love affair.

We've got to flirt and fall in love and come forward with her. We get to that place where the image of God or the photograph looks back at us and the eyes start to move. This is a very important moment. The tendency is to swoon back and not look because it's looking at us. It's important that we look into it. It's like flirting with someone. We catch the stranger's eyes. Now what? The tendency is to look away. But the way to make the flirtation go into the love affair is to meet the gaze. We all want to be known. God wants to know us. He wants us to know him. There's a relationship here. It's romantic love. It's really simple. This is the truth. This is how it really works. This is the big magic. This is how the rocks talk to me and the trees talk to me. When I go outside and I'm loving Hanuman, this huge wind whips up right at that moment. Hanuman the monkey God is the son of the wind.

It always comes back to just letting go with love. Just put love in it, whatever it is, and if you can't put love in it, don't do it. If you do it without love it doesn't have any power. It gets down to that. You've got to get the earth magic going. You've got to get the elemental earth mother backing your play. Then you get the power of the spot where you are. You acknowledge the spot. You sit in your house and say, "Thank you Mother for this spot. Thank you for this house. Thank you for my bed. Thank you for my chair. Thank you for my life. Thank you." This is the way. It's simple, it's the way of the child. If you become a little child, you shall enter the kingdom of heaven. That's really what it is. It's finding that childlike, spontaneous connection to the feeling tone, without putting a label on it. Just let it be, like raw sensations, experience the freshness of the feeling. Just celebrate the body instead of all the trips we have about our bodies.

We are love. Start really letting go, being in your bodies, and seeing the divine in the body. Tantra is worshiping the body as the divine. Not just your body, all bodies. Everyone's it. That feeling that every time we see someone, we really are looking at the Divine Mother; and she will play within their eyes for you. This is my experience all the time. She constantly plays with me, lets me know, constantly winking at me in the crowd, and constantly being seen. That's the ecstatic dance of the lover.

We all have a choice. Mother lets us have it our way. If we want to have God by being president of our company then that's our God. If we want to have God as that Mercedes with the great sound system, then that's our God. I think we need a new brand of God. We need the Mother. Kali is such a perfect screen for what's going on right now in the world. Kali absorbs it all, all the harshness and ugliness of life and all the suffering; she brings us back again so we can get it. Get what? Get the love. Life comes out of death. The sex act is totally divine and holy—regardless of whether we think it is or not. Allow yourself to discover what it is. Stop getting in the way of it. Get out of our own way and let the way be. There is no way, you can't have a way, because if you have a way you're going to block the way. If you have a plan you're going to block the big plan, and you're going to be working your plan. And then Mother's curse is that she will give you your plan. She curses us by giving us our own desires so we end up imprisoned within our own illusions.

An attitude of sincerity and humility is the first prerequisite on the spiritual path. We've got to know that we don't know. We've got to know that there's nothing to know, that there's only being. That's it. We've got to keep the momentum of bringing the mind back to God, and that's what a daily spiritual practice does. If we can use the world as our puja table, then everywhere we go is the puja table. These ordinary things put us back into the stream of awareness. That's what a mantra does. It's the sound body of God.

The mantra is the name of our lover. That's his or her name, whatever name touches our heart. It's a very intimate, deeply passionate, erotic love affair that has to keep us engaged so that we're all excited when God calls us. This is the real Romance.

Mother brings us home on so many different paths and lanes, we do not know where she will lead us, how she will bring us there, or what circumstances will come about. Why second guess God? The best attitude is to be very grateful and thankful and constantly generous. What can I give, not what can I get. Just let the lightness of the moment be what it is. That's a great thing to do, that's the way we can save the planet, the children, the whales: Save yourself. What do you have but yourself? Do you have anything else? We own nothing. We don't even own our bodies. It's only the breath and name of God.

Get into the breath. The breath is the seat that we sit on. It is something we can get hold of. If we get hold of the physical in an attitude of devotion and adoration and real humility and real sense of wonderment, then it's going to open up and reveal itself to us. Things will fall away and we'll wake up and discover the truth. It was there all the time. We can search the whole world for the treasure that is buried in our own backyard. Still the journey needs to be taken.

If you can get that atmosphere of devotion going, then the spiritual path is fun and exciting. You won't even have to try, it will no longer be work but a part of your everyday life—a part of every moment. Everything is just what it is. It can be as light or as heavy as we want to make it moment to moment. We get to choose each moment and how we want to live in it. How do you want it? It's the biggest deal of all, and yet it's not a big deal. It's just life and death. The joy in the enlightened beings I've been around is just incredible. It seems like this is what we all want—to be happy. You're going to be a lot happier if you don't have a plan. Because then, magical things can happen. You're open to people coming up to you because you know that everyone is God, so God's going to come up to you, give you a message, bring light to you, and inspire you. This is what the dakinis are. It's the external world awakening us. They circle around us when we become the upright stone, when we become still out of devotion. We show our love by stillness, by being heartfelt, by just getting into a divine mood. The divine mood is everything. Without the divine mood, none of this can happen. I think that's what's missing in the New Age. There's not a lot of divine mood going on. There's only a lot of hustle going on, more buying and selling.

Nurture the inner, and the outer will take care of itself. The outer is always a reflection of the inner. Animals and young children can tell when you lie. Other people can fake it, but children know, they feel the vibe, they feel that fun, and so do animals, they feel the love. So does all life around us. We are what our experience is, all the time.

I HAVE DONE it all. I have done the deepest, most intense spiritual practices. When I was doing my one hundred thousand prostrations at Bodh Gaya, I had my board and I was out there at four in the morning for three hours, one hundred thousand prostrations. You can count, too. Use rocks. Every time you do a prostration you move a stone over, you have ten stones you set up. You go into a kind of trance with your body. In other words, sixty thousand to seventy thousand prostrations into doing this, I did a prostration, and I completely slid off the board into infinity. I went into this complete realm of golden light and bliss, I saw nothing but golden Buddhas shining a light upon me. And I opened into a whole realm. And then I got up and did the next prostration.

In a way, that's what life is. Life is like doing prostrations. Everybody wants to prostrate, everybody wants to bow, we just don't know how to bow. How about bowing to the ground? How about kissing the earth and saying, "Thank you Ma for being here." How about bowing to gravity? Let's get into that feeling when we bow, really keep laying down our bodies—it creates an incredible happiness.

The point I'm getting to is that it takes one hundred thousand prostrations to get one good one. To get results from japa, you need to do twenty thousand malas a day. No one does this. This is not a hobby. Spirituality is not a hobby. If it's a hobby, you're going to get the results of a hobby. Don't expect to get many results after doing your hobby for twenty or thirty years. There are workshops here. Ammachi comes once a year. If you've got a picture of her up on the wall, don't expect much. You've got to really make the sacrifice. She wants ego sacrifice. Mother wants real blood, the depth of your feeling tone. It's like having a baby. It doesn't get much more sincere. This is what it is to have God. Do you want to have God? Do you want to know God? Then you have to be

God because God dwells in you. It's not an ego trip, it's not a power trip—it's just the opposite. All that power leaves you. It's an amazing experience to feel your body as big as the universe and transparently empty, to feel your body as small as an atom, just a little speck of dust.

Life is a journey to death, a journey home. The more we can die now, the more we are prepared for the journey. Let go of the fear—Kali wants the blood of our heart. She is the pump of our heart, she is the breath, the power of the breath, the moment of the life energy. She's devouring the blood as it flows through us. Everything is that. So get generous, that's what it amounts to—real generosity of your life. It isn't your life, it's Her life. We are living Her. She's deeply compassionate, and she is wisdom. We live in duality, yet her wisdom is nondual. So start from where you are, start with desire. If you're a man and you have a lot of lust, and lust is your problem, she's a beautiful young girl. Make God a beautiful naked girl, and go for it. Guess what? God will come to you as a beautiful young naked girl and take you right through the lust into the love. That's been my experience.

The problem with all these different traditions is that we start taking on Tibetan heaven or Muslim heaven, and if we're not a Tibetan or Muslim, it gets confusing. I think we need to bring all this wisdom into a real American context. Find God in the shopping mall. Let the earth of existence and the Mother support us. Let it be. Stop trying to mess with it. It's very mystical, like making fire. The way you make a fire is to let the energy of the fire make itself. It's like cooking. You've got to know just when to mess with it and when to leave it alone. It's okay to go all the way. When you learn how to leave it alone and let it be, then the divine shines through it, and you stop fiddling with it. Every gesture becomes authentic instead of being half-way. You learn how to get behind it and have more space in simplicity.

Then you have the meditation of being in the light, but it needs to come through that bindu experience. It's got to come out of emotional passion and love. That's where the divine flows from. What's your thing? Do you like the ocean, do you like the mountains, do you like to work on the computer, do you like to write? Whatever it is, find that way and the divine will shine through it for you. Mother will show you, because she will write the story through you and you will see it manifesting through you. That will increase your devotion.

Over and over again I've been in these experiences, particularly when I'm talking with people. You probably have, too, and you really surrender to her, and words come upon your tongue and they're the right, appropriate thing for that moment. I pray to Mother that I can be of help to people spiritually. People come to me and tell me their secret visions. They trust me. In those moments of intimacy, because I'm loving them as Ma, I see how that one thing will come out of my mouth that's just for them. I watch them get it. It's wonderful to have that experience. It's total fulfillment. That one thing, because it's authentic, is not something we read and memorized, it's not a phrase. We're making it come together in the moment through love.

First you learn to concentrate. The easiest thing to concentrate on is music, sound. You get one-pointed. Then spontaneously, through your love, that will lead you into meditation. It's a gift, a state of grace. Meditation comes. I don't sit to meditate, I sit to love. I'm hopping in bed with the Divine Mother. Let's play Ma! Let's have fun! How are you? What's going on? You've got to get really simple with it. It's like a little girl playing with dolls. Love them and kiss them, and they come alive. And when they look at you, you look back and you feel that joy and love in your heart.

Take it out of the heavy trip and make it into a light trip. Let the light be God for you. When I offer the flower to Ma, I put the flower down and step back; I look at the light coming off the edge of the flower, a scene so beautiful it explodes my mind in ecstasy. It's just the flower, but it's a flower given with love. So she accepts it and then the boon she gives is the light on the edge of the petals. I will come in that flower for you because you love me. Love is enough. Presence is enough. Presence is all that we have and all that we are. So let's just experience the presence and let ourselves have it. That's all it is. All these spiritual practices, sadhanas, disciplines, ashrams, and chanting is for purification so we can drop into that childlike state of wonder and surrender to existence.

How much do you want? How much freedom, how much liberation do you want? How much God do you want? Most people want about 2 percent. Maybe 1 percent. It's always going to be the few who really want to go all the way. But we're all going all the way anyway, whether we want to or not, because we're all really Here.

How to get here? How to show up for life? That's what it's all about. You have to be present to win. In one mind moment, it's gone. To be able to catch the wind, to be able to have the birds land in your hair, you have to be very still. When the birds chirp on top of your head, it's a great, blissful experience. It's being one with nature. We are the trees and we are the earth and we are the fire and the water and the air. We are all of this.

To see ourselves in others—all others—and to be ourselves in others until there are no others is what it's all about. There is only love, only One.

Printed in the United States
by Baker & Taylor Publisher Services